HRH
THE PRINCESS
ANNE

HRH
THE PRINCESS
ANNE
A Biography

Brian Hoey

COUNTRY LIFE
BOOKS

Published by Country Life Books,
an imprint of Newnes Books,
a Division of The Hamlyn Publishing Group Limited,
84–88 The Centre, Feltham, Middlesex, England,
and distributed for them by
The Hamlyn Publishing Group Limited,
Rushden, Northants, England
Copyright © Brian Hoey, 1984

First published 1984
ISBN 0 600 35715 5
Printed in England

CONTENTS

AUTHOR'S NOTE

Princess Anne is the Queen's only daughter, second child and sixth in line of succession to the Throne, yet fewer books have been written about her than almost any other senior member of the Royal Family. Dozens of biographies containing millions of words have been devoted to the lives and times of the Queen, the Duke of Edinburgh and Queen Elizabeth, the Queen Mother, and in 1981, the marriage of the Prince of Wales to Lady Diana Spencer caused the couple to become the world's most talked about and written about newlyweds.

Prince Andrew and Prince Edward, the Queen's younger sons, have both been the subject of recent biographies, but as far as Princess Anne is concerned the half dozen or so books which have been written about her since her birth in 1950, ended around the time of her marriage in 1973. Why should this be? Her activities still attract a tremendous amount of attention from the world's press. She carries out a large number of public engagements and in royal terms she has what they call a 'high profile'. In other words Princess Anne is 'news'. In recent years there has been a concerted public relations attempt on the part of the Buckingham Palace Press Office to improve her image and she has become more accessible to journalists and photographers, a number of whom have been invited to Gatcombe Park, her Gloucestershire home, to talk to her and see for themselves what sort of lifestyle she enjoys. Throughout 1981 (with the exception of the period when she was having her second child) she allowed a camera team from Thames Television, to follow her around and film her at work on her public engagements both at home and abroad. The resulting programme was shown on the I.T.V. network at peak time on 23rd December, 1981, and created a precedent by being the first programme of its length – one and a quarter hours – to be transmitted without any commercial breaks.

Yet with all this attention from television and press nobody has produced a book about her in the past ten years, during which time she has become the mother of two children, runs a large country estate and still assumes a wide variety of public engagements. This book is intended to bring up to date the story of Princess Anne's life and to try and explain her role in the Royal Family of today.

INTRODUCTION

I first met Princess Anne on a sunny Sunday afternoon in September 1971, in the grounds of Burghley House in Lincolnshire. The home of the Marquess of Exeter was the venue for the European Three Day Event Championships, one of the world's leading competitions in the equestrian calendar. Her Royal Highness, at the age of twenty-one, was about to burst on to the world sporting stage by becoming the first member of the Royal Family to win an international title.

Riding the Queen's horse Doublet, Princess Anne had performed brilliantly in the dressage stage on the opening day and she had shown electrifying courage over the toughest cross-country course during the speed and endurance test on the Saturday. So now she needed a clear round to win the European Crown. I stood with an old friend and colleague of the Princess, Richard Meade, arguably the most accomplished horseman Britain has ever produced. He was already out of the running as far as winning was concerned, but together with team-mates Lucinda Prior-Palmer and Chris Collins he stood talking quietly to Princess Anne as she waited with Alison Oliver for her turn to enter the arena. The atmosphere was tense as the vast crowd, impatient to see the Queen's only daughter, silently urged the other riders to complete their rounds. Princess Anne didn't watch the competition; she concentrated her attention on getting Doublet ready for his big moment.

Then quite suddenly, after what seemed an interminable wait, it was time. It is now, of course, a matter of history that horse and rider performed impeccably and we had a royal European champion.

The Queen was there to present the award to her daughter and I was fortunate enough to be among the first to congratulate her and then interview her for B.B.C. television news.

Since then I have talked to her on many occasions, and was present, again with television cameras in evidence, when her engagement to the then Lieutenant Mark Phillips was announced. I was sent to Balmoral to be given details of the betrothal and then the following morning after an overnight journey from Scotland, I went to Buckingham Palace with Reginald Bosanquet of I.T.N. for the official engagement interview. Later that same year I met Princess Anne at the Army Horse Trials at Tidworth where she offered me a drink served from the back of her shooting brake, and in 1981 I spent the best part of a year following her around at home and abroad, in order to make a film about her working life. She was the complete professional, co-operative with the camera crew and willing to do anything within reason if it would help the programme. Perhaps one of the most revealing aspects of Princess Anne's character came to light when we had completed the filming. She took the trouble to find out the names and addresses of every member of the film team and a personal invitation to a Royal Garden Party at Buckingham Palace followed. Not only that, but she also made sure when the day arrived, that she met and spoke to everyone she had invited – the whole television crew and their families.

Her courage has never been in doubt. The week after the kidnap attempt in The Mall in 1974 she was competing in a local horse show in Cirencester, because she had promised the organisers she would turn up. When she suffered severe concussion after a bad fall during the European Three Day Event Championships in Kiev in the Soviet Union, she insisted on visiting the stables to see that her horse was all right, before she would see the doctor about her own injuries.

She combines a wide variety of roles in her public and personal lives. She is a Counsellor of State and a working farmer's wife. She is President of the British Academy of Film and Television Arts and Patron of the Riding for the Disabled Association. Her Royal Highness is President of The Save the Children Fund, for whom in 1982 she went on an eight-country tour of Africa and the Middle East visiting refugee camps, and she is Chancellor of the University of London, although she does not have a degree herself. Two aspects of her life might appear to be contradictions. She rides with a number of fashionable hunts, yet she is also Patron of the Jersey Wildlife Preservation Fund. She is Colonel-in-Chief of a number of regiments in the Army and Chief Commandant of the Women's Royal Naval Service. She is the first member of the Royal Family to have competed in an Olympic Games – Montreal 1976, and the first Royal Princess to have been voted Sports Personality of the Year, by both the B.B.C. and the Sports Writers' Association of Great Britain.

Her mother is Queen but neither of Princess Anne's two children is titled. She is sixth in line of succession to the Throne but married to a commoner. If she wasn't who she is, she says she would probably be a long-distance lorry driver. It's a job she is well qualified to take on because she already has a licence to drive heavy goods vehicles, which she does frequently, at the wheel of her ten-ton horsebox, going from competition to competition during the eventing season.

If she is not driving her horsebox she will probably be behind the wheel of her own car, a Reliant Scimitar sports saloon, which, with its three-litre engine, is capable of, and has many times been driven at, speeds in excess of 100 m.p.h. It's an easy car to recognise: the colour is royal blue and it bears the distinctive number plate 1420 H; the number was a personal gift from the 14th/20th Hussars, one of the regiments of which her Royal Highness is Colonel-in-Chief. The others are the Worcestershire and Sherwood Foresters, the Royal Corps of Signals, the Royal Scots and the 8th Canadian Hussars.

She carries out around 200 official engagements a year for which she receives a little over £100,000 from the Civil List. She is emphatic, however, that this is not 'her pay' and every penny goes on expenses. Princess Anne has been brought up as a member of the world's leading family, taking as a matter of right, the privilege and position this has accorded her. Those who know her well and have been in her company on informal occasions, sometimes have to pinch themselves to remember to whom they are talking: she can be so friendly and disarmingly candid. Yet within seconds the royal mask is restored if there is the slightest hint of familiarity. This then is the young lady, still in her early thirties, who can be said to be at the crossroads of her life. As a young and glamorous Princess of Wales begins to take an increasing part in royal duties and Princess Anne's two younger brothers, Andrew and Edward, also start to take on public engagements in their own right, what part can she expect, or want, to play in the Royal Family in the future?

Will she retreat into the country life of the shires, sharing the rural interests of her farmer husband? Will she continue to occupy the unique position she holds as the Queen's only daughter and carry on the tradition of royal patronage of those organisations where she feels she can do most good? As she reaches full maturity, will she be offered, and accept, the title that many feel should have been hers years ago, that of Princess Royal?

So in writing this biography, I plead guilty to a bias in favour of my subject. I know she has been called uncooperative by the world's press, but how many of them know what it's like to be at the wrong end of a lens as they approach a water jump to find fifty photographers all waiting to get that picture of them going in head first? I've heard all the stories of how she doesn't earn her money from the Civil List, but I've also seen her spending hours with handicapped children at a Riding for the Disabled show when there have been no reporters or cameramen around.

One example of her work pattern occurred in January 1984, when Princess Anne flew to Houston, Texas, as President of The British

Olympic Association. This was the first of sixteen public engagements which she was to undertake in the period leading up to the Games in Los Angeles in July – more than she would do for any of her other organisations during the year.

The purpose of the visit was to raise funds to send British athletes to the Olympic Games.

The two main functions of the short two-day visit were to be a reception held in the ballroom of the Four Seasons Hotel, where 500 guests paid $50 each for the privilege of rubbing shoulders with the royal guest, and an exclusive dinner in the nearby Petroleum Club restricted to 150 guests who had been fortunate enough to be allocated one of the $500 tickets. At the early evening cocktail reception, with press and television cameras recording every moment, the Princess 'worked the room' making sure that she spoke to every group present. She was particularly pleased to meet a British real-estate agent, Mike Mahoney, who had that day learned that he had been selected to compete for Britain in the Olympic Sailing Squad. As she told him 'you are the reason we are all here anyway.'

The evening function at Houston's exclusive Petroleum Club, turned into an outstanding success with more than $75,000 going into the Olympic kitty. Michael Ashley, the organiser, said that Texans didn't mind giving money but that it was necessary to 'get bucks with a bang' and that the Princess had certainly done. Bob Scarborough, another local millionaire, who had acted as host for part of the evening, felt he had 'got every red cents worth' while yet another tycoon said 'with Princess Anne on my team I could sell anything to anyone.'

Houston was just one of the many stops on the fund-raising tour at the start of Olympic Year. The Princess would also visit Galveston and New Orleans, travel the length and breadth of the United Kingdom, in addition to attending the Winter Olympics in Sarajevo, Yugoslavia, and the summer Olympics in Los Angeles. She was determined that no British athlete was going to be denied the chance of competing because of a shortage of money.

Princess Anne travels the world in a style which seems an anachronism to some in these days. She uses the Royal Yacht, aircraft and helicopters of The Queen's Flight, chauffeur-driven limousines and gilded, horse-drawn coaches, attended by bewigged and liveried servants when the occasion demands. In private, she prefers to drive herself, with a sometimes arrogant disregard for speed restrictions and traffic regulations. She is used to people calling her 'Ma'am' and very few are allowed to use her Christian name. She can be infuriating and affectionate; totally regal one minute, completely relaxed and informal the next. She is Princess Anne Elizabeth Alice Louise.

Chapter 1

THE PRESENT

It's 8.15 in the morning and at Harrods, the 'top people's' favourite store, they have been up and about for hours. It's a red-letter day in the life of the world's leading shop. Today Princess Anne is coming to open officially their new Food Hall and inaugurate British Food Week.

Throughout the night the sales staff have been arranging their wares in a series of exhibits, each one seeking to outdo the one next to it, and there's an air of excitement as floor managers and heads of departments scurry around checking on the last-minute details to make sure that everything is in order for the royal visitor.

Around the number 10 entrance, at the rear of the building, a small knot of people has gathered, all wearing their Sunday-best clothes as if they are going to be personally inspected by the Princess. Looking somewhat incongruous in their midst are two workmen in jeans and sweatshirts, standing guard over a roll of carpet. This is the red carpet which will be unrolled only at the last minute so that non-royal footprints do not sully its pristine condition.

In the building across the street from the entrance, windows have been opened and residents of the flats, and early-morning office workers, are claiming their grandstand positions for the arrival of the Princess. Most of them don't know who is coming, but from the activity below it's obvious that someone important is expected.

A group of 'Royal' photographers and reporters turn up and take their positions at the exact point where they know, from experience, the royal car will come to a halt. Some of them are wearing round cardboard labels attached to their lapels bearing the words 'Royal Rota'. These are the official press party who will be allowed – at a distance – to accompany the Princess throughout the visit. The area immediately around the entrance is kept clear of vehicles by the police, but traffic is allowed to use the road until the very moment of the approach of the royal car. Police officers are stationed at all the road junctions along the route and every few minutes one of them whispers into a miniature radio transmitter he has attached to his uniform jacket.

At Buckingham Palace another small group is waiting in the corridor on the second floor where Princess Anne has her small suite of rooms. Lt. Col. Peter Gibbs, the Private Secretary, and Miss Victoria Legge-Bourke, the Lady-in-Waiting who has been designated the companion for this visit, hover patiently around the door which is marked with a small white pasteboard bearing the legend: H.R.H. The Princess Anne.

They do not knock to let her know they are waiting. Their job is to be ready to leave when she is ready. As they wait they chat about the engagement ahead. Peter Gibbs has driven up from his home in Wiltshire in the early hours of the morning, while Victoria has come in from her flat nearby. She is going to do only part of today's diary, which is due to go on until late in the evening, because she has to get back to her full-time job.

Before they start to look anxiously at their watches, the door opens and the Princess comes out. Victoria curtseys and Peter Gibbs bows from the neck. Princess Anne wishes them a good morning and they are off down the crimson-carpeted corridor to the lift. The Princess is wearing an outfit of emerald green and she seems to be in good humour though obviously suffering from a heavy cold. She has a busy day ahead with four separate engagements which will take her from London to Worcestershire, and last night she had a late evening when she was on duty to present awards at the Royal International Horse Show at Wembley.

A Rolls Royce from the Royal Mews is waiting in the quadrangle and so too is Inspector Philip Robinson, one of the Princess's three personal police officers. The Princess gets into the car, sitting as she always does, in the seat immediately behind the driver; next to her is the Lady-in-Waiting and Peter Gibbs takes the folding jump seat. The detective sits alongside the driver, while following close behind is the police 'back-up' car. It's an unmarked blue Rover with two pin-stripe suited detectives who are in constant radio contact with the car in front, and also with their colleagues who are manning the junctions along the route. They also carry the emergency first-aid bag which always lies between their seats. Someone has already been over the route from Buckingham Palace to Harrods and they know that even at this time of the day it will only take them five minutes. The original plan was for the Princess to arrive at 9 a.m., but when the Private Secretary pointed out that this would coincide with the opening of the store to the public, it was brought forward half an hour. Organisation of the royal progress through London's peak hour traffic is now so smooth that other motorists are barely aware of any disruption and right at the appointed minute the royal limousine glides to a halt and the Princess steps out on to the red carpet which has been laid across the pavement.

There is a minimum of formalities, a few waves from the people in the windows overlooking the entrance to the store, and she is into the round of handshaking and presentations which will continue until nearly midnight. Inside Harrods hundreds of staff are lined up; most of them seem to have been issued with straw boaters bearing the green and gold colours of the store.

Princess Anne is accompanied by the chief executive who introduces the heads of the various sections, who in turn describe in great detail the part of the Food Hall for which they are responsible. If the Princess is bemused, at this time of the morning, by the technical and detailed explanations of how to prepare oysters or spin sugar into intricate designs, she doesn't show it. In fact her progress through the department is getting slower and slower as she is obviously fascinated by some of the stands. She stops occasionally to speak to members of the staff who have not been designated to be presented, and if they are a bit nervous she soon puts them at ease. There's a lot of laughing going on and the youngsters are finding that she's very easy to talk to. As she passes by, one young man in his early twenties whispers to a colleague 'she's a lot prettier than she looks in pictures'. It's a fairly common comment from those who are seeing her in the flesh for the first time. Philip Robinson and another of the police officers are ever watchful and, acting as extra press secretaries this morning, make sure that no photographer gets too close, or that microphones are not 'shoved under the Princess's nose'.

Victoria Legge-Bourke is within a few feet of her employer at all times, talking to one of the managers and reassuring him that everything is fine and going according to plan. It isn't really going according to plan, because the Princess is so interested in what she is seeing, and is spending more time than was envisaged in talking to people along the way, that the programme is getting seriously behind. Breakfast is organised in the restaurant on the third floor, and there is a second engagement timed to start in another part of London at 10.15.

Eventually the Princess has seen all there is to see in the new Food Hall and she goes upstairs to join the other guests. It's a traditional English breakfast of fruit juice, scrambled eggs, sausages, bacon, sauté potatoes, toast and coffee or tea. Her Royal Highness makes a brief but humorous speech in which she refers to the enticing smell of the Food Hall which has brought back pleasant childhood memories in spite of her cold. She speaks without notes, in a firm clear voice, and then sits to enjoy her breakfast, showing a healthy appetite for everything that's put in front of her.

The hidden sense of timing that almost seems to be a sixth sense among all the Royal Family tells her when it's time to leave for the next job, and with a final handshake for her hosts she's back into the car heading for Bond Street. Harrods have spent £2·5 million on their new Food Hall. Princess Anne has added the icing to this very expensive cake and ensured wide press coverage for the store the following day. For them it has been an unqualified success for their investment; for her an early start to what will be a very full day.

On the way to Bond Street where she is to attend the centenary celebrations of a well-known art gallery, Princess Anne decides to make a quick call at Buckingham Palace. The policemen *en route* are told by radio what's happening and she is inside the Palace for less than three minutes before the motorcade sweeps back out through the North Centre Gate, into St. James's and finally down a very crowded Bond Street, where a large crowd has gathered outside Ackerman's the art dealers.

It's a tiny gallery with what appear to be over a hundred guests crammed into the ground floor showrooms and basements. Spotlights placed strategically to show the prints to their best advantage have turned the gallery into a sauna bath, but the Princess still looks the coolest person in the room as she tours the exhibits, mingling with the Marchioness of Tavistock and television quizmaster, Bamber Gascoigne, who are among the guests.

Peter Gibbs and Victoria Legge-Bourke are concerned that too many people are crowded together downstairs and the police officers are being rather 'firm' with the press photographers who never seem to be satisfied that they have got enough pictures.

After an hour spent in the gallery Her Royal Highness signs the distinguished visitors' book – it's always a fresh page with only her name on it – and then it's back to the Palace for a change of clothes before leaving for a formal lunchtime engagement with one of the Livery Companies in the City.

The Livery Companies are exclusive organisations going back many centuries and originally consisted of members of the same trade or profession who formed themselves into associations for the purpose of mutual benefit. Hence, the Farriers, Saddlers, Carmen, Fishmongers and so on. Today the members may not practise the trade of their particular livery company in quite the same way as their ancestors, but to be elected to one of the Livery Companies of the City of London is a highly sought after and rare privilege. Princess Anne is an Honorary Freeman or Yeoman of six Livery Companies and honours each with her presence at least once a year.

On this occasion she will have to sit through a number of speeches, eat lunch, which she probably doesn't feel like after a late hearty breakfast, and have a long line of people presented to her. Meanwhile Peter Gibbs has returned to his office in Buckingham Palace to spend the afternoon working on the details for the Princess's future programme.

Once the luncheon in the City is finished, Princess Anne goes back to the Palace where she changes into less formal clothes and tries to catch up with some of the administrative work that has piled up on her desk. She works for an hour or so with Brenda Hodgson, her Personal Secretary, and then she and Inspector Robinson climb into her Reliant Scimitar sports saloon and she drives them the 112 miles to Gatcombe Park. By now her Lady-in-Waiting has changed, Victoria Legge-Bourke having gone back to her other job and Mary Carew Pole taking over. At home she is able to spend a little time with her two children, Peter and Zara, and have a brief rest before dressing for the final engagement of the day. This is to attend a fashion show at Malvern in Worcestershire as part of the centenary celebrations of the Savile Row tailors, Gieves and Hawkes. This is another venue to which she decides to drive herself. At the show, which is being held in aid of a local charity, the Princess meets a line-up of civic dignitaries and workers for the cause and then sits through the two-hour fashion show apparently unaware that most of the other guests are watching her rather than watching the models. There is a reception after the display, with the Princess circulating and making small talk with a large number of people she has not met before, nor is likely to meet again. Each one is received with courtesy and friendliness and Princess Anne is the one who has to keep the conversation going. She has shown a keen interest in the evening's proceedings with no hint of the fatigue she must have been feeling after having driven more than 150 miles and as the fourth engagement draws to a close. At last she is able to make her farewells and she and her small party are free to leave for the drive back to Gatcombe.

Once inside her own front door she bids goodnight to her Lady-in-Waiting and to the detective. The day began before seven when she arose at Buckingham Palace; it ends after midnight at Gatcombe Park in Gloucestershire. This has been Princess Anne's working day, fairly typical and repeated time after time throughout the working year. In all she carries out approximately 200 engagements every year, which places her very near the top of the table of 'working Royals'. She may be asked to present prizes to disabled children in the North of Scotland or degrees to graduating students at London University. She could be asked to represent the Queen at an independence celebration in Fiji or visit a refugee camp in Ethiopia. Her presence is required at State occasions at Buckingham Palace and when the Queen is abroad she acts as a Counsellor of State dealing with 'the boxes' as they are delivered daily.

Counsellors of State are appointed by the Queen to act on her behalf whenever she is incapacitated or out of the country for more than a few days. Under the present arrangements, there are six Counsellors of State appointed – the Duke of Edinburgh, the Queen Mother, and the four adults next in line of succession: the Prince of Wales, Prince Andrew, Princess Anne and Princess Margaret. Prince Edward will be appointed when he reaches the age of twenty-one.

Any two of the Counsellors are eligible to sign official documents normally requiring the Sovereign's signature and to carry out certain other duties in the U.K. and the Commonwealth. They do not have the power to dissolve Parliament (except on the Sovereign's instructions) and neither are they able to create peers. However, when Princess Anne represented the Queen in Fiji in 1980, she did carry out an investiture and bestowed the honour of knighthood on a number of recipients.

There has never been a royal princess who has worked harder than Princess Anne and for her there has never been any question of changing her role. She accepts that by an accident of birth there are certain responsibilities to which she is committed, and as far as she herself is concerned that commitment is for life. As she has put it: 'The idea of opting out is a non-starter.' Had she been born a hundred years ago her role in life would have been far different. Her public appearances would have been rare, her circle of friends severely restricted. Today she is a modern, knowledgeable woman with a great zest for living and unlimited curiosity about the rest of the world. As one of her police officers, the people who spend more time with her than anyone else, has said: 'She's a hundred per cent, this girl.'

An unusually gruelling tour followed the 1984 Winter Olympics in Sarajevo when the Princess flew immediately to West Africa for a 1500-mile journey through the Gambia and Upper Volta. As President of The Save the Children Fund, she lived rough, travelled hard and saw sights to touch the toughest heart. In temperatures soaring way above 100°, in the area known as the poorest region in the world, every other baby is destined to die before the age of three. Here she focused world attention on scenes of almost unrelieved and unbelievable misery. This was the Princess at her best, doing the job she knows and cares about so much. At the end everyone, including a Press party of twenty, was convinced of the worth of what she was doing. As the *Sunday People* said 'This is the Real Anne. A Princess we can be proud of'.

Chapter 2

1950 – THE BIRTH

If ever a royal princess could be said to have ushered in the second half of a century, that person must surely be Princess Anne. She was born ten minutes before noon on the 15th August, 1950, and weighed exactly 6 lbs.

Within minutes of her birth a bulletin was issued from Clarence House:

> *Her Royal Highness the Princess Elizabeth, Duchess of Edinburgh, was safely delivered of a Princess at 11.50 am today. Her Royal Highness and her daughter are doing well.*
>
> (signed) WILLIAM GILLIATT
> JOHN H. PEEL
> VERNON F. HALL
> JOHN WEIR

Copies of the bulletin were posted on the gates of Clarence House, outside the Home Office in Whitehall and at the Mansion House in the City of London.

The Duke of Edinburgh announced the news at Clarence House and invited members of the Household to toast the health of the new Princess in champagne. Next to be informed was the King, George VI, who was on holiday at Balmoral. When Prince Philip telephoned the Scottish castle the King was out shooting on the estate and the news was conveyed to him by an aide. The Queen already knew. She had remained in London to be near her daughter for the birth and five minutes before the baby was born the Queen was seen being driven into Clarence House.

Queen Mary, the Queen Mother, was staying at Sandringham and she was also informed immediately, as was the Duke of Edinburgh's mother, Princess Andrew of Greece. She was staying as a guest of the Dowager Marchioness of Milford Haven, Prince Philip's grandmother, in her apartments at Kensington Palace. Messages were sent to Princess Margaret, who was in Scotland at the home of the Duke and Duchess of Buccleuch in Dumfriesshire, and to the other members of the Royal Family who were scattered all over the world.

After the family had been told, Mr. Chuter Ede, the Home Secretary, was notified officially and he passed on the information to the Lord Mayor of London. At the same time, all the Governors General of the Dominions were informed and the Ambassadors to the Court of St. James's, so that they could relay the news to their countries.

A forty-one gun salute was fired in Hyde Park, by the King's Troop, Royal Horse Artillery, and this was answered by a salute of sixty-two guns from the 1st Regiment, Honourable Artillery Company, based at the Tower of London. In Plymouth, royal salutes were fired from the battleship H.M.S. *Howe*, the aircraft carrier *Illustrious*, and from the Royal Citadel on the Hoe.

In accordance with ancient custom the Secretary of State for Scotland, Mr. Hector McNeil, despatched letters to the Scottish capital addressed to the Lord Provost of Edinburgh, the Lord President of the Court of Session, the Lord Advocate and the Lord Justice Clerk, advising them of the birth of the infant Princess. This practice of informing high personages in Scottish life had grown from the days when communications were difficult, and it was considered important that authoritative information on matters of national interest should reach areas remote from London.

Back in London meanwhile the Test Match between England and the West Indies at The Oval had been briefly interrupted just before the luncheon interval, to announce that 'Ladies and Gentlemen, we have a new baby Princess.' There was loud applause from the crowd on that brilliant summer day. All that morning there had been crowds of people waiting outside Clarence House for news. They were in great humour, many of them holiday-makers watching with interest the comings and goings of the various members of the Royal Family.

As soon as the announcement had been made and the news spread, people poured into the area around Clarence House and long queues formed to read the official bulletin which had been posted outside the house. By mid-afternoon the crowds were so dense that police reinforcements had to be called out to help control them. Post Office messenger boys were bringing bundles of congratulatory telegrams and dozens of bunches of flowers arrived.

In reply to a message of congratulations from the Lord Mayor of London, Princess Elizabeth and Prince Philip sent this telegram:

We thank you, My Lord Mayor, and through you the citizens of London, most sincerely for the kind message of congratulation on the birth of our daughter – Elizabeth and Philip.

Princess Elizabeth had been attended at the birth by the four royal doctors who had signed the bulletin. However, there was no government minister in attendance as had been the custom until the time of Prince Charles's birth in 1948. Just before Prince Charles was born the King had expressed the view that it was no longer necessary for a Minister of the Crown to be present at a birth in the Royal Family: it was an archaic custom for which there was no legal requirement.

At the same time that this view was given, the *London Gazette* announced the King's decree that 'the children of Princess Elizabeth and the Duke of Edinburgh were to enjoy the style and titular dignity of Prince or Princess before their Christian names.' If the King had not issued such a Royal Decree, the infant daughter of Princess Elizabeth might have been known simply as Lady Anne Mountbatten, the family surname, until 1952.

King George V had issued a Royal Proclamation on July 17th, 1917, which had restricted the titles Prince and Princess to a Sovereign's children and grandchildren in the male line only. Of course this was in the days when 'Bertie', the King's second son, was not expected in the normal course of events to succeed to the Throne, and his future daughter's position as Heiress Presumptive had not been envisaged.

The new infant Princess – she had not been named yet – made history from the moment she was born. She was the first baby to have been born in Clarence House since its conversion by Nash from the old portion of St James's Palace in Stable Yard in 1825.

However, the house had been used as a royal residence before this. William IV, as Duke of Clarence, occupied an apartment on the same site before the conversion and it was here that his second daughter, Princess Elizabeth, was born on December 4th, 1820. A daughter born the previous year had lived only one day, and Princess Elizabeth survived less than a year; she died in March, 1821. If she had lived she would have succeeded to the Throne, and the course of history would have been mightily changed. As it was, her cousin became Sovereign and, as Queen Victoria, ruled for longer than any other British monarch.

Queen Victoria's mother, the Duchess of Kent, used Clarence House as a home for some years, and then from 1866 to 1893, the Queen's second son, the Duke of Edinburgh, lived here. He spent a great deal of money enlarging and improving the house and in 1900 it passed to Queen Victoria's youngest son, the Duke of Connaught, who remained in residence for the rest of his life. He occupied the house throughout the years of the First World War and for the first three years of the Second World War until his death in 1942.

For the remainder of the war years Clarence House served as

headquarters for the Red Cross and St. John's Ambulance Brigade and it wasn't until 1949, eighteen months after they were married, that Princess Elizabeth and Prince Philip moved in.

This then was home for the new royal baby. No elaborate arrangements had been made to accommodate the new arrival. She was to share the top-floor nursery already used by Prince Charles, and the two ladies who cared for him, nurse Helen Lightbody and nursery maid Mabel Anderson, would take on the additional duties of looking after the new baby. No extra staff were engaged.

August 15th was a day for double celebrations as far as the Duke of Edinburgh was concerned. As well as becoming the father of a blue-eyed, blonde-haired baby daughter, he was promoted to the rank of Lieutenant Commander in the Navy on the same day. So it was with a light step indeed that he set off to journey to Balmoral, to deliver in person to the King, the news he had already conveyed by telephone.

Two weeks after the baby was born, the names she was to be given were announced and the birth registered. Her full names were Anne Elizabeth Alice Louise. Anne was an old Stuart name long favoured in the Royal Family, but not, however, liked by the infant Princess's late great-grandfather, King George V. Sir John Wheeler-Bennett wrote in his official biography of George VI (Macmillan), of the birth of Princess Margaret: ' . . . the naming of the new Princess was a matter for grave consideration. "I am anxious to call her Ann Margaret [the Duchess wrote to Queen Mary] as I think Ann of York sounds pretty." King George however was averse to the name of Ann and though disappointed the parents bowed to his wishes in the matter and chose instead the names Margaret Rose.' Elizabeth is of course a name shared by Princess Anne's mother and grandmother. Alice was chosen as a tribute to the Duke of Edinburgh's mother, Princess Alice of Greece, and Louise was the Christian name of the Duchess of Fife, eldest daughter of Edward VII who was Princess Royal from 1905 to 1931. The name is also the female derivative of Louis, the name of Lord Mountbatten, the Royal Family's favourite 'uncle'.

The full names and title would be: Her Royal Highness, Princess Anne Elizabeth Alice Louise of Edinburgh. She would not be known yet as *The* Princess Anne. The definite article is reserved for the children of the Sovereign and it was to be another eighteen months before Princess Anne would be entitled to use this distinctive article before her name. At 11 a.m. on the 19th August. 1950, the Registrar of Births and Deaths for the Sub-District of Westminster North East, Mr. D. A. Boreham, called at Clarence House to register the royal birth. He was accompanied by two ladies from the Westminster Food Office, Mrs. Lillian Smith and Mrs. Vera Jarvis, because even though the war had been over for five years, it was a time of austerity and there was still food rationing in Britain and everybody, even members of the Royal Family, had to have a ration book.

Prince Philip received them in his study and signed the register 'Philip'. Then he signed the National Registration Form 33/31 and handed it to the food officials. In return he was given a yellow identity card for the Princess with the number MAPM/396, a green ration book which entitled her to an allowance of bread, milk, eggs, sugar, butter, margarine and meat, a bottle of orange juice and a bottle of cod liver oil. The formalities took a little over fifteen minutes to complete, and the following day the Duke of Edinburgh flew to Malta to take command of the frigate H.M.S. *Magpie*, a posting which had followed his promotion.

Princess Anne, second child of Princess Elizabeth, Heiress-Presumptive, was third in succession to the Throne, behind her mother and brother Prince Charles, under the Act of Settlement 1701. For the first few weeks of her life she stayed in a dressing-room alongside Princess Elizabeth's bedroom in order to be near her mother. Then she moved to the nursery on the top floor of Clarence House along with her brother who, until then, had been the sole focus of attention, both from within the Royal Family and from the world outside.

Such was the interest in the royal children, that when Princess Anne made her first public appearance, just a month after she was born, more than 200 people waited for several hours in the forecourt of King's Cross Station in London, to get their first glimpse of her. Princess Elizabeth was taking her baby daughter to Scotland by train, so that the King, who was waiting at Balmoral with the Queen, could see his new granddaughter for the first time. The infant Princess, wrapped in a white shawl and wearing a knitted bonnet, was carried by her mother through the station entrance to the waiting train, and there Princess Elizabeth pulled down the covering shawl to give onlookers a glimpse of her daughter's face. For the journey they used a special sleeping coach which had been attached to 'The Aberdonian', one of British Rail's crack overnight express trains. The Princess's coach had been made originally for the Duke of Windsor when he was Prince of Wales. It consisted of a double bedroom and a sitting-room, which was adapted to provide sleeping accommodation for Prince Charles and a place for Princess Anne's cot.

The following morning the first news photographs of the infant Princess appeared and so started what was to be a lifetime of press interest in anything and everything she did. In Scotland, Princess Elizabeth and her two children moved into Birkhall on the Balmoral estate, the house now used by Queen Elizabeth, the Queen Mother, whenever the Royal Family is in residence at Balmoral. The King's reaction when he saw his granddaughter for the first time was that she was 'delectable'.

In the weeks following the royal birth, gifts poured into Clarence House from all over the world. Hand-knitted garments of every description, shade and colour, a complete wardrobe presented by the children of Swindon in Wiltshire; five dolls, each nine inches high, representing Princess Elizabeth, Prince Philip, Princess Margaret and the pages at the Royal Wedding, were sent from Ontario, Canada; hundreds of toys ranging from dolls to train sets were received and almost immediately redistributed to children's hospitals throughout the country. A bale of cotton was sent from Edinburgh, Texas, with a message from the Mayor, Mr. F. McDonald saying that Princess Anne had been made an honorary citizen of the town and proclaimed 'Princess of Edinburgh, Texas'. Princess Elizabeth accepted the gift on her daughter's behalf and replied saying that she knew that Princess Anne would come to value the proclamation as one of her most treasured possessions.

One of Australia's oldest woollen mills designed and made a pair of blankets emblazoned with the Duke of Edinburgh's coat of arms for the Princess. The employees at the mill had competed for the right to work on the blankets and those chosen each had more than forty years service in the woollen industry. Among the more unusual gifts were a number of songs which were composed specially for the infant Princess. Two waltzes were written by the then Assistant Head of Music for the Midland Region of the B.B.C., Mr. Kenneth Pakemen. He called the dances 'Waltzes for a Princess' and they were included in a broadcast in December, 1950.

The first gift to be presented to the Princess, and one which she was not to appreciate for many years, arrived just half an hour after her birth. At 12.30 p.m. on 15th August, 1950, Princess Anne was elected the millionth member of the Automobile Association. The Chairman of the organisation said the fact that membership had reached one million on the very day of the royal birth was coincidence, but there was a unaminous decision to elect the Princess when it was realised how closely the two events had occurred. By another remarkable coincidence it was also at this time that the speed limit was abolished in Britain – something which no doubt would have been appreciated by the Princess when she was stopped for speeding some years later, after the restriction had been reimposed.

It's a golden rule within the Royal Family that every letter receives a reply and every gift an acknowledgement, so for weeks after the birth of the Princess, ladies-in-waiting and secretaries were kept busy writing thousands of thank-you letters to all those people around the world who had written or sent presents.

The christening of the royal baby took place on 21st October at Buckingham Palace. The Music Room was used because the private chapel in the Palace had been badly damaged by bombs during the war and was still not repaired. Prince Charles had also been christened in the Music Room and, like him, Princess Anne wore the historic royal christening robe of Honiton lace over a satin petticoat, which had been used by all Queen Victoria's children, by the King and his brothers, by Princess Elizabeth and Princess Margaret, by the children of the Duke of Gloucester and the late Duke of Kent, and was to be worn in future by Princess Anne's brothers, Andrew and Edward, her own children, Peter and Zara, and Prince William of Wales.

For the christening, which took place at three o'clock on a Saturday afternoon, the silver gilt font which was another tradition at royal christenings, was brought from Windsor Castle. The ceremony was performed by Dr. Garbett, Archbishop of York, because the Archbishop of Canterbury, Dr. Fisher, who had christened Prince Charles and who would normally have had charge of such a royal event, was on a three-month tour of Australia and New Zealand. But the Duke of Edinburgh, who was also abroad at the time with his new command H.M.S. *Magpie*, flew home specially for the occasion. Princess Elizabeth and the Duke of Edinburgh had invited five relatives to be godparents. One of these was the Queen herself, a choice which would have been unthinkable until two years previously, when the King had set a precedent by suggesting himself as godfather to Prince Charles. So both grandmothers acted as sponsors with Princess Andrew of Greece, who was abroad and unable to attend, being represented by proxy in the person of Princess Alice. The remaining sponsors were Princess Margarita of Hohenlohe-Langenburg, the Duke of Edinburgh's eldest sister; Lord Mountbatten, great uncle to Princess Anne; and the Hon. Andrew Elphinstone, first cousin to Princess Elizabeth.

The white and gold Music Room had been decorated for the ceremony with sprigs of oak grown from acorns planted on the day Princess Elizabeth and the Duke of Edinburgh were married, and according to reports at the time, the centre of attention at the christening 'behaved impeccably'. It was an historic occasion with four generations of royalty present. Even Queen Mary, then approaching her eighty-fifth birthday, had been driven from Sandringham and joined the fifty or so guests who had been invited to witness the christening. Cecil Beaton captured the occasion in a series of memorable photographs which included one of Queen Mary holding the baby, while flanked by the Queen and Princess Elizabeth.

Within a few short months mother and child were to be separated for the first of many times. Prince Philip was still serving overseas with his ship and Princess Elizabeth flew to meet him and spend Christmas with him in Malta. The parting could not have meant anything to the infant Anne but it was a cruel wrench for her mother. The baby was, of course, well cared for by the doting staff at Clarence House, and one or other of the grandmothers was in almost daily attendance to make sure there was no lack of attention to the youngest members of the family. It was a pattern that the young Princess was to know for the rest of her childhood – her parents being away for long periods and her companions being her brother, grandparents and the ever watchful nursery staff.

The King's health had been giving cause for concern for some time, and his eldest daughter, Princess Elizabeth, took on more public duties than usual in 1950 and 1951, in an effort to give her father as many opportunities as possible to rest. Instead of a year away from royal duties, as was the case when Prince Charles was born, Princess Anne's mother went back to the daily routine of investitures, official visits and affairs of State almost immediately after the birth of her daughter.

Princess Anne was just a year old when her parents left for engagements in Canada and The United States, and then in the early days of 1952 came the events that were to mean that she was not just the daughter of the heir to the Throne, but much closer to the succession.

On the 6th February, 1952, just seven days after Princess Elizabeth and the Duke of Edinburgh had embarked on a long tour of the Commonwealth, King George VI died in his sleep. So the young mother who had really had very little time to enjoy her children, returned to Britain as Queen, and she and her family moved from the comfort and cosiness of Clarence House, to the far more austere and, strangely, more cramped accommodation across the road in Buckingham Palace.

At first the Queen and Prince Philip had considered staying on at Clarence House and using Buckingham Palace only for formal occasions, as certain Prime Ministers had done with 10, Downing Street, but Sir Winston Churchill was strongly opposed to the idea. He felt that it was essential for the Sovereign to be seen to be in residence at Buckingham Palace and persuaded the Queen.

At the age of nearly eighteen months then, Princess Anne became second in line of succession to the Throne and from the date of her mother's accession, she became known as H.R.H. *The* Princess Anne, not that she of course was aware of any change in her status at the time, or even of the change of address. Since the day of her birth she had been so used to the seasonal moves from one royal house to another – weekends at Windsor, Balmoral in August, Sandringham (at that time) for Christmas and the New Year – that the move to Buckingham Palace meant little to her, apart from the fact that all the nursery furniture had to be moved across, and instead of taking with her just the few essential toys that invariably accompanied her wherever she went, this time the whole lot were removed, lock, stock and barrel.

Had she been born a generation earlier, she might have noticed one major change in her lifestyle: the attitude to her parents. Until Queen Elizabeth II came to the Throne, royal princes and princesses were always required to bow or curtsey to their parents, the King and Queen, from an early age. Prince Charles and Princess Anne were excused this customary convention because their mother was most anxious that the children should be brought up for as long as possible, without the knowledge of their exalted positions.

There was one exception to the 'no bowing or curtseying' rule, and that was the Dowager Queen Mary. She was a stickler for protocol and court etiquette and insisted that her great-grandchildren should pay her these formal compliments whenever they met. There were no problems with Prince Charles, but on more than one occasion Princess Anne had to be shown what was required when she, some thought deliberately, misunderstood and refused to curtsey.

Queen Mary had of course been brought up in the old school and one of her pet aversions was the telephone. Throughout her life she never once used this form of communication, right up to the time of her death shortly before the Coronation, which was in the year following the Queen's accession to the Throne. Queen Mary had insisted on being the first member of the Royal Family to pay obeisance to the young Queen on her arrival back in London. And shortly before her death in March 1953 she made it known to Buckingham Palace that she wished the Coronation to proceed on the scheduled date despite the normal period of Court mourning. Princess Anne, not yet three years old, was considered to be too young to attend the ceremony at Westminster Abbey and was left behind in Buckingham Palace with her nanny to watch the proceedings on television. Prince Charles, two years older, was taken to the Abbey by his grandmother, Queen Elizabeth, the Queen Mother, but even he found it difficult to remain still for the three hours of the crowning ceremony and was taken out by a side door before the end.

The only thing Princess Anne even vaguely remembers about the day in June, 1953, was being taken on to the balcony of Buckingham Palace, together with the rest of the family and being told to 'wave to the people'.

It was around this time that Princess Anne began her life-long passion for horses. A strawberry roan pony named William was delivered to the Royal Mews to be shared by both children, partly as an introduction to the equestrian life but more probably to take their minds off the fact that their parents were to be absent for even longer than ever before. The Commonwealth Tour which had been interrupted in February, 1952, after only a week, because of the death of the King, became the Queen's Coronation Tour of 1953.

Prince Charles found little difficulty in adapting to the saddle, even as a five year old, but his approach was conventional and taken in easy stages. His sister, on the other hand, with her mercurial temperament and habit of never walking when she could run, gave early hints of the prowess and fearlessness that were to come. She demanded to be lifted into the saddle at every opportunity. Not for her the sedate walk at the end of a tether: she wanted to trot and even gallop almost from the first lesson. So even though the pony was a shared treat, it was Princess Anne who took the lion's share, but there is no evidence that this in any way dismayed her brother who preferred the quieter pastimes of the nursery and schoolroom.

He of course never had any need to compete with anyone. Although both he and his sister were brought up in their earlier years to behave as normally as was thought possible, nobody within Palace circles, including the family themselves was ever left in any doubt about his position. As the first-born child he would inevitably have a great deal of attention focused on him anyway, and he has always occupied a special place in his grandmother's heart. But even though the Queen and the Duke of Edinburgh made great efforts not to differentiate between their children, Princess Anne always felt, from an early age, that she was less important than her brother.

In an interview with Kenneth Harris, of the *Observer* newspaper in 1980 she said, 'I've always accepted the role of being second in everything from quite an early age. You adopt that position as part of your experience. You start off in life very much a tail-end Charlie, at the back of the line.'

Perhaps it was this feeling of being second all the time that subconsciously prompted her as a young child to push her way to the front whenever she and Prince Charles were together. If he held back when they appeared in public, Princess Anne would be first out of the car or train, determined that no one would miss her. A total reversal of her attitude these days when she cares little for personal publicity and is not in the least put out if the press completely ignores her. In fact, there are many occasions when she would prefer it.

In the early years of the Queen's reign, the demands of State meant that there was little time available to be spent with the children. The Queen and the Duke of Edinburgh – when he was home – usually saw the children for half an hour in the morning, then again perhaps at four in the afternoon for tea. The domestic life of the young Prince and Princess remained in the capable hands of their nanny, Miss Helen Lightbody, who had come to the Palace after presiding over the nursery of the Gloucester children, Princes William and Richard, and her willing assistant Mabel Anderson. These two ladies continued the tradition of royal nannies coming from Scottish stock, which had begun with the Queen's own favourite nanny, Bobo MacDonald, many years earlier.

Indeed the Scottish connection among royal servants was strengthened even more when a governess was appointed to take charge of Prince Charles's early education. She was Miss Catherine Peebles who came from Glasgow, who also had graduated to Buckingham Palace through service to another branch of the Royal Family. Before taking on the responsibilities of the Palace schoolroom she had worked for Princess Marina, Duchess of Kent, with the young Prince Michael as her charge.

People ask how one gets to work for members of the Royal Family. Do you have to be personally recommended? Is there a secret recruiting service with a private supply of suitable applicants? The answers are far more prosaic. Although it's true there used to be a great deal of traffic between the various branches of the family, with a nanny or governess or nursemaid being passed from one to the other when children got beyond the age of needing nursery staff, the initial introduction into the royal houses is more usually through the normal channels by which wealthy people recruit their domestic staff.

For example, Mabel Anderson advertised her services in a nursing magazine and one of the replies came from the then Princess Elizabeth, who after a personal interview and taking up the required references, offered her the job of assistant nursemaid to the royal children. Other members of the Royal Family have themselves advertised for staff, usually under a box number, and when the position involved is as a personal servant the applicant is invariably interviewed by the employer herself, even when that person might be the Queen.

Chapter 3

PALACE SCHOOLDAYS

When Prince Charles was five years old Miss Peebles began giving him lessons in the Palace schoolroom and Princess Anne recalls, 'She started with my brother and I went along I suppose, none of which I fortunately remember.' Her Royal Highness also puts paid to the myth that one of the ways in which she was trained for all the arduous hours of standing that she was going to have to endure later in life, was by having to do all her lessons standing up. She says 'Who could possibly have thought of that? Short of actually the odd hours of punishment, it was all done in the conventional manner, sitting.' She does not deny, though, that there were 'odd hours' of punishment, usually as a result of some minor breach of the rules of the nursery or schoolroom. If Prince Charles was to be a quiet, studious pupil, his sister sometimes showed her rebellious nature, which was probably a natural way for a little sister to behave when trying to attract the attention of a brother two years older.

For two years Princess Anne 'tagged along' to the lessons with her brother, but when she was five Charles was sent away to school at Cheam and she became the sole object of Miss Peebles' educational attention.

After discussion with the Queen and the Duke of Edinburgh it was decided that it would be better if a couple of other little girls of similar age could be brought into the schoolroom to share the lessons, so in May, 1957, two children who were related to former retainers of the House of Windsor were placed in the unique position of having their lessons with a school friend who was second in line of succession to the Throne.

The chosen pair were Susan (Sukie) Babington-Smith, a grand-daughter of Admiral the Honourable Sir Herbert Meade-Feather-stonehaugh, a former equerry to King George V, and Caroline Hamilton, granddaughter of the Dean of Windsor. The importance of introducing these children into Princess Anne's life was not so much the fact that her horizons were being broadened by meeting 'ordinary youngsters' – indeed those chosen could hardly be said to come from anything other than the privileged classes. The fact that they were at least her own age was important. For the early part of their lives both Prince Charles and Princess Anne had spent nearly all their time in the company of adults. Apart from each other and the odd occasion when they might meet some of their cousins, their days were spent with nannies, nursemaids and chauffeurs, plus the few hours which they were permitted to spend with their parents. So Susan and Caroline were the first contemporaries that Princess Anne was to spend any real time with, and the arrangement at Buckingham Palace was to continue for the next seven years, until all three children were twelve and the next stage in their education had to be considered.

Susan Babington-Smith is now Mrs. John Hemming, wife of the Director and Secretary of the National Geographic Society, who is also one of the world's leading authorities on the culture of the South American Inca Indians. Mrs. Hemming leads a busy life looking after two small children as well as acting as information officer at the London headquarters of the National Trust.

She has almost total recall of the days when she and Caroline Hamilton were first taken to Buckingham Palace – their mothers operating an alternating 'school run' in the mornings and afternoons. She remembers being taken in by the Privy Purse Door and put into a lift on the ground floor, which had mirrors on the walls and a red plush bench to sit on. On the second floor they were taken along the widest corridor they had ever seen to join Princess Anne in the schoolroom. Each of them was given a tiny desk and introduced to Miss Peebles who was to be the most important figure in their lives for the next seven years.

The scholastic day was divided into formal study in the schoolroom in the mornings, either with Miss Peebles or one of the specialist tutors who were engaged to teach subjects like music and languages, and special outings to places of interest in the afternoons. There were two French tutors, one of whom even spent part of the summer holidays at Balmoral so that the young Princess could practise conversation, but Princess Anne claims that particular lesson was 'a dubious necessity', and even though this gave her a basic grounding, it was some years before she became proficient in French.

Mrs Hemming says that she and Caroline Hamilton were treated in exactly the same way as Princess Anne, and if she was taken to be shown something special happening in the Palace, they would automatically be included. 'It was lovely when the Queen was going to open Parliament or there was a State Visit – we would be taken out into the Courtyard to see the Procession leaving and if the Queen saw us, she would always wave.' Because such care was being taken with the Princess's education, the benefits rubbed off on the other two children to such an extent that Susan Hemming now recalls 'It was practically teaching on a one-to-one basis. If one had to pay for it, it would have cost the earth.' Miss Peebles had a small suite of rooms next door to the schoolroom and the children's meals were brought to them there. Every morning at 11.30 they would be able to hear the bands playing in the forecourt as the Changing of the Guard took place.

There were always important guests arriving at the Palace, and whenever someone particularly interesting was expected Miss Peebles would take the three girls around to the main entrance, which is hidden from the public view, so that they could get a good look. Susan Hemming reflects that 'there was great excitement when Yuri Gagarin, the first Russian spaceman, came – we all crowded round thinking he might look like a Martian.'

The school year was divided up into the usual three terms with one variation. The first four weeks of the autumn term were always spent at Balmoral where the Royal Family was completing its summer holiday, so Susan and Caroline were taken by Miss Peebles on the overnight train to Aberdeen, from where one of the royal cars would drive them to the Castle. Lessons were confined to the mornings at Balmoral; during the afternoon all three girls would go out with the guns of the royal shooting party.

Just before the outbreak of the Second World War, King George VI and Queen Elizabeth had decided that their two daughters should join the Brownies, the junior branch of the worldwide Girl Guide/Girl Scout movement. So the 'B'ham Palace Pack' was formed with the daughters of members of the Household and children of staff at the Palace invited to join their employers' daughters at their weekly meetings. Princess Margaret who took a special interest in her niece, especially when the Queen and Prince Philip were abroad, thought it would be a good idea for Princess Anne to widen her circle of friends even more and suggested that the pack be re-formed. It was, and not only were the daughters of the senior Household members allowed to participate, but also those belonging to the domestic staff and the many craftsmen who were employed in and around the Palace. Not the least of the benefits of having a number of other children of similar age around was the fact that whenever they went outside the Palace, to the zoo, the Planetarium, Richmond Ice Rink or the Tower of London, the sight of three young girls, or in the case of the Brownie pack, seven or eight, was not likely to excite the curiosity of the public nearly so much as a single figure with nanny and security guard in attendance.

It must have been the most cosseted Brownie pack in the world in terms of the facilities they enjoyed. Not for them a draughty village hall on winter evenings or trudging miles out into the country to search for somewhere to pitch a tent. They met in the comfort of the Palace and when they went out of doors to practise lighting fires and cooking, they were taken to Windsor Park where the most private of camp and picnic sites were available. Still they were supervised by qualified Guiders and they all achieved the necessary standards to bring them up to 'badge' level in the various disciplines. They even went to camp in Essex where they all had a marvellous time living under canvas.

The Girl Guide/Girl Scout movement is among the world's most democratic, and if Princess Anne was pre-eminent in many of their activities, it was not because the group was meeting in 'her house', but because, at the time, she had so much energy that her natural enthusiasm for each new interest pushed her to the forefront – even casting her in the unlikely title role of Cinderella in a Brownie production of a Palace Christmas pantomine.

I asked Susan Hemming if there were any great advantages she could think of to having her early lessons with Princess Anne. She replied: 'One of the things I mostly remember is the marvellous trips we had. As we got older we were all keen on tennis and we were taken several times to Wimbledon where of course we were given the best seats. In fact Wimbledon was the only place where the press bothered us. They would always want pictures of the Princess and her companions watching the tennis. Then we had a craze on ice-skating so we were given individual tuition at Richmond Ice Rink. We took it all for granted, thinking that everyone got the same treatment as we did. It wasn't until we each went our separate ways that I began to learn how to do things for myself.'

But were they aware even at that early age that Princess Anne was any different from them? 'Of course we knew that she was royal. Not by anything she consciously did or said, it was simply something about her that made us realise that she was different. The Palace was somewhere we went every day, but at the end of the afternoon we went home and she, of course, remained. I can never remember a single occasion when she was treated any differently from us in the schoolroom, apart from the odd time when Miss Peebles would be stricter with her than she was with us. One would see the Queen quite a lot around the Palace but she never came to the schoolroom. If she wanted to know how we were getting on she would send for our notebooks.'

Having a father like Prince Philip made it inevitable that the royal children would be introduced to a variety of outdoor pursuits at an early age. The Duke of Edinburgh had excelled from early childhood in a number of sports such as swimming, athletics, sailing and cricket. His equestrian prowess was to come later in life.

From almost as far back as she can remember, Princess Anne has been able to ride and to sail. Mention has already been made of the strawberry roan pony, William, on which both she and Prince Charles took their first tentative lessons on horseback, at the age of three and five respectively. It was only a little later that Princess Anne was introduced to the sport of sailing. Every year the month of August is sacrosanct as far as the Royal Family is concerned. They embark on the Royal Yacht *Britannia* for a cruise up the west coast of Britain, *en route* to Balmoral where the main summer holiday is always spent, usually managing to arrive off the coastline surrounding the Castle of Mey just as the Queen Mother begins her summer break. Even today if Princess Anne is asked what she would regard as the ideal summer holiday she will reply 'a couple of weeks with the family at Balmoral'. Unfortunately, in recent years because of the demands of her own family and the fact that August is right in the middle of the competition season for 'eventers', she hasn't been able to join the rest of the Royal Family as often as she would wish.

Loch Muick near Balmoral is one of the safest and most beautiful lakes in Scotland and was a perfect place on which to get to grips with the intricacies of dinghy sailing, and it was here that Prince Philip first introduced his daughter to the sport. She also tried her hand at fishing, but, unlike Prince Charles, this never became one of her great sporting loves.

From the age of about nine she was able to handle a small boat on her own and Prince Philip also had his ocean-going yawl *Bloodhound* brought into Scottish waters so that the family could go 'island-hopping' during their summer holiday. It was on *Bloodhound* that Princess Anne learned some of the skills needed to crew larger yachts, such as furling sails and coiling ropes. So the years of early childhood continued with Miss Peebles supervising the formal education in the classroom and Prince Philip making sure his daughter received her share of tuition in the outdoor activities which were to occupy such a large part of her later life.

If Princess Anne was being brought up to believe she was no different from other children, there was no doubt that she was being given the advantages of being the daughter of extremely wealthy parents. For example, when she showed signs of wanting to play tennis, the former Wimbledon player and later doyen of tennis commentators, Dan Maskell, was engaged to coach her. Perhaps he saw glimpses of the determination that was to take her to the top of another sport years later, because he said in retrospect that had

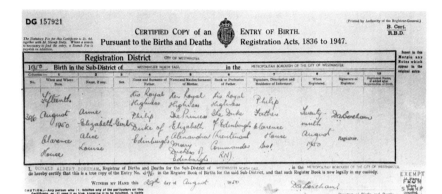

1. Princess Anne's birth certificate (*top*). Two weeks after the royal birth, the registrar of births and deaths of the City of Westminster visited Clarence House where Prince Philip signed the Register.

2. The christening (*above*) was an historic occasion with four generations of royalty present. Queen Mary, then approaching her eighty-fifth birthday, had been driven from Sandringham.

3. (*Above*) The Princess
spent her first birthday
with the Royal Family at
Balmoral and while being
held by her mother, then
Princess Elizabeth, she
evidently found the
brooch of her aunt,
Princess Margaret, a
fascinating toy.

4. Coronation Day (*right*):
The Queen and the Duke
of Edinburgh,
surrounded by members
of their family, pose for
the first official
photograph in the Throne
Room of Buckingham
Palace.

5. Still two months short of her third birthday, Princess Anne was thought to be too young to attend the Coronation ceremony in Westminster Abbey, so she remained at Buckingham Palace. But she smiled happily for this special Coronation Day photograph with her grandmother, Queen Elizabeth, the Queen Mother.

6. (*Above*) The Picture Gallery at Buckingham Palace was the setting for this evocative photograph showing Princess Anne and her brother, Prince Charles, sitting on the floor – a favourite place to read.

7. (*Opposite top*) Excitement or a little yawn? Princess Anne with her great aunt, the Princess Royal, watches the Trooping the Colour Ceremony in June, 1957.

8. Summer holidays (*right*) were always taken at Balmoral where Prince Charles and Prince Philip joined in the fun of Princess Anne's fifth birthday.

9. (*Top*) Princess Anne arriving back in London from Balmoral with Miss Peebles, her governess, and Susan Babington-Smith (*left*) and Caroline Hamilton (*right*) who shared the schoolroom.

10. (*Above*) The ten-year-old Princess and her twelve-year-old brother, Charles, pull baby Andrew along in his pram at Balmoral.

11. April, 1963 and the Princess competes in the Ascot Gymkhana
Jumping Events to raise funds for the St. Francis School Building,
one of many events she was to take part in, in the Windsor area,
during the next five years.

12. First day at school: when Princess Anne arrived at Benenden
School in Kent all 300 girls turned out to meet her. It was the only
occasion on which she was given any special treatment. Here the
Queen talks to Miss Elizabeth Clarke, the Headmistress, while the
Princess meets her housemistress, Miss Cynthia Gee, for the first
time. Princess Anne was one of sixty new girls and wore the
regulation uniform of a blue suit with a red tie. Girls at Benenden
called her 'Anne', while the staff addressed her as Princess Anne.

she concentrated exclusively on her game she could have played at Wimbledon – as indeed her grandfather George VI had done in the 1920s. When I put this to Princess Anne recently she said 'I think he's wrong actually. I'm temperamentally unsuited to tennis, especially in this day and age. I quite enjoyed it but that's all really.'

From the age of three Princess Anne had travelled with her parents on occasional visits abroad. In 1953 she and Prince Charles had the distinction of being the first royal passengers to be carried by the newly completed *Britannia*. Her maiden voyage saw the Royal Yacht cruising to North Africa where the children were to be reunited with their parents after a State visit to Uganda and the Middle East. So the business of being 'Royal' and of being aware of it came as naturally to the young Princess as walking and talking. She says she knew that people would be around to take photographs wherever she went and that she was taught to shake hands with whoever was presented, but she didn't realise it was any different for any other child. After all how could a child of three or four know that it wasn't a normal thing for a Lord Lieutenant resplendent in full ceremonial dress to turn up to greet you whenever and wherever you tagged along with the rest of the family?

The whole business of royal training seems to come about more by association than actual design. When I asked Princess Anne if her parents had broken her in gradually by taking her with them on official functions, she gave a somewhat surprising reply: 'I don't ever remember doing an official engagement in this country with them apart from as a very young child we once went to Cardiff and Milford Haven in order to get on the yacht, then we tagged along, but that was the only time I remember doing that in this country. Otherwise it was only when we were abroad.'

The stories of rivalry and competition between Prince Charles and Princess Anne as youngsters have been fanned by the press and those who claim to be 'in the know', but as far as the two people themselves are concerned there is very little evidence that any such rivalry existed beyond the usual brother-and-sister relationship. Certainly neither of them can recall any particular instances when they felt a special need to compete with the other. One thing is certain: when Prince Charles left to go to his preparatory school for the first time, his sister missed him enormously.

The year 1958 was of historic significance for the Royal Family. The British Empire and Commonwealth Games were held in Cardiff and the Queen took the opportunity at the closing ceremony to announce that she intended to create her son Prince of Wales. The announcement was made via a tape-recording played to the assembled crowds and Princess Anne had been let in on the secret a few hours earlier at Buckingham Palace.

This was the year she also made her first presentation as a member of the Royal Family. It was at the Royal Windsor Horse Show when she made the award for one of the classes of harness horses. The year might also have seen a date which equestrian historians would have noted in later years: the first visit to Badminton Horse Trials by a young Princess who was to make it a regular venue for many years to come. But the childish complaint of chicken-pox was passed from brother to sister during the Easter holidays and the moment passed with the spotty eight year old prowling around the rooms of Windsor Castle, instead of 'walking the course' at the world's leading three day event.

The following year was also an eventful one for Princess Anne. The confidences she was able to share with her two classmates included the news that her mother was having a baby, her aunt, Princess Margaret, was getting engaged to a Welsh photographer, Anthony Armstrong-Jones, and her cousin Lady Pamela Mountbatten, was about to marry one of the country's leading interior designers, David Hicks. This last piece of news was perhaps the most exciting of all, because Lady Pamela had invited her eight-year-old royal cousin to be bridesmaid, a duty she carried out with great seriousness at Romsey Abbey near the family home, Broadlands in Hampshire.

This was the first time that Princess Anne had acted as bridesmaid, but in the following eighteen months she was to do so again on two important occasions. First in May at Westminster Abbey when she was the senior of eight young attendants who were bridesmaids to Princess Margaret, and then the following year, 1961, saw her carrying out the same duties when the Duke of Kent married Miss Katherine Worsley. This last ceremony must have made a great impression on the young Princess because twelve years later, at her own wedding, she chose as a wedding march the self-same piece of music: Vidor's Toccata.

After a gap of ten years the Queen's third child, Prince Andrew, was born on February 19th, 1960. He was born in mid-afternoon and his sister was so anxious to see him that Miss Peebles decided to call off the remainder of the day's lessons and allow her inattentive pupil to satisfy her curiosity. Within an hour of Prince Andrew being born, Princess Anne was taken by her father to visit the infant Prince, and it was not many weeks before she was offering to take a share of his nanny's duties by pushing him around the Palace gardens in his old-fashioned, high-wheeled pram.

The loneliness that Princess Anne had felt when Prince Charles went to school was partly offset by the introduction of the two companions into the Palace schoolroom, and when at the age of ten, by which time she had pursued many of her childish enthusiasms, the new baby arrived, he was to prove an excitement that would last for her remaining two years under the eye of her governess.

Then came the moment when it was felt that she would benefit from going away to school. Her grandfather, King George VI, even though he had been brought up in the rigid tradition of private tuition within the Palace walls, was far-sighted enough to advise his own daughters that times were changing and it would be better if their children were to mix with others their own age and so get a feel of the outside world at an early age.

Both the Queen and Princess Margaret had received their education from governesses and tutors, but their husbands, Prince Philip and Lord Snowdon, had been at boarding school and were known to favour their children doing so.

Princess Alexandra had been the first British princess to break with royal tradition when her mother, Princess Marina, sent her to Heathfield, but no daughter of a reigning Sovereign had ever attended school, and so it was left to Princess Anne to add another 'first' to her list of achievements. The only things Princess Anne knew about school life were what she learned from Prince Charles when he came home from Cheam at the end of term. Until then she had not been aware of the restricted life she led; but her brother's tales added to her normally restless nature and she was curious to find out for herself what life 'on the outside' was really like. So her reasons for wanting to go to school were somewhat different from those of her parents, who felt that a princess's preparation for life in the modern world of the second half of the twentieth century needed a broader education than she would receive in the confines of the Palace schoolroom.

The Queen and the Duke of Edinburgh did ask Princess Anne if she wanted to go away to school but even though she replied in the affirmative, some years later she reflected that it probably wouldn't have made much difference anyway if she had said no. The decision about the continuing education of the Queen's only daughter had been made and the school she was to attend for the next five years had been chosen, after a great deal of subtle investigation and discussion among the Household and family and friends.

Benenden School for Girls in Kent was finally decided upon and it was there that Princess Anne went a few weeks after her thirteenth birthday which she had celebrated with the family at Balmoral in the summer of 1963.

When the decision to send Princess Anne to boarding school had been reached it meant the end of the Buckingham Palace schoolroom and the Girl Guide Company. The three girls who had been constant companions for five years, sharing their lessons, confidences and hopes for the future, were split up and sent to different schools. There was a complete cut-off which Sukie Hemming believes was quite deliberate. 'I'm sure it was laid down by the Queen and her advisers that we should be split up and I'm equally sure that it was the right thing to do, even though at the time it seemed rather brutal. We were each moving on to the next phase in our lives, and to try and hang on to the old ways would have made life very difficult for Princess Anne in her new environment. We never wrote to each other after leaving the Palace; we didn't even have a farewell party; there was no contact. It was just the end of one part of one's life and the beginning of the next. Looking back I realise now what a wonderful experience it all was and I shall always be very grateful for what turned out to be the most important part of my education. In my case at least, it was certainly better than what followed.'

The Princess herself had no reservations about wanting to get away from the Palace schoolroom and into the mainstream of life at a public school. She had always been aware of the fact that Miss Peebles doted on Prince Charles and when he went away to Cheam, something went out of her life. There were many occasions when Princess Anne was treated, if not badly, then with a severity that was perhaps a little unwarranted, simply because Miss Peebles felt that with Prince Charles gone, anyone else was 'second best'.

Prince Charles returned his governess's affection in full measure, and couldn't wait to get back to Buckingham Palace to tell her all about the latest happenings at Cheam, and receiving every sympathy when he explained that things were not always going as he wished. When Miss Peebles was found dead in her room at the Palace two years later, Prince Charles was inconsolable, but perhaps the emotion Princess Anne felt was guilt over the fact that she and her first teacher had not always got along.

Going away to school also meant that for the first time, she would be mixing with girls of her own age who had not been specially chosen. Through no fault of their own Caroline Hamilton and Susan Babington-Smith had become associated with a period in the Princess's life which she was anxious to put behind her, and she looked forward to the challenge of Benenden.

Nothing she had experienced before in her short life had prepared her for the shock to her system that was to follow when she first entered the communal life of a girls' boarding school.

Chapter 4

1963 – BENENDEN SCHOOL FOR GIRLS

Princess Anne celebrated her thirteenth birthday as she had celebrated nearly all the ones before, with her family at Balmoral. But this was to be a significant milestone in the young Princess's life because a few weeks later she was to leave the comfort and security of living her year in the various royal residences, surrounded by willing servants to carry out every wish and cosseted from the outside world by governesses, tutors and friends who had been specially chosen because they were 'suitable'. She was to become a boarder at a girls' school in Kent, where she would be required to wear school uniform at all times and where she would share a dormitory with three other girls.

Benenden in Kent was the school chosen and the Headmistress, Miss Elizabeth Clarke, now retired and living in a delightful cottage just a few miles away from the school, explained how the decision was made known to her. 'I received an invitation to lunch at Windsor Castle and realising it was not because of my scintillating convers-ation and sparkling personality, I guessed it might have something to do with education,' she says. 'When I arrived at the castle there was just the family, the Queen, the Duke of Edinburgh, Princess Anne and myself. But far from being a formal, uncomfortable occa-sion it turned out to be a pleasant, easy meal of the sort that one might have enjoyed with the parents of any other girl who was being thought of as a prospective pupil.' Several days later Miss Clarke received a telephone call from the Queen informing her that it had been decided to send Princess Anne to Benenden if she was acceptable.

To get into the school, girls normally take an entrance examination, but Princess Anne was excused this formality because, as Miss Clarke explained, she then spoke to the Princess's tutors at Buckingham Palace and they satisfied her that her new student was up to the required standard.

'It was important,' says Miss Clarke, 'because if she had not been at the same level as the other girls coming in it would have been unfair to the school and we would not have been doing her any favours by making an exception. Anyway the problem didn't arise. I was confident that she would be perfectly capable of coping with the work and subsequently of course this was found to be the case.'

Benenden is situated in the High Weald of Kent near the small town of Cranbrook. The house itself is a large rambling mock-tudor mansion built in the 1860s and one of its most illustrious owners has been the former newspaper proprietor, Viscount Rothermere. It is set in 200 acres of parkland dotted with giant chestnut trees and copper beeches and its most striking feature, an avenue of lime trees. Benenden School moved there from its original location in nearby Bromley just a year after the school was founded in 1923, and when Princess Anne first went there, the fees were £525 a year.

On September 20th, 1963, there were sixty new girls going to Benenden and they were nearly all accompanied by their mothers to see them safely settled in. Princess Anne was no exception. She and the Queen had travelled down overnight from Balmoral in the Royal Train, and on the morning of the opening day of term they drove the short distance from London.

The royal car was late arriving at the school and this caused a certain amount of concern to the 300 pupils and 40 staff who had lined the drive into Benenden to welcome their new colleague. Royal motor cars do not break down, and if punctuality is the virtue of kings it is also one of the basic rules applying to the life of the Queen. She is always on time.

Many years later Miss Clarke tells the story of the reason for the late arrival. Apparently Princess Anne was so nervous at the prospect of starting her new life that she had been physically sick on the way, hence the delay. But there was no sign of any nerves or discomfort when the Princess met the staff and several of the pupils before going to her new home to see her room-mates. She did not inform the matron or make any excuses about feeling 'off-colour'. Miss Clarke found out only by accident some time later and she gave the details as an early example of the extraordinary discipline Princess Anne had learned even at that age.

The welcoming ceremony was the only occasion when Princess Anne was treated as 'Royal'. From then on she became just another new girl and was expected to 'muck in' like the rest.

Her Royal Highness had been enrolled into the Lower Fifth and assigned to Guldeford House, one of the six at Benenden. Her first dormitory was Magnolia, a room shared by four girls on the first floor of the main house. Benenden has a very pleasant and practical way of looking after new girls. They are allocated a 'housemother' – a girl of around the same age who has been at the school for a couple of terms and so is able to help the newcomer settle in and find her way around. Every school has its own peculiar traditions and unwritten rules and Benenden was no different in this respect. They even have their own language. For example, it's no use asking for the 'ladies' or the 'loo' or the 'toilet' at Benenden – their word for it is the 'honk'. If a girl wants one of her friends to join her she will invite her to 'have a side' – if she feels like one of the iced buns that are allowed twice a week, she will ask for a 'greased rat'. All harmless enough little peculiarities, but important for the newcomer to learn if she is quickly to feel at ease.

Princess Anne's 'housemother' was Elizabeth Somershield who showed the newest member of Magnolia dormitory where to put her clothes, how to make her bed and generally gave a lot of help in showing her the layout of what must have seemed, in those early days, a very confusing way of life. Some years after she had left Benenden I asked Princess Anne what her first impression had been. She told me: 'The continuous noise and the fact that everywhere you turned there were so many people.' All very understandable when you consider that until she went to Benenden she had spent her life surrounded by adults in an atmosphere of peace and tranquillity in the vast and silent palaces which had been her home for thirteen years.

But Princess Anne adapted to school life in a remarkably short time and the school authorities quite sensibly decided that in order to make sure that nobody would have the opportunity of cultivating and perhaps exploiting a relationship with their royal pupil, they would give all the girls a chance to 'get it out of their systems'. There was already in existence a seating plan at the dining tables in Guldeford House which involved rotation every few days so that in a very short time every girl in the house had sat with Princess Anne, and no one could claim a 'special relationship'. Indeed as Princess Anne herself said years later, 'fortunately children aren't so stupid. They accept people for what they are rather quicker than adults do. They have no preconceived ideas, because how could they have? They accepted people for what they were and they had other things to do, so they weren't bothered.' Nevertheless, friendships were made and some have lasted ever since; in fact one of the Princess's earliest acquaintances at Benenden was Victoria Legge-Bourke who has remained one of her friends, and is now one of the Ladies-in-Waiting.

Princess Anne quickly settled into the routine at her new school and no special instructions were given regarding her education or her lifestyle. Like the other girls she wore a dark blue tunic in winter and for out of doors a blue hooded cape lined with orange, the colour of Guldeford House. In the summer, dresses of a lighter shade of blue were worn, and these were described as the very 'depths' of fashion by most of the girls.

It was a world of timetables, school magazines, games and activities which began when the bell went at 7 a.m. for the girls to get up. The first duty of the day was to make the beds – each girl making her own before going to breakfast at 7.40. Immediately after the first meal of the day there was a compulsory run down the drive and back again to give the girls some exercise before settling down to the morning's lessons. Princess Anne took English, Maths, History, French, Geography, Latin, Biology, Chemistry, Physics, Art, Gym, Handiwork and Dancing. The day was divided up between formal lessons in the morning and games in the afternoon – lacrosse in the winter and swimming and tennis in the summer. Supper was taken at 7.20 in the evening and afterwards there was a relaxation period when the girls could listen to their own records – they were allowed to bring their record collections, but could listen to them only in the music room, record players were forbidden in the dormitories. It was a full twelve-hour day with strict timetables and firm discipline throughout. The girls took it in turns to lay the tables for the evening meals, and at weekends when the domestic staff were off duty, they also washed and dried the dishes – and nobody, royal or otherwise, was excused.

Visits outside the school were rare and then only under strict supervision. The girls never went to the cinema but they did have occasional concerts and film shows inside the school. They were allowed out at weekends if their parents had agreed, but only if the school knew where they were going and with whom.

One of the reasons why Benenden had been thought to be suitable for Princess Anne was that it was located near the Sussex home of Lord Rupert Nevill and his wife, Lady Anne, who were old friends of the Queen and the Duke of Edinburgh, and so it would be convenient for the Princess to make weekend visits. In the early months at Benenden Princess Anne did make use of the nearness of the Nevills' home for weekends, but eventually as she became more and more involved with the everyday life of the school, she stayed behind with the rest of her friends, and weekends were spent on one or other of the many activities they found occupied nearly all their spare moments.

Elizabeth Clarke recalls two incidents which she feels were significant in Princess Anne's early experiences at school. The first occurred within a couple of days of the new term. At Benenden the housemistresses usually end the day by reading aloud to the girls, after which one shakes hands before going to bed. The reading takes place in a comfortable sitting room in which there are a variety of chairs, sofas and cushions. There is an unwritten rule that the more senior the girl, the better the seat. Princess Anne, unaware of the system, arrived one evening and promptly sat in one of the most comfortable chairs in the room. When another girl, senior to her, turned up, she told Princess Anne to vacate the chair, which to her credit, she did without any fuss. Being royal did not mean being able to jump the queue, and Princess Anne accepted the rebuke. However, as she moved up the ladder of seniority she made sure that she occupied her rightful place. She neither asked for nor received any more, or any less, than any other girl.

The other incident Miss Clarke remembers concerns the handling of money. At the beginning of each term parents would allocate a certain sum which the housemistress would hand over to the girls in instalments as weekly pocket money. On Thursdays and Saturdays they would be allowed to go into the nearby village shop for small items of stationery, sweets and chocolates. Miss Clarke recalls that in the first few weeks of Princess Anne's time at Benenden she became aware that Her Royal Highness had very little idea of the value of money and was comparatively unused to making purchases on her own behalf. This was one of the few ways in which she was different from the other girls, but she soon came to terms with the practicalities of school life and in other ways she was able to show an example to her fellow boarders. Princess Anne gives a different version of the 'pocket money' story. She says: 'We had £2 a term and as I had been brought up by a careful Scots nanny to appreciate the value of money, I simply didn't spend my allotment. I've always been mean with money and as far as I know, I was the only girl in the school who had any left at the end of term.'

Princess Anne was not the only royal princess to join Benenden in the autumn of 1963. In fact there were three others, two being the granddaughters of Emperor Haile Selassie of Ethiopia and the third Princess Basma of Jordan. The parents of the Ethiopian princesses visited the school on one occasion when they joined the girls for evening worship in the chapel. As the girls were leaving after service Princess Anne saw the royal couple sitting in a distant pew. It would have been easy for her to have left with the rest of the congregation, but realising that she had met the Prince and Princess at Buckingham Palace some years earlier Princess Anne went over and reintroduced herself and chatted sociably for a few minutes. Miss Clarke says this was a perfect demonstration of her good manners and previous training, even as a thirteen-year-old.

As part of her early upbringing the Princess had learned the intricacies of Scottish highland dancing – one of the Queen Mother's favourite pastimes – and at Benenden she soon became one of the leaders of the Dancing Club. Pottery was another of the pleasures which she enjoyed in the company of her classmates, but the greatest joy for Princess Anne was the weekly session at the nearby stables at Moat House. The riding school was organised by Mrs. Hatton-Hall, better known in the equestrian world as Cherry Kendall, who in the early 1950s was a highly successful competitor at three day events and horse trials throughout the country, even to the standard of Badminton – then, as now, the premier event of the equestrian world. Princess Anne had, of course, shown early promise and enthusiasm from the days when she and Prince Charles shared their first pony, but the fact that she was allowed to stable her own horse, High Jinks, at Moat House within a few months of arriving at Benenden, meant that she was able to concentrate a great deal from the age of thirteen, on the sport that was to become one of the most important parts of her life later.

But riding, at that time, was allocated only a small amount of time during the school term and there were plenty of other activities requiring the attention of a young boarder. Benenden has twelve tennis courts and the Princess played herself into the Guldeford House Pairs where she did extremely well.

She obviously was suited to the robust competitiveness of lacrosse, and eventually ended up in the school's second team, where in her final year she became a member of the team which won the finals of the All England tournament. Princess Anne was as pleased as any other player at the success of the team but she also had a special private reason for jubilation – she had managed to play throughout the entire tournament without being recognised as the Queen's daughter, something which would never happen these days.

Academically Princess Anne had an easy time at Benenden. She excelled in the subjects she liked, such as English, History and Geography, and simply didn't bother with those that did not hold her interest. Basic arithmetic held few fears for her but the higher reaches of geometric problems and algebraic equations defeated her, mainly because if she did not grasp a subject immediately she lost interest, and the teachers at the school did not push her as perhaps they might have any other girl.

Her inquisitive nature found a natural outlet in chemistry and some of the experiments she conducted, on occasion with more imagination than skill, filled her teachers with alarm, and her fellow pupils with amusement.

Princess Anne was a naturally bright pupil and her upbringing and background had given her the confidence to ask questions on any and every subject. It there was something she wanted to know she simply asked someone. Whereas other girls might be hesitant to ask in case it displayed their own lack of knowledge, she did not have the same reservations; indeed, this is a trait shared by all the Royal Family even today. If they want to know something – they ask.

Her headmistress felt, however, that the Princess needed a firm hand as far as her studies were concerned, and there were occasions when she had to be given a bit of a jolt in one or two subjects. The Queen and the Duke of Edinburgh were anxious to be kept informed of their daughter's progress and at times they would turn up at the school, usually being driven in an unmarked, unobtrusive Ford, to discuss Princess Anne's development.

One of the reasons why the Queen and the Duke of Edinburgh had decided to send Princess Anne away to school was that they wanted her to experience the rough and tumble of life away from the protective claustrophobia of Buckingham Palace, and in this respect Benenden achieved the target it had been set. After the initial shock of being immersed in the noise and clatter that characterizes any boarding school, Princess Anne threw herself wholeheartedly into the many varied activities and her royal upbringing, which had instilled in her the need to fill every minute of every hour, combined with her natural toughness, enabled her to come to terms with the school's regime much faster than her brother had been able to do when he first went to Cheam.

This does not mean that the early days at Benenden were completely without problems for the young princess. She suffered from the normal nervous habits any young girl in a new environment might experience, such as biting her nails and 'first night' nerves when she appeared in a number of school productions, including the comic role of Alfred in Christopher Fry's *The Boy and the Cart*, which was performed on Speech Day, with the Queen in the audience – so the school regarded the play quite unofficially as a 'Royal Command Performance'. Princess Anne also threw herself heart and soul into the part of a drunken sailor in *Dido and Aeneas* and was realistically sea-sick as one of the animals on board Noah's Ark in the school production of *The Flood*. She also had to remember all the time to be on her guard if anyone enquired too closely about her family. The other girls would chatter on about their parents and brothers and sisters, but it was noticeable that Princess Anne said very little about her 'home life'. Parents were allowed to visit the school two or three times a term, and the Queen and Prince Philip took advantage of these facilities whenever they could, arriving unofficially and parking like all the other parents somewhere along the drive that leads to the school.

But of course her parents were not just like all the others. They were always accompanied by detectives, and police forces along their route were always notified that the royal car was passing through. Princess Anne might well have been accepted by the other girls as just 'Anne' – which is what they called her, the staff referring to her as Princess Anne – but she, too, had a bodyguard who lived just outside the main gates and she was never allowed outside the school without him being in the background. Her weekends might mean lunch with the Archbishop of Canterbury or a visit to Fairlawns, the Queen Mother's stables nearby, so even though every effort was made, by her and for her, to become 'one of the girls', nobody was in any doubt that in their midst was a young lady of immensely privileged position.

Another occasional visitor to the school during term time was Commander Perkins, the Queen's private detective. The police officers detailed to protect Princess Anne were the responsibility of Mr. Perkins and he would frequently turn up at Benenden to check that all was well. But even though his visits were unannounced he was always expected because, just as the school authorities were advised by police stations on the route when the Queen or the Duke were coming, they performed the same service when Commander Perkins was in the area. Miss Clarke recalls there was one definite advantage to having a detective around the place: 'Whenever we played an away match against another school or Princess Anne was included in an outside expedition, it was very convenient to have that extra car around.'

Princess Anne has always been an uninhibited, forthright person with tremendous enthusiasms, and by the time she had spent two years at Benenden she had tried just about every activity there was to try and joined every club and society the school had to offer. She was eventually persuaded to narrow her pastimes down a little, but was willing to lend a hand with any venture that was projected. All the time she was a prolific writer of letters to her parents, telling them of the latest escapades, and the Queen had to be reassured when she learnt that her daughter had joined in a rock-climbing expedition and been seen scaling a fifty-foot cliff as part of an 'outward bound' adventure scheme. The exercise was not repeated.

During the five years the Princess spent at Benenden there were occasions when she was required to attend her parents at royal events, and whenever this happened Miss Clarke would be asked to excuse her royal pupil for the day. It didn't happen very frequently, but the headmistress was determined that it was only on the most important occasions that permission should be granted. She remembers receiving a letter requesting that Princess Anne be relieved from school duties for what was regarded as a matter not related to her position within the Royal Family. Miss Clarke wrote to the Queen, pointing out respectfully but firmly that if Princess Anne were to be granted an exeat on this occasion it would create a precedent and set Her Royal Highness apart in a way Her Majesty had indicated she did not wish. There was immediate understanding on the part of the Queen and the request was withdrawn.

Miss Clarke felt it was important at the time: 'If I had given her special leave for this exeat it would have given her a special privilege not granted to her fellows. Others would have felt hard done by if I had allowed this; they could hardly have done so for the Opening of Parliament. The creation of precedents has to be watched in school life.'

Elizabeth Clarke had been given instructions on how she should get in touch with the Palace in case of emergency, and throughout the entire period of Princess Anne's stay at Benenden there was only one occasion when this was necessary. The Princess had been riding Jiminy, one of the sixty horses kept at Moat House stables, when she lost her balance and broke a bone in her little finger. It wasn't a major accident of course, but one that required the Princess to be driven to London for the finger to be set.

The emergency procedure was carried out according to instructions and much later that evening the Queen herself telephoned Miss Clarke for a personal report on the incident.

Miss Clarke recalls there were occasions when the Queen would telephone personally to discuss some aspect of her daughter's education. 'Once one had got over the initial shock of realising that it really was the Queen on the telephone, the conversation became very informal and relaxed.' On one Sunday evening Her Majesty arrived at Benenden for a visit and during the conversation in the Headmistress's study, Miss Clarke mentioned something about the examination system with which another parent would have been familiar. The Queen however was perplexed and gently reminded her: 'You'll have to explain that a little more fully, Miss Clarke, remember I never went to school.'

The other girls at Benenden accepted Princess Anne into their midst almost from the beginning and she went on all the outside expeditions with her class without ever being recognised, including a school trip to Davos in Switzerland for a winter sports vacation.

During the school holidays the Princess was allowed to accept invitations to join family parties arranged by her school friends' parents, and when the Queen and the Duke gave a party at Windsor Castle a large contingent of Benenden girls was included on the guest list.

Throughout her years at Benenden, Princess Anne was being prepared gradually for her introduction to public life. Her parents included her on a number of official duties, some of which could not have delighted the young Princess more, especially on occasions like the Opening Ceremony of the Commonwealth Games at Kingston, Jamaica, in 1966. Prince Philip performed the Opening Ceremony and decided it would be an ideal opportunity for Princess Anne to meet some of the world's leading young athletes. It also gave the young Princess an opportunity for a quick stop-over in New York where, for once, she was not recognised by the press. Four years later she was to find on a visit to Washington as a guest of President Nixon that the American press corps expected 'instant headlines' and total accessibility at all times, even to a princess. But this was all very much in the future when she arrived in Kingston to join the festivities that were part of the Commonwealth Games.

Prince Charles joined the party from his school in Australia, and the social gatherings and informal parties they attended provided a fund of stories for the girls back at Benenden when the new term began. There were a number of barbecues on the beautiful Jamaican beaches where the Princess was usually among the last to leave, no matter how late the hour. She threw herself enthusiastically into the spirit of the Games, enjoying the company of some of the fittest and most individualistic athletes in the world.

Royal weddings also claimed a share of the Princess's time in the mid-1960s and there was great excitement when she was invited to act as bridesmaid at the Duke and Duchess of Kent's wedding in Westminster Abbey and again in Athens in the same role for Princess Anne-Marie of Denmark, for her marriage to King Constantine.

But as the Princess moved up through the school towards her final years the pressures of forthcoming examinations and the added responsibility of being a member of the upper school brought with them a new sense of duty. She became a monitor, which meant that she was responsible for the welfare of a number of young girls and Miss Clarke, who had kept a watchful eye on her royal pupil without the Princess being aware of it, noticed that she adopted a compassionate yet firm stance when dealing with the thirteen and fourteen year olds in her care. 'She was a good monitor and later a very capable Captain of House who was able to exert her authority in a natural manner without being aggressive. If there was any failing at all it was possibly her impatience. She was extremely quick to grasp things herself and couldn't understand anyone else not being able to do so.'

The final term at Benenden was spent in the company of all the other Upper Sixth Formers, cramming furiously for her 'A' level examinations. She had already decided not to apply for entrance to university. As she put it: 'I think it's a highly overrated pastime.' But when the results were published it was found that she could have gained a place if she had wished. She secured passes in History and Geography which would have been sufficient for most universities outside Oxford and Cambridge.

Miss Clarke had no doubt at all about her ability to have continued her education. 'If you look at the acceptance levels for university entrance in 1968 I think you'll find that she could easily have gone if she had wanted to. The fact that she didn't apply was her own decision as far as I am aware, but I believe that academically she could have gained a place on her own merits.'

In June 1968, Princess Anne left Benenden after spending five years of living like any other girl of her age. What had she learnt? In the first place she had learnt to cope with the pressures of a life spent controlled by bells and timetables. She had experienced the give and take needed to exist with 300 of her fellows. The school had made sure she attended lectures and seminars on social work and environmental care. Sport had played an important part in her life and the hours spent at Moat House were to stand her in good stead when she embarked on the next stage of her equestrian career. She had learnt how some of the most simple pleasures of life were not to be taken for granted and she had made one or two friendships that were to remain with her. The school had taught her about the careers that other girls were to follow and as a Prefect she had learnt that authority and position bring with them a need for a sense of responsibility.

As far as the school itself was concerned, having Princess Anne as a pupil was something of a double-edged sword. It was considered a great honour for the Queen's only daughter to be taught at Benenden, but it had also attracted tremendous attention to the school, not always of the kind they might have sought. Perhaps the words of her Headmistress Elizabeth Clarke best sum up the overall feeling: 'She made a definite contribution to the school and I think we all felt that in spite of the press and television attention, which we could have done without, the benefits of having her here outweighed any disadvantages. I hope we in our turn contributed something to her training for her future role in public life.'

Chapter 5

PUBLIC LIFE – THE BEGINNING

The year 1968 was to prove an exciting and significant year for Princess Anne. Following her 'A'-level examinations, she had to undergo what for many people is a much more nerve-wracking event. She took her driving test in April and passed first time, with flying colours. In fact as far as Princess Anne was concerned, the test was really little more than a formality. Not that she was given any concessions because of her royal birth, but because, like all the other royal children, she had been driving over the private roads of Windsor, Balmoral and Sandringham ever since she was tall enough to handle a car. So whereas most youngsters have to wait until their seventeenth birthday before venturing on the roads behind the wheel of the family car under the watchful eye of a driving instructor, by the time the Princess was old enough to drive legally, she already had years of experience behind her.

Still it was another hurdle to be cleared and she was thankful when the ordeal was over. But she had to wait another six months before she was able to drive a car of her own. In October of that year the Queen and the Duke gave her a blue Rover 2000 saloon as a belated present for her eighteenth birthday the previous August.

So the year progressed with her school days coming to an end and the young adult princess getting ready to begin her role in public life the following year. There were still one or two things that had to be taken care of by way of preparation, and one of them was that Princess Anne herself decided it was time for her to learn to speak French properly. She had received a grounding in the basics of the language from an early age, with the tutors at Buckingham Palace and later at Benenden, but like most students there was a world of difference between knowing the grammar and sentence construction of a foreign language as taught at that time in schools and actually being able to converse fluently.

The Princess made enquiries about various language courses and finally decided on the world famous Berlitz school which has its London headquarters just off Oxford Street. The school uses the 'saturation' or 'total immersion' technique which involves lessons for up to ten hours a day in which the only language spoken is the one being taught. In addition every pupil is given a substantial amount of homework to complete every evening after classes end and much of the work is carried out on a one-to-one basis, with the tutor and pupil talking together with no chance of the escape which might be possible if there were other people in the class. The course lasts for six weeks and at the end of it Berlitz guarantee that you will be able to conduct a reasonable conversation in whatever language you have chosen. The course is very expensive and it was typical of Princess Anne that once she had made up her mind to get to grips with French, she went at it in her own determined fashion. As she described the process: 'It was a necessary evil and I wanted to get it over with.'

Perhaps also one of the other main reasons why she decided to go through with the 'total immersion' course was that she was aware of the linguistic abilities of other members of her family, particularly her father who is fluent in several languages including French and German. At the end of the six-week course Princess Anne succeeded in satisfying her tutors at Berlitz but even more significantly, after a gruelling hour-long conversation, the Duke of Edinburgh expressed himself well pleased. Lady Susan Hussey, who was acting as companion to the Princess, used to meet her for lunch and they would visit many of the shops in Oxford Street, trying on dresses and never being recognised. Then Princess Anne would return to her studies and Lady Susan, who looks back on these days as among the happiest she spent with Her Royal Highness, would go back to Buckingham Palace where she was a Lady-in-Waiting to the Queen.

But the year was not all study and books. It was also the year of the Mexico Olympics, and the British Equestrian Team of Derek Allhusen, Jane Bullen, Richard Meade and Ben Jones was accompanied by a young reserve rider, Mark Phillips. The British quartet, in the most atrocious conditions ever experienced in an Olympic Games, conquered all and emerged as the Gold Medal winners. Mark Phillips didn't get a ride in Mexico but he was an official member of the team.

Back in London at the end of the Games, Whitbread's, the famous brewers, who had long been supporters of equestrian sports, invited the entire team to a celebration party at their renowned cellars near Ludgate Circus in London. Her Majesty Queen Elizabeth, the Queen Mother was to be the guest of honour and she decided to take Princess Anne with her, knowing her granddaughter's passion for anything to do with horses.

This was apparently the first time that the Princess and her future husband met and by all accounts it was a pleasant informal evening with Mark making up the numbers at the small dinner party which followed in a London club. As most of the company were people who had grown up around horses there are no prizes for guessing what was the main topic of conversation. But as a first meeting, although it was congenial and relaxed, there was no apparent 'immediate chemistry' between the two young riders, apart from a mutual interest in eventing. Mark Phillips returned to Sandhurst where he was still an officer cadet and the Princess continued with her preparations for 1969 which was to be the first year of her solo public duties.

Princess Anne was very much aware of her own public image right from the start, and as soon as she left Benenden she set about putting right those aspects of her appearance she felt could be improved. The stodgy food at school had left her a few pounds overweight, so she went on a course of diet and exercise that soon brought her weight and measurements back to the slim proportions she has retained ever since. Even after the birth of her two children, the Princess immediately worked to get her figure back, each time with complete success.

Make-up and hair were the next things that needed attention, so she went to the best professional beautician she could find to learn how to apply her own make-up to best effect. Princess Anne realised that hers was going to be a busy life and that there would not always be time to go to a beauty parlour or attend a hairdresser, or even to have one on call at the Palace, so she decided that she would look after her hair herself.

This she has done ever since with the styles changing to suit the occasion and her moods. One day she will wear her hair piled high in an elegant, upswept fashion, the next day, or even later the same day, she may let it hang down her back, swinging loosely. She is acknowledged by other members of the family to have the best head of hair of any of the royal ladies and she still washes and sets it herself.

In 1982 when the Princess was on a tour of Africa on behalf of The Save the Children Fund, she was visiting Victoria Falls when a number of photographers asked her to move closer to the Falls so that they could get a more dramatic picture. She had already posed at several other locations and she refused this final request: not because she was nervous of being too close to the Falls or because she was being uncooperative. It was simply that at this point she was wearing a plastic head cover to protect her hair which she didn't want to remove. What appeared to be stubbornness was, in fact, merely female good sense on the part of a Princess who does her own hair.

This was still the age of the so-called 'Swinging 60s' in Britain and

London was the fashion centre of the world. A young Welsh designer named Mary Quant had introduced the mini-skirt and no fashion-conscious teenager would have dreamt of wearing a dress that wasn't at least four inches above the knee.

Princess Anne was no exception; she browsed among the trendy boutiques of the King's Road, Chelsea, and some of the large chain stores where she indulged her tastes for high leather boots and mini-dresses. There were no restrictions placed on her by her parents as far as dress went, even though most of the other members of the Royal Family were, and are, most conservative in their choice of clothes. Her wardrobe at Buckingham Palace quickly became filled with the latest fashions, and if she had started by following the trends set by the pace-setters of the 'Swinging 60s', she soon became an innovator herself. No sooner did she appear wearing one of her wide-brimmed 'cowboy' hats than every eighteen year old in the country followed suit. When pictures of the young princess appeared showing her wearing a mini skirt, it was a sign that the outfit had been given royal approval and sales blossomed. Even the Queen and Princess Margaret, who had influenced her niece's choice of clothes, to a certain extent, began to wear their dresses a little shorter; not perhaps exactly mini-length but at least as near knee length as royal decorum would allow.

Outwardly then she was very much a progressive young lady of the time and in other ways her tastes reflected the styles of the era. The Liverpool sound of the Beatles was very much in its heyday and all their records were played on the sophisticated stereo system that was installed in the joint sitting room at Buckingham Palace shared by the Princess and Prince Charles. She still enjoys pop music a great deal and when she is driving her own car between Gatcombe and Buckingham Palace, the journeys are often enlivened by the latest hits of Abba or Elton John booming out of the cassette player.

It seemed to be an ideal life for Princess Anne. She had all the comforts money could buy; she had passed her driving test and been given her own car; the pressures of school examinations were over for good, and she had started out in the sport that was to take up so much of her time. She was in no hurry to move on to the next phase of her life, in fact at that time she would have been quite content to have continued in the same mould, with most of her time being taken up with trying to reach her goal as an international horsewoman. But the Royal Family these days doesn't work like that. As soon as one reaches the age of maturity one is expected to take on certain responsibilities and enter public life, and for Princess Anne it came sooner rather than later.

On March 1st every year a member of the Royal Family is present at the St. David's Day Parade of the Welsh Guards, in order to present leeks, the traditional Welsh emblem, to members of the regiment. In 1969 the Duke of Edinburgh had agreed to take part in the ceremony but at almost the last minute it was found that owing to a conflict of engagements he could not attend and so Princess Anne was asked if she would take on the duty in his place.

In retrospect it does seem hardly credible that it was a last-minute decision, because royal diaries simply do not get 'overbooked'. Each member of the family has a highly efficient office who plan engagements many months ahead, and it's a rare occasion indeed for anything to go wrong. This was probably just a novel and thoughtful way for the Queen and the Duke to introduce their daughter into public life without giving her too long to think about it and perhaps become a little nervous.

There was certainly no need to worry. The Princess carried out her first solo public engagement with an assurance and confidence which far belied her years and she found that she enjoyed the attention being focussed on her. Until then she had always stood in the shadow of her parents; this was the first time when all eyes were on her, and the salutes and greetings were directed at her alone. It was a heady experience for an eighteen year old and the guardsmen at Pirbright in Surrey were delighted to be inspected by someone quite near their own ages, wearing a mini-skirt and a wide-brimmed green hat. As an introduction to public life it was an unqualified success and boded well for the future relationships which the Princess would establish with other branches of the armed forces.

This was also the period when the Princess caused something of a stir by dancing with the cast and other members of the audience on the stage at the end of the nude musical *Hair*. But Her Royal Highness herself appeared fully clothed in a purple trouser suit.

After the initial engagement, Princess Anne's diary filled up rapidly. She toured part of the Rover car factory in Birmingham, with particular interest as she was then driving one of their products, and visited the newly opened National Equestrian Centre at Kenilworth in Warwickshire before going to Wembley Stadium to attend her first F.A. Cup Final, an experience she found slightly beyond her comprehension. The sight and sound of a hundred thousand fans in full volume was, as she put it, 'somewhat astonishing'.

This was also the year when the Princess launched her first ship. Again the occasion came about as a result of one of her parents, this time the Queen, having to withdraw, and Princess Anne stepped in to substitute when the S.S. *Northumbria*, at that time the biggest tanker ever to be built in Britain, was launched at the Tyneside yard of Swan Hunter. Launchings are events when things are quite likely to go wrong and it takes an experienced person to carry out the duties properly, especially if the champagne bottle won't break or the button releasing the ship from the launch platform gets stuck. But the Princess, acting as if she had been doing it all her life, not only successfully launched the massive tanker smoothly, but enchanted the 600 guests at the tea party which followed.

In all during that first year of public duties Princess Anne carried out thirty engagements on her own. At many of them she was required to deliver a speech and she set a precedent which has been followed in her case ever since. She wrote all her own speeches. I asked her about the practice of writing speeches, realising that other members of the Royal Family of necessity have many of their speeches written for them. She replied: 'I do all my own and always have done. Writing a speech is always a chore even if you know what you are talking about, although obviously it's easier if you do.'

Princess Anne tends to play down the amount of homework she does before going to an engagement, but the evidence is there that she has always taken her job very seriously, and the very fact that she makes it look as if there is nothing to it shows just how professional she is.

At the end of that first year of public duties the Princess emerged as an attractive, enthusiastic personality and a welcome addition to the close circle of Royals who are available to be of assistance to the Queen in her ever-increasing number of commitments. Towards the end of the year she began an association with the armed forces which was eventually to encompass all the Services, but there's little doubt that, as with any first love, her first regiment in the British Army was to occupy a special niche of its own – a relationship that would grow stronger year by year.

In common with all the other members of the Royal Family, Princess Anne now has strong connections with the Services. The Queen, of course, is Commander-in-Chief of all the Services, the Army, Navy and Royal Air Force, but her immediate family have responsibilities to individual ships, regiments and squadrons which over the years have grown into warm, personal relationships. Princess Anne is associated with the Royal Navy as Chief Commandant of the Women's Royal Naval Service (WRNS) and with the Army as Colonel-in-Chief of five regiments: the 14th/20th King's Hussars, the Worcestershire and Sherwood Foresters, the Royal Signals, the 8th Canadian Hussars and, the most recent, the Royal Scots, whose last Colonel-in-Chief was the late Princess Royal. Princess Anne also became Commandant-in-Chief of the Women's Transport Service (FANY's) in 1981.

As with other bodies with which she is associated, Her Royal Highness does not lightly accept a Service appointment. She takes her responsibilities very seriously and before agreeing to become Colonel-in-Chief or Commandant she researches the organisation thoroughly and finds out everything she can before she commits herself. Once she does accept an appointment she throws herself into it heart and soul with a dedication and enthusiasm second to none. Her earliest association with the Services began when she was appointed by Her Majesty to become Colonel-in-Chief of the 14th/20th King's Hussars, one of the most prestigious regiments of the British Army. Princess Anne was just nineteen years old when she joined this cavalry regiment of great distinction, the Battle Honours of which go back before the Napoleonic Wars.

The year 1969 was a year of great activity for the Royal Family with the most notable event taking place in August when Prince Charles was invested as Prince of Wales at Caernarvon Castle.

For Princess Anne, October was to be a month she would remember. This was the month chosen for her first official visit to Germany to meet the members of her first regiment. It was also a first for the regiment itself: Princess Anne was their first Colonel-in-Chief and as the then Commanding Officer, Lieutenant-Colonel J.M. Palmer recorded, 'To be the Princess's first regiment is a singular honour, and one which fills us with both pride and humility.'

The regiment was based in Paderborn, West Germany, and as, at that time, Princess Anne did not have a Lady-in-Waiting of her own, she was 'lent' one by her mother, the Queen. Lady Susan Hussey, an experienced Court attendant, was chosen and her helpful advice to both the Princess and her hosts, on what could have been a somewhat tricky assignment, proved to be invaluable. The only other member of Princess Anne's party was her personal detective, Inspector David Coleman, a pleasant, efficient police officer who sadly died of cancer a few years later, at a tragically early age.

As it was the first time that Princess Anne had been to Germany on an official visit, the regiment was determined that she would not forget it! Between 3 p.m. on Wednesday, when she arrived at R.A.F. Gutersloh, to 2.15 on Friday afternoon when she left, a total of seventeen engagements had been arranged, ranging from dances in the sergeants' and officers' messes, a coffee party with the soldiers' wives, a visit to the British families' school, and firing a Sterling sub-machine gun on the range, to watching a display of the regiment's tanks – an occasion she could not allow to pass without jumping into the driving seat herself for a high-speed drive.

Like all other cavalry regiments, the 14th/20th is now an armoured unit, with giant fifty-ton Chieftain tanks replacing the chargers of old, and the flamboyance of the former mounted troopers has carried over into the technological disciplines of the modern, twentieth-century Army, so Her Royal Highness was able to sample for herself one of the most fearsome weapons of modern warfare.

In spite of utilising many of the most up-to-date aspects of military life the regiment has retained a number of ancient customs and traditions, and at a regimental dinner given in her honour on the first night of her visit, Princess Anne was initiated into the regiment in a unique and colourful ceremony. One of the 'spoils of war' enjoyed by the 14th/20th is a solid silver chamberpot captured from its original owner Napoleon III in the early nineteenth century. On dining-in nights it is a tradition that the vessel is filled to the brim with champagne and then passed around the table with every officer taking a sip until it is empty. Regimental records show that on Thursday, October 30th, 1969, the ritual was carried out in fine form and the Colonel-in-Chief participated 'without a qualm'. If Princess Anne needed to, she won the hearts of every member of the regiment with this simple gesture and it's a mutual admiration society that has grown in intensity with each passing year. The 14th/20th Hussars regard themselves as being a Lancashire Regiment – that's where most of their recruiting takes place – and as such they have a strictly 'no nonsense' approach to things. They are not easily impressed, no matter what a person's rank might be, but once they decide to accept you, you are a friend for life, so when the young Princess showed them that she was truly one of them, they took to her immediately, and to a man; so it would be a foolish person indeed who was rash enough to speak disparagingly of her in the hearing of any member of the regiment. And this feeling of admiration, which amounts in some cases to near worship, is not confined to the officers' mess. It permeates the regiment down to the most junior trooper. I wonder how many barracks will admit to having photographs of the Colonel-in-Chief adorning the walls as 'pin-ups'.

The hierarchy of the regimental life in the British Army consists of what appears to be a number of contradictory items. For example, the Commanding Officer is usually a Lieutenant-Colonel; the Colonel of the Regiment is at present a General and the Colonel-in-Chief (not every regiment has one) is almost always a member of the Royal Family who has probably never previously served in the regiment.

When Princess Anne became Colonel-in-Chief of the 14th/20th King's Hussars, the Commanding Officer was Lieutenant-Colonel J. M. (Mike) Palmer. Now a Major-General, he has maintained his connection with the Royal Family through his appointment as Defence Services Secretary, with responsibilities for advising on the conduct of the Queen's affairs, and to a lesser extent, those of other members of the Royal Family, as far as they concern the three Services. He carries out these duties from an office in Buckingham Palace.

As Commanding Officer of the 14th/20th Hussars, Mike Palmer acted as host to Princess Anne on the first two visits that she made to Germany in 1969 and 1970. He and his wife, Jilly, occupied a pleasant but modest four-bedroomed house on the camp at Paderborn, where Princess Anne was to stay. The Palmers gladly vacated their own double bedroom for their guest, and moved to a room in the attic. The problem was there was only one bathroom in the house, so the hosts decided to use the facilities of next door where the regimental dentist lived. A story is told of how at 6 o'clock one cold morning Colonel Palmer decided to take his morning bath and, wrapped only in a towel, dashed the few yards between the houses – only to be apprehended by a vigilant and over-enthusiastic German detective who had been assigned by the civil authorities to guard the royal visitor. Just who was the most surprised and what happened next, has not been recorded!

Princess Anne, of course, was completely unaware of these happenings and indeed of the domestic arrangements that had been made to accommodate her. She was, however, fully aware of an incident during another visit which could have been embarrassing had not her sense of humour come to the rescue. The entire party, royal guest and her retinue, had attended another function, leaving the house fully locked and secure against their return. However, when they did eventually return to their quarters very late at night, it was found that no one had a key and they were all locked out. The initiative of Inspector Coleman saved the day – or night: he noticed an open window in a bathroom, promptly climbed a drainpipe – in evening dress – and let the remainder of the party in through the front door; to the relief of her hosts, Princess Anne saw the funny side of the situation. It's not very often that things go wrong on a royal tour; when they do, it provides welcome relief on occasion, especially when it doesn't upset the programme too much and nobody is made to feel uncomfortable.

This first visit to her first regiment was an outstanding success and Princess Anne made sure that she met as many people as possible. She toured every department and when she was preparing to drive a tank for the first time the Quartermaster's Stores were asked to provide a pair of denims for her to wear. This gave them the opportunity to designate themselves – entirely unofficially, of course – as By

Appointment – Suppliers of Finest Denim Cloth to H.R.H. The Princess Anne.

Since that first visit the Colonel-in-Chief has been to see her regiment at least once every year because as she says: 'I like to keep up with what's happening as they move around from place to place, and also because of the changes in personnel it's as important for them to see me, as it is for me to see them. I've long since passed the time when I inspect the troops simply for the sake of inspecting them. If there's a particular parade I will inspect them, and it is far easier to be seen by more people on a parade than it is moving around a crowded room.'

There is never any danger that Princess Anne could forget her first regiment for a moment. Mike Palmer made sure of that during her first visit when he guessed that somewhere in Britain there must be a vehicle bearing the registration number 1420 H. So he did what any Commanding Officer would have done by instructing his extremely efficient and competent Second-in-Command, Major Chris Ross, simply to locate and obtain the licence plate. The operation was carried out as a military exercise, and, with some help from the Crown Equerry, was brilliant in concept, preparation and execution. The number plate was located in the London Borough of Ealing where for some years it had adorned an electric milk float. Negotiations were conducted with the owner, the details of which were not asked for, nor revealed, and the distinctive number plate became the property of H.R.H. The Princess Anne. The Princess was delighted with the highly original present and the regiment was assured of a permanent reminder of their connection with Her Royal Highness.

During the same year Princess Anne was appointed Colonel-in-Chief of the Worcestershire and Sherwood Foresters Regiment on their amalgamation. This is a mechanised infantry regiment of the line whose motto is 'Firm' and whose soldiers are recruited from Worcestershire, Nottinghamshire and Derbyshire. They serve on rotation in West Germany and Northern Ireland, where they have suffered a number of fatalities over the years.

The Princess visits them at least once a year and presented new colours in 1981. They are not regarded as one of the glamorous regiments of the British Army and they are particularly pleased to have a member of the Royal Family as their Colonel-in-Chief. As their regimental secretary put it: 'It's a great morale booster, especially when Her Royal Highness meets the soldiers face to face on her walkabouts. She spends more time with the soldiers and their families than she does with the officers, and that always goes down well.'

Chapter 6

THE PRINCESS AND HORSES

If 1968 was to prove the year that Princess Anne was launched into her first round of public duties, it was also the year when she decided that eventing was the sport at which she wanted more than anything else to excel, and in typical fashion she set about finding the best person she could to help her in her quest.

She had already competed in a number of Pony Club events around Windsor with a certain amount of success. What was needed now was someone with the proper authority and knowledge to channel her enthusiasm and undoubted courage in the right direction. She had been riding, of course, almost since she was able to walk, and her courage had never been in doubt. Even when she took a bad fall and broke her nose it didn't put her off, and shortly after leaving King Edward VII Hospital for Officers in London she was back in the saddle anxious to make up for any lost time.

She had been encouraged in her ambitions by the Crown Equerry, Lt. Col. (now Sir) John Miller, the man who controls the Royal Mews and is himself a horseman of considerable note as a former member of the British three-day event team. Col. Miller was an important member of the Queen's Household with many duties, and although he turned up at most of the events the young Princess took part in and would continue to do so, his was a full-time job and he could neither spare the time for more instruction of the Princess nor did he feel qualified to specialise in the demanding world of three-day event coaching. The requirement was for a thorough professional: one who would not be influenced by the royal 'qualifications' of the Princess and who would not be overawed by being in the presence of the Sovereign's daughter. Fortunately the equestrian world is peopled by those who tend to judge solely on performance and respect has to be earned, whether it be a farmer's son or an earl's daughter, even though there's an easy camaraderie among the competitors.

Princess Anne already knew several of the leading riders in Britain, but as an aspiring champion she was obviously not as yet accepted on equal terms by such as Richard Meade, Jane Bullen, Chris Collins and Mark Phillips. It's not that there is any particular snobbery among the upper echelons of the world of show jumping and eventing, it's simply that it is such a competitive business that those at the top fight harder to remain there and just do not have the time to notice anyone who is not an immediate threat.

There have been many theories about why Princess Anne chose the toughest of all equestrian sports on which to concentrate her ambitions. At that time eventing was a comparatively unknown sport, its participants being, for the main part, young men and women from a particular section of society who had grown up with horses in the rural counties of England. They were people who knew each other generally and who mixed socially, as well as on the field of competition. Public knowledge of the sport was negligible and even the world's leading three-day event at Badminton would only attract a few thousand spectators. A far cry from these days when a quarter of a million supporters will pay to watch Badminton or Burghley, and millions more will be glued to their television sets for the entire three days. Those who run the sport freely admit that the present popularity of eventing is due, to a great extent, to the success of one woman – Princess Anne – though she of course would disclaim this. But this was all very much in the future, when in 1968–9 she set about making it almost a full-time occupation.

Some observers have said that Princess Anne chose eventing because she had always been the 'loner' of the Royal Family and she enjoyed doing something as an individual rather than as part of a team. Others claim that it was because she was fed up with always being number two to her brother, Prince Charles, and was determined to show that she could be number one in her own right. My own favourite theory is that she chose eventing because, as someone who had ridden from an early age, there was a natural progression to this more advanced form of equestrianism and it was the one sport where, if she succeeded, it would be because of her own ability and not because of the accident of her birth. As she herself put it: 'When I'm approaching a water-jump with dozens of photographers waiting for me to fall in, and hundreds of spectators wondering what's going to happen next, the horse is just about the only one who doesn't know I am royal.' Although she has been dumped into the lake only once at Badminton and in fact only four times in fifteen years at other courses, her observation that horses are no respecters of rank has been proved right time and time again; either you can ride a horse or you cannot.

Mrs. Alison Oliver had already achieved distinction as one of the most brilliant and successful riding instructors in the country by the time Princess Anne was ready to take her career a step further. She also had the reputation of being a most independent woman and was known not to waste her time with pupils simply because they could afford the fees. If the talent was not there Mrs. Oliver did not want to know and quickly got rid of anyone she felt would not benefit from her tuition or was not prepared to work as hard as she did herself. When it was first suggested that she take on Princess Anne as a pupil she did not jump at the chance immediately as might have been expected. She was anxious to find out what sort of potential there was in the young Princess before committing herself. The initial call to Mrs. Oliver came from Col. Miller; he knew she was the sort of teacher who would get the best out of Princess Anne and he telephoned to get her reaction. Alison Oliver recalls that instead of asking to meet the Princess immediately, she wanted to find out more about the horses she would ride, so Col. Miller sent one of his own mounts, Blue Star, to the stables. This was the son of one of his Olympic horses, Stella, who had been ridden into seventh place in Helsinki in 1952. However, the horse was found to be technically unsound and Mrs. Oliver sent him back. His brother then made the journey to Warfield and he showed enormous potential. He was given to Princess Anne and so began her association with her first leading event horse – Purple Star.

Princess Anne then drove herself to the Oliver stables at Brookfield Farm in Buckinghamshire to be 'looked over'. She was under no illusions about the reasons for the visit; she knew Mrs. Oliver's reputation and in fact it was partly for this reason Mrs. Oliver was chosen in the first place. It was a case of mutual 'sizing up'. Princess Anne knew that she would have to be accepted on her own merits and Alison Oliver wanted to be sure that the Princess would accept the disciplines that were needed if she was to get to the top.

The initial meeting proved to be successful and Alison Oliver agreed enthusiastically to become the Princess's trainer. For the young rider there started the daily round of non-stop training that would take her to the top in a remarkably short time. It could have been too great a task, as the beginning of the association with Alison Oliver coincided with the Princess's introduction to public duties. But her determination to succeed, meant that she was able to do three hours a day at the stables, if she left Buckingham Palace at seven o'clock in the morning, and still be back in time to change and leave for an engagement by lunchtime. If there was still time left after the day's official duties were over, it was back into her Rover 2000 and heading west for Buckinghamshire where she could usually be found until the early evening.

It's a tribute to her ability and eagerness to learn that she so quickly got to grips with the essentials of eventing: dressage, cross country and show jumping. But in addition there were the basic skills of schooling and training her horses to be learnt. Although the Princess was a more than adequate horsewoman already, all she had been required to do in the past was actually ride the horses. Now she had the additional responsibility for schooling and training, and even though her horse, Doublet, was to prove himself one of the best event horses in the world in a short while, like his rider he was a complete novice when he first went to Brookfield Farm Stables. So it was a busy time, to say the least, but the harder the Princess was pushed by Alison Oliver the more she seemed to thrive.

Three day events are considered to be the ultimate test for horse and rider. The first stage is dressage, a phase which is designed to test the rider's skill in controlling his mount without commands by word of mouth, and the horse's sense of obedience and suppleness. Next comes the gruelling speed and endurance test, which is popularly known as the cross-country section, where the horses have to complete a circuit of several miles within a given time limit, at the same time clearing a large number of fixed obstacles of varying degrees of difficulty, and then, on the final day, there is the show-jumping phase, which does not in any way compare with the fences encountered in the world of show jumping proper, but is really a test of the horse's fitness after the trials of the previous day's cross country. Most eventers agree that competitions are won and lost on the speed and endurance test, but if there are several riders who are close at the start of the final day, it can mean an exciting finish.

Princess Anne's programme and development were carefully planned from the beginning. She had three fine horses in Doublet, Purple Star and the most recent acquisition, Royal Ocean, an Irish thoroughbred standing at 16.2 hands, and she had the determination to work and work until she satisfied herself and, more importantly, Alison Oliver.

Mrs. Oliver now lives in a charming farmhouse in a tiny village in Oxfordshire, with pride of place in the drawing room going to a delightful photograph of a young Princess Anne enclosed in a blue leather frame and signed personally by the subject. Alison Oliver told me that once it had been agreed that Princess Anne would join her, the first problem to get resolved was how the Princess should be addressed. 'It would have been impossible for me to keep shouting instructions all the time if I had had to remember to say Your Royal Highness every time,' she recalls. Princess Anne herself came up with the only answer: 'Call me Anne,' she said, 'that's what they did at school.' So Anne it was and Anne it has remained ever since.

Mrs. Oliver says that she had never before taught a pupil who had such dedication. She was anxious to learn and there was no aspect of horsemanship that she didn't want to know about. 'There were a number of other young riders around at the time and Princess Anne mucked in with them completely. Everyone was aware, of course, of who she was – it was impossible to forget – but I cannot remember a single occasion when she reminded us that she was a princess, or a single occasion when she used her position to refuse an unpleasant task.' At the end of a hard day's work most of the youngsters would repair to the Olivers' kitchen to drink coffee from heavy mugs and gossip about the latest goings on in the equestrian world. The Princess would always join them and she was an avid listener to the latest stories.

I asked Alison Oliver if she recognized immediately the talent of her royal pupil. She hesitated before replying: 'I knew there was something there right from the start, but I didn't think, at the beginning, that she would become a champion as quickly as she did. No one could have foreseen her rapid rise to fame at that time.'

Doublet was being brought along quietly in the early days of 1969 but it was her Irish horse, Royal Ocean, that Princess Anne rode in the Windsor Horse Trials at the end of April. Mrs. Oliver had decided that section D of the Novices Trials would be the right competition. By coincidence Mark Phillips on Great Ovation was also riding in the same section. Princess Anne finished in the lead over the twenty-six other starters and her victory caused a certain amount of adverse criticism from the non-equestrian press who had started to take an interest in her career. They claimed that because Windsor was her home course she had an unfair advantage over the other competitors. In fact she had not ridden the course for more than a year, and, of course, the other riders were not in the least concerned. But it did show that the Princess was going to have to get used to being sniped at by the press, and it was particularly irksome that it was the gossip columnists and self-appointed 'Royal watchers' among the journalists who were usually trying to provoke trouble, while the serious equestrian correspondents concentrated on the technical aspects of her performance and only criticised her, as they did the other riders, on her ability as a horsewoman.

So for the Princess it was a busy and exciting year, travelling up and down the country with Alison Oliver, from their base near Ascot to horse trials at Eridge, Taplow, Wylye, where Lady Hugh Russell, who had been severely injured in a hunting accident, terrified competitors and spectators alike by driving madly around the course in her specially adapted mini-moke vehicle. Then came Powderham Castle in Devon, up to Warwickshire to Stoneleigh Abbey, then on to Stokechurch, Tweseldown and Chatsworth, the home of the Duke and Duchess of Devonshire.

It was an exhilarating time and Alison Oliver recalls that even though they were concentrating a great deal on each individual performance, analysing all the faults and trying, time and time again, to reach perfection, it wasn't all work and no play. Princess Anne began to include the Olivers – husband Alan, of course, had been an extremely successful show-jumper in his own right – in a number of social engagements at Buckingham Palace and Windsor Castle. It was a new world for them and Mrs. Oliver explained: 'We were seeing places and meeting people which, a few years before, would have been absolutely impossible.'

By this time people throughout the equestrian world were beginning to take Princess Anne's riding career seriously. What had previously been good-natured tolerance towards the Queen's only daughter as she pursued what many thought was merely a diverting hobby, turned to considerable respect as her determination to succeed became reflected in the increasing success she was achieving in trials throughout the country.

The success continued during 1970 and the relationship between rider and trainer became even closer. By this time Alison Oliver had taken on an assistant at her stables so that she was able to concentrate almost solely on Princess Anne, and in a remarkably short time they were to become a formidable team.

Doublet had by now become the number one horse in the royal partnership and the first major event for which they tried to qualify was the Badminton Three Day Event trials in April, 1971, a competition which attracts riders not only from Great Britain, but also from the U.S.A., Canada, Australia and Europe.

A month before Badminton was held it was announced that Princess Anne had qualified and she would ride in the world's premier three day event. Alison Oliver says she and Princess Anne realized that a great many people thought they were being over-ambitious and few expected the Princess and Doublet to complete the testing cross-country course on the second day, over thirty-one obstacles ranging from tree trunks, solid walls and cunningly constructed traps, to the ever waiting depths of the lake, where even the most experienced riders had been known to take a ducking.

In addition to the course itself there were also forty-seven of the world's leading riders to contend with, and none of them was going to give an inch to their newest rival – royal princess or not. Among the competitors were the World Champion, Mary Gordon-Watson, who would, some years later, go on to become the first lady jockey in Britain; plus Olympic riders Richard Meade and Mark Phillips, with intense pressure coming from Lorna Sutherland, Debbie West and Hazel Booth, all three day eventers of tremendous experience and world-class ability.

When the day arrived the Queen, the Duke of Edinburgh, the Queen Mother and Princess Margaret all turned up to support the Princess. Badminton had long been a royal occasion and the Duke of Beaufort, as Master of the Horse, was well used to acting as host to the Royal Party every April. This time it really was a full house because when the news of Princess Anne's qualification became known, her three brothers, Charles, Andrew and Edward, all turned up to swell the ranks of the Royal Family.

Princess Anne could not have made a better start. At the end of the first day's dressage stage she was in the lead. While the rest of the Royal Party enjoyed the splendour of Badminton House's magnificent dining room, downstairs in the old kitchens the Princess and Alison Oliver were eating with the stable lads and planning how they would attack the daunting cross-country section the following day. Overnight torrential rain had turned Badminton into a quagmire when the time came for the Princess to ride the course. Twelve years later Alison Oliver recalled the round saying 'she rode the course in a way which I can only describe as innocent. There was a delight to her riding which was fresh and enthusiastic which was absolutely rare in competition at that level. She appeared to be enjoying herself all the way around and she was a joy to watch. Even though she was ambitious even at that stage, there wasn't apparent the some-times bitter single-mindedness that characterizes so many of the world's leading sportsmen.'

At the end of the second day Princess Anne and Doublet were in fourth place, a magnificent performance by any standards, but even more so for a young rider in her first major international event.

When she entered the arena for the show-jumping finale to the trials on Sunday it was virtually impossible for Princess Anne to win; it would have meant the three riders in front of her all having to hit three fences or more. As it turned out she herself had one of them down and the end result was that she finished in fifth place; the winner being Mark Phillips on his horse, Great Ovation. It was an amazing performance from a rider who had entered senior competition so recently and Alison Oliver's eyes still shine as she remembers the feeling of jubilation they shared. What was important to them was that they should be satisfied with the way in which Princess Anne rode. They were aware of the scepticism with which certain members of the establishment greeted the entry, and for them it was

13. The christening of Princess Anne took place on 21st October, 1950, in the Music Room at Buckingham Palace, because the private chapel had been damaged by bombs during the war. The Duke of Edinburgh was given special leave from his ship, H.M.S. *Magpie*, to fly home for the ceremony.

14. Princess Anne's ninth birthday, 15th August, 1959, was spent with the rest of the Royal Family at Balmoral. Many years later the Princess was to say that her idea of a perfect holiday was still a few weeks spent with the rest of the family in Scotland. This birthday photograph, with one of the Queen's corgis, was taken at Windsor.

15. From an early age the Princess became a regular visitor to the Badminton Horse Trials. The nine-year-old enthusiast joined her great aunt, the Princess Royal, and the Duke of Beaufort before setting out to walk the course.

16. In May, 1960, Princess Margaret asked her niece to be chief bridesmaid when she married Welsh photographer Anthony Armstrong-Jones, who was later created Earl of Snowdon. Princess Anne acted as the senior of eight young attendants at the ceremony which was held in Westminster Abbey.

17. (*Above*) The blossoming teenager among the flowers in the gardens at Buckingham Palace. Princess Anne in the official photograph which was released on her sixteenth birthday. By this time the Princess had spent three years at Benenden School in Kent and was starting to show the poise and confidence which she would display in later years. Throughout the school years the Queen was anxious that her daughter should be left alone as much as possible to enjoy the normal pursuits of her fellow students. Only on official occasions did the Princess pose for photographers.

18. (*Above right*) The Trooping the Colour ceremony was the last formal engagement at which the Princess joined her parents before going away to school in the autumn of 1963. The Duke of Edinburgh always rides in the parade behind the Queen, and afterwards the Royal Family gathers on the balcony at Buckingham Palace to watch the traditional fly-past by aircraft of the Royal Air Force.

19. (*Above*) The State Opening of Parliament, 1967. The Princess is with the three most senior of the Queen's Ladies-in-Waiting: (*left to right*) The Countess of Euston, the Countess of Cromer and Mrs. (now Lady) Abel-Smith.

20. (*Left*) With a father like the Duke of Edinburgh, it was inevitable that Princess Anne would be introduced to outdoor sports at an early age. From almost as far back as she can remember the Princess has been able to sail, both dinghies and larger ocean-going yachts. Prince Philip taught his daughter how to furl sails and coil ropes on board *Bloodhound* which he had brought into Scottish waters so that they could use her during the long summer holidays, when they would go island-hopping. In fact, if Princess Anne had not become an international rider she would probably have ended up crewing for her father in yachting events.

21. (*Opposite, top*) In 1969 at a children's home in Scotland. The Princess has always had a marvellous rapport with children.

22. (*Opposite, bottom*) St. David's Day 1969 and the nineteen-year-old Princess carries out her first solo public engagement – presenting leeks to members of the Welsh Guards at Pirbright in Surrey.

23. (*Above*) The year 1969 also saw a British champion at Wimbledon as Ann Jones received her trophy.

24. The year 1971 was an outstanding one for British sport. Princess Anne had won the Individual title in the European Three Day Event Championships at Burghley and Jackie Stewart had become World Champion motor racing driver for the first time. Awards were heaped on the two sports personalities, including being voted Sportsman and Sportswoman of the year by the B.B.C. and by the Sportswriters' Association of Great Britain. When they attended one of the first presentation ceremonies, they found they had a great deal in common. From that date their friendship has grown to include their respective families.

as important to be accepted as a serious competitor as it was for the Princess to be highly placed. On all counts it was a complete vindication of their decision to enter Badminton and for the moment Princess Anne could do no wrong. The press, with no spectacular falls to photograph or other disasters to record, were unanimous in their enthusiasm for the Princess's courage and skill and observers were already speculating how far she could go. The European Championships were to follow in September and some were even looking as far ahead as the following year's Olympic Games which were to be held in Munich.

Both Princess Anne and Alison Oliver were aware that the early success could backfire; on the one hand it did focus attention on the Princess and bring to the notice of the leaders of the eventing world the fact that here was a new entrant for international honours; but also there was a danger that those selfsame leaders would harden their attitude, feeling that they were being pressured by the newspaper comments and the public assumption that Princess Anne was the new 'golden girl' of eventing. Nevertheless, within a month after Badminton, Princess Anne was told that she had been selected to ride at Burghley as an individual, but not as a member of the official team.

The selectors took the unusual step of issuing a public statement about their decision to exclude the Princess from the official team in the light of the enormous number of queries they were anticipating from the world's press:

The selectors were greatly impressed by Princess Anne's performance on Doublet at Badminton. However, since this was the first international competition for both of them, and in view of the very large number of experienced combinations available, it was not thought advisable to include Her Royal Highness in the shortlist from which the team will be chosen. But Great Britain will be allowed to enter approximately twelve individuals, in addition to the team, as the host nation. Princess Anne is being invited to fill one of these vacancies.

What it meant was that she had been accepted by the establishment as a competitor in her own right and she was able to continue her preparations for the European Championships secure in that knowledge.

Then in July something occurred which could have meant disaster. Princess Anne had to go into hospital to undergo surgery for the removal of an ovarian cyst. It's a fairly commonplace abdominal operation, but debilitating none the less. When Alison Oliver visited her in King Edward VII Hospital for Officers to commiserate, she was astonished to find the Princess sitting up in a chair already making plans to get fit in time for Burghley. Mrs. Oliver had been prepared to forget the European Championships for that year, but even she had reckoned without the determination of her Royal charge.

Princess Anne immediately went back to Balmoral where she spent the days leading up to her twenty-first birthday in taking long hikes and undergoing strenuous mountain climbing in order to regain her strength.

There was a brief respite on August 15th when a very special twenty-first birthday celebration was held on board the Royal Yacht *Britannia*. Mrs. Oliver was invited and the next day she and Princess Anne returned to Warfield to prepare for the Eridge Trials which were to be held the following week. So within four weeks of the operation, Princess Anne was back in the saddle with no apparent after effects.

Eridge proved to be another of the many horse trials in which the future husband-and-wife team would find themselves in close competition. Their respective positions changed with the dressage and show-jumping sections and then in the cross-country phase Princess Anne and Doublet parted company having jumped up out of the watersplash and over a big log.

The run-up to the European Championships was a testing period for the Princess and her trainer recalls that she wasn't always on her best behaviour. If a session had gone wrong she lashed out in all directions with her tongue and no one escaped if they were within earshot. Mrs. Oliver says: 'I warned everyone to keep out of her way if the signs were ominous and on more than one occasion I led her to a horsebox with instructions to stay there until she had cooled down.' Fortunately these were fairly rare happenings and the Princess is not one to sulk. Once she has got her temper out of her system it's back to normal very quickly and she does not bear grudges. This whole question of nervous tension is one that has plagued athletes and world-class performers of every description. Some sportsmen get physically sick before an event, others cannot eat for days leading up to a competition. These days some leading sports personalities use their talent as an excuse for the most appalling manners and there are still more who like to be left alone before a contest.

Before Burghley Princess Anne did not sleep for three nights and maybe it was the lack of rest that keyed her up to give the sporting performance of her life.

What happened during the four days between September 2nd and 5th, 1971 is now a matter of equestrian history. Princess Anne and Doublet went into an early lead on the first day and after the dressage section had been completed they were in first position with 41.5 penalty points. The most experienced rider in the official team, Richard Meade on The Poacher, was the only other British rider to get below 50 penalty points.

Princess Anne and Doublet went into the second day as leaders and they attacked the cross country fences like veterans. There were a couple of fences where, by taking a calculated risk, several seconds could be saved; Princess Anne, who had walked the course several times with her trainer, considered the risks worth taking and she returned the second fastest time of the day. In fact she was several seconds faster than any member of the official British team, Debbie West and the reigning champion, Mary Gordon-Watson, coming second and third. So as the Trials entered their third and final phase the British riders could not have been in a better position. Princess Anne was in individual first place and the British four were leading the rest of the world in the team event.

We have already mentioned that most three-day events are won and lost over the cross-country section and when Princess Anne entered the show-jumping phase on the Sunday afternoon she was in a virtually unassailable position. She could afford to have two fences down and still win, but nonetheless it was a tense atmosphere at the packed arena with both the Queen and the Duke of Edinburgh sitting in the stands waiting for their daughter to appear. The crowd was good-humoured but obviously impatient, wanting only to see Princess Anne. For a young rider of such relatively little experience at this level it was a nerve-wracking couple of hours. She stood quietly with Alison Oliver, outwardly calm but inside her stomach was in knots. At last her turn came and when she rode into the arena she was greeted by wild applause and even that, well-meaning as it was, could have had an adverse effect on Doublet but the little chestnut behaved as he had throughout the Trials, impeccably, and they set off for the first of the twelve fences that stood between Princess Anne and the European Crown.

There was a hush as the thousands of spectators silently willed Doublet over each obstacle and when they came to the last, by which time they were unbeatable, the vast crowd went wild and Princess Anne finished her clear round in a cacophony of sound so loud that even the announcer's voice coming over the public address system was lost.

Only three short years after she made her first appearance in a horse trial she was the European Champion, which meant in effect, World Champion at the time. The Queen presented the Raleigh Trophy, a gold medal and a cheque for £250, and with this single victory eventing became a sport known to millions throughout the world.

Alison Oliver and John Miller were the first to congratulate the Princess and when I interviewed her for B.B.C. television news a few minutes later she was delighted to acknowledge how much these two had contributed to her success. Princess Anne had shown a fearless outlook, ridden with supreme confidence and beaten the best in the world. The fact that every move she made, on and off the course, had been watched and noted by reporters and photographers, had made no difference at all to her performance. She had proved that when it came to the crunch she had the determination and the talent to succeed in a sport where money and position is no guarantee of victory.

For Alison Oliver it was the crowning moment of a brilliant career and the endless hours of training and schooling were forgotten as they celebrated. Yet already in the midst of the jubilation, they were thinking about the next obstacle to be overcome. Equestrian writers the following day were unanimous in their opinion that Princess Anne and Doublet must be included in the British team for the Olympic Games in Munich the following year.

When I spoke to the Princess about the possibility, it was obvious that she had thought about it even though she modestly said that the Games were a long way off and it was too soon to start planning that far ahead.

If Princess Anne had been the first to acknowledge her debt to Alison Oliver, the trainer herself was equally anxious to put the record straight about the partnership. 'People have given me credit for producing Doublet,' she says, 'but I could not have done it without Princess Anne's determination. What singles her out as a competitor is her burning desire to be in the winner's enclosure.'

That year Burghley was an overall triumph for British riders. Princess Anne's success had quite naturally attracted most of the attention of the television cameras and press photographers, but the official British team had also won the team event, something that was almost overlooked in the euphoria following the individual result. Debbie West had come second on Baccarat, Mary Gordon-Watson fourth on Cornishman V, Richard Meade fifth on The Poacher and Mark Phillips sixth on Great Ovation.

The fact that Princess Anne had beaten the reigning World Champion, the current winner of Badminton and an Olympic Gold Medallist, was not lost on either the British public or the sports journalists who soon began to heap awards on her.

She was named as B.B.C. Sports Personality of the Year and

received the trophy in a televised programme that was seen by millions of viewers to B.B.C. 1, who had voted for her. Then she was named by the *Daily Express* as Sportswoman of 1971, the Sportsman of the same year being racing driver Jackie Stewart who has since become one of the Princess's closest friends, and finally the hardbitten reporters whose task it was to follow sport throughout the world, voted her as their number one personality and she received the Sportswriters' Award.

Quite a number of people tried to jump on the publicity band-wagon and bask in the reflected glory surrounding the Princess. One of them, Harvey Smith, a leading show-jumper who had also tried his hand at all-in wrestling and pop singing in order to attract more attention, publicly attacked her performance saying 'In her own class she is the best there is, but that is nowhere near Olympic standards.' He went on to include most of the other competitors in three day eventing in his general condemnation, claiming that 'any fourth-rate professional show-jumper could enter any event and win it every time'. He may have had his tongue firmly in cheek at the time or he could have been referring to the show-jumping phase of eventing which everyone admits is not intended to be compared with show jumping in its purest form. Or he could simply have been doing it for publicity; if so, it was a huge success because the press took up the story with great glee.

Richard Meade took it upon himself to become Princess Anne's champion and publicly issued a challenge to Smith to ride against him at Badminton. The challenge was not accepted as far as the public knew, and what could have been an intriguing comparison between the two forms of equestrianism never took place.

Obviously the next big hurdle was the Olympic Games and Princess Anne and Alison Oliver were determined that they would put up a good show at Badminton the following April to consolidate their position and make sure of Olympic selection. Doublet was given every preparation and it was a bitter blow when just a week short of the Trials he broke down with a sprained tendon and he was withdrawn. So Princess Anne's hopes of an Olympic place were dashed for another four years, but there was consolation in the fact that another of the Queen's horses, Columbus, was coming along nicely and would subsequently replace Doublet as the Princess's partner, if only for a short while, before it was decided to ask Mark Phillips if he would like to take him on. The Princess rode Columbus in the defence of the Raleigh Trophy which she had won the previous year, but it was an unsatisfactory partnership and the horse clearly needed the muscles of a man to control his enormous strength.

So after Burghley in 1972 Mark Phillips became Columbus's jockey and Princess Anne began her association with another of the Queen's horses which was eventually to prove worthy of an Olympic place – Goodwill. The horse was a 16.2 brown gelding bought by the Queen from Trevor Banks on the advice of Alison Oliver, and Princess Anne began riding him after Burghley in 1972, with the object of entering Badminton the following April.

That year Badminton was to have all the ingredients of a Dick Francis thriller plot. Mark Phillips was attempting to set a new record by becoming the first man to win the Trials three times, on Great Ovation, and Princess Anne, after the frustrations and disappointments of the previous year, was seeking to re-establish herself on her new mount. In addition the speculation on a possible romance between the two riders had attracted the gossip writers and news reporters in even greater numbers than before.

As it happened, Badminton may well have been the decision point as far as getting married was concerned, but on the equestrian side there was a definite anti-climax. Great Ovation went lame and was withdrawn on the second day, denying Mark Phillips his third championship, for that year at least, but Princess Anne and Alison Oliver were satisfied, if not elated, at the performance of Goodwill, who finished in eighth place. It meant that if the problem with Doublet should prove to be more serious than it appeared at the time, there was every chance that Goodwill could replace him as the Princess's partner at the forthcoming European Championships which were to be held in Kiev the following September.

Within a month of Badminton the engagement was announced between the Princess and Mark Phillips and their joint efforts to prepare for Burghley and Kiev were carried out under the unrelenting glare of the world's press. By now the attention had grown to fever pitch and if they had been concerned by what had happened before they became engaged, it was nothing to what followed in the six months before they were married. There were arrangements to be made for the wedding, houses had to be viewed at Sandhurst where Mark was to be posted immediately after they returned from honeymoon, interviews with the press, radio and television, and all the while Princess Anne was uncertain which of her two horses was going to partner her when she defended her European title.

Doublet was given a final trial at Osberton where he was eliminated for refusals at one of the water jumps and it was obvious that he was never going to be fit to compete at Kiev, so Goodwill got his chance to be in the limelight.

A defending champion automatically attracts a great deal of attention, but when that champion is a Royal Princess who is about to get married, the spotlight burns with an even greater intensity. The presence of the Princess captured the imagination of the Russian people, even though they were not told officially who she was, and they were intrigued by the immaculate turn-out of the British team at the opening ceremony and during the dressage phase of the competition. The incongruity of the situation, which appeared to illustrate the difference between the old style aristocracy epitomised by the British and German teams in their formal dress, and the Russian spectators in their sober working clothes, was not lost on either the competitors or the watching reporters from the West.

The Princess finished the opening day in sixteenth place after the dressage phase and she returned to the hotel where she was staying with the rest of the team reasonably confident about the cross-country section to follow. She explained to reporters that she did not consider she was under great pressure because she was the reigning champion, as she was not partnering the same horse: 'I am not riding Doublet, so there is really no pressure.'

The cross-country course had been built some five miles outside Kiev and some experts claimed it was tougher than the Olympic course had been at Munich. Princess Anne's defence of her title was to end sharply and dramatically. The second fence on the cross-country course consisted of telegraph poles nailed together over a ditch, approached by a slippery, winding grass track descending from a hill. The spectators had obviously decided that this was where the most spectacular falls were going to be seen and hundreds of Ukrainians gathered on the hillside waiting for the inevitable.

By the time Princess Anne came to ride, Debbie West on Baccarat, one of the official British team, had had three refusals at the second fence and a number of other riders had been eliminated. Princess Anne recalls, 'I was told to jump it a different way from the way I had walked it – and got it wrong.' The Princess joined the list of casualties at fence number 2 and later she described how it felt. 'It was like hitting tarmac as far as I was concerned. I had never hit the ground as hard or as fast. The main impact was on the side of my leg and, when I got up, it was numb from mid-thigh to mid-calf; I couldn't feel a thing. I wasn't, at that stage, aware that there was anything wrong with my shoulder – but I couldn't walk – I could stand on one leg, that was about all. I didn't think I'd broken anything, but Goodwill looked completely stunned and I couldn't walk, so I decided there wasn't a great deal of point in going on. I was only riding as an individual, so there didn't seem to be a great deal of honour at stake.'

When Princess Anne got to her feet after the fall she received loud cheers and applause from the watching crowd who, throughout the day, were to see no fewer than thirty-five victims claimed by the now notorious fence. The Princess was worried about Goodwill and insisted on returning with him to the stables to see if he was all right before she would go back to the Moscow Hotel where she was staying. The doctor at the British Embassy gave her a check for broken bones. Dr. David Woodhead decided that something had gone but that an X-ray would be needed to show the full extent of the injury. The Princess remained in Kiev to witness her title going to the Russian rider, Alexander Yevdokimov, and then flew with the Duke of Edinburgh, who had been at the championships in his capacity as President of the International Equestrian Federation, to Balmoral. When X-rays had been taken, it was revealed that she had chipped a bone in her shoulder and almost dislocated her collar-bone. With her superb fitness she was soon on the mend, but a long-lasting result of the injury has meant a slight unevenness in her shoulder ever since.

The year 1974 was to prove to be one in which Doublet would ride in his last competition and some weeks later have to be put down. Princess Anne entered both her leading horses, Doublet and Good-will, for Badminton in April and Mark Phillips was again seeking his third title, riding Columbus. Doublet, who never again recovered his title-winning form of 1971, was retired after the steeplechase section, but Goodwill, who had finished the day in fifth place, jumped clear in the show-jumping phase, to finish a very creditable fourth. Mark Phillips on Columbus was unbeatable that year and he went on to take the title for the third time.

A few weeks later Alison Oliver was riding in Windsor Great Park with Princess Anne who was on Doublet. There had been no hint of the tragedy that was to come. Mrs. Oliver recalls that she was a half mile or so away from the Princess when she saw her come to an abrupt halt and dismount. 'I rode up to her and she was white-faced. She had heard the horse's leg break and realized immediately that there was little she could do.' They both waited while a vet was summoned to the scene with Doublet apparently unconcerned by the pain, grazing peacefully. The vet took one look at the horse and confirmed what they both had feared. There was nothing to be done. Doublet was painlessly put down and both Princess Anne and Alison Oliver knew that it was the end of a short but brilliant era.

Princess Anne was asked some time after the event what the loss of Doublet had meant to her. She replied: 'He was a rather difficult horse to get to know. He wasn't a particularly friendly horse. He was a rather aloof character and one rather admired him for it. But he wasn't a horse you could go and chat to.' Nevertheless she described the day he was put down as 'quite the most ghastly experience of my entire life.' Lady Susan Hussey recalls that 'I've never been so sorry for anyone in my life. She was inconsolable and completely shattered when I saw her later that day.'

The remainder of that year and the early part of 1975 were taken up with competitions at home and abroad including a short trip to the United States to compete in the Ledyard Three Day Event in which Captain Phillips was eliminated and Princess Anne finished in tenth place on Arthur of Troy. Goodwill had by now reached the premier position in Princess Anne's stable and when the official British team to compete in the European Championships at Lumuhlen in West Germany was announced, they were selected as part of the first all-female team, which was completed by Janet Hodgson on Larkspur, Sue Hatherly on Harley and Lucinda Prior-Palmer on Be Fair.

The *chef d'équipe* was Col. Bill Lithgow, the man who, as an instructor at Sandhurst, had arranged for officer cadet Mark Phillips to ride in his first Burghley Event. Colonel Bill remembers that there was no problem as far as he was concerned with having a member of the Royal Family in his charge for the first time. 'The problem was that they were all girls and one had to remember to moderate one's tone a little. Luckily I did have some moral support from Mike Tucker who had been invited to take part as an individual.' The ladies fully lived up to Col. Lithgow's expectations and their combined performances proved to be the most successful ever in these championships, Lucinda Prior-Palmer winning the individual Gold Medal, Princess Anne taking the Silver and in so doing becoming only the second woman in eventing history to achieve success in the European Championships on different horses, while the four riders together won the Team Silver Medal. Bill Lithgow returned to Britain full of praise for his team and they had killed off once and for all any suggestion that women are physically unsuited to the rough and tumble of international competition.

Obviously the main target for all the international riders in the world as 1976 approached was a place in the Olympic Games, which were to be held in Montreal. When the list of five 'probables' was announced, Anne and Mark became the first husband-and-wife team to be included on an Olympic shortlist, along with Richard Meade on Jacob Jones, Hugh Thomas on Playamar and Lucinda Prior-Palmer on Be Fair. Lucinda had undergone the traumatic experience of winning Badminton that year only to have her horse Wide Awake drop dead in the arena just a quarter of an hour after the Queen had presented the winning trophy.

When five riders are selected for four places there is bound to be one who is going to be disappointed and on this occasion it was Mark Phillips who was relegated to the position of reserve rider, as he had been in Mexico in 1968. He had, of course, already won his Olympic Gold Medal in Munich in 1972. If Mark Phillips was bitterly disappointed at not being selected to ride, he gave no hint of his frustration, concerning himself instead with supporting the rest of the team and devoting a great deal of his time to working with his wife. They flew to Canada with the rest of the squad, travelling economy class which raised no eyebrows among their team-mates, who would have expected nothing else, but the press, ever watchful for a headline, made much of the fact that Princess Anne was flying 'just like an ordinary person'.

They were even more amazed when the royal couple stayed in the Olympic Village in Bromont, using exactly the same accommodation as all the other athletes and queuing up for their meals at the self-service counter along with everyone else. If any attempt had been made to separate Princess Anne from the rest of the team and treat her any differently, she would have been the first to protest, and indeed she had made it perfectly clear that she was no different from any of the other competitors. If the officials had tried to make it so, she would have refused to comply with their arrangements.

As it was, she described the accommodation at Windsor Place, the aptly named Olympic Village, as 'excellent' and Col. Bill Lithgow, the team manager, said that 'all Her Royal Highness wanted was to be regarded as an ordinary member of the team, and that's exactly what she is.'

Security at the village was extremely heavy, not just because of the presence of a member of the Royal Family, but because of the tragedy at the previous Olympics in Munich, when a terrorist gang invaded the Israeli headquarters and killed eleven of the athletes.

When the time for the competition came around it must have been a particularly frustrating period for Mark Phillips, who just a few months earlier had seemed to have the pick of a number of sound horses in good form. Two of the British horses, Be Fair and Playamar, proved to be unfit and this resulted in the team being eliminated, leaving only Richard Meade and Princess Anne to ride for individual medals.

After the dressage stage, Richard Meade was twelfth on Jacob Jones, with Princess Anne in twenty-sixth place; not particularly encouraging, but a good round in the cross-country section could have meant either of them being among the leaders on the final day. As it was the second day proved to be a disaster. Hugh Thomas falling at the Lake ended up with Playamar lame and Lucinda Prior-Palmer, who had ridden magnificently clear on Be Fair, had the disappointment of finding her horse had slipped a tendon off his hock and for them the Olympic Games were over. Richard Meade calling on the experience and expertise that have made him one of the most consistent riders in the world went clear on Jacob Jones, but Princess Anne was another casualty, falling at the nineteenth.

It was a spectacular fall which left the Princess concussed and her mother and husband anxiously waiting when they heard the news over the public address system. The Princess was advised to retire as she was technically unconscious, but she refused to give up and remounted to complete the course, arriving at the finishing line in a daze. When Princess Anne had fallen at Kiev she had retired because, as she said, 'competing as an individual there was little honour at stake'; in Montreal she was aware, even in her concussed state, that she was riding for Britain, and as far as she was concerned there was no question of quitting.

The Princess was of course well out of the running for a medal, but she did complete the final show-jumping phase to finish in the twenty-fourth place with Richard Meade narrowly missing a Bronze Medal and coming in fourth.

For the Princess the Olympic Games had proved to be a true test of courage, determination and stamina. She had said earlier that being on the short list was an achievement, to get into the squad was another achievement and actually to ride in the Olympics was 'really something'. So as far as her personal ambitions were concerned she must have been satisfied to a large extent. But competition at this level is all about winning and no doubt she and her husband returned to Britain reflecting on what might have been.

Of course the 1976 Olympic Games were not the end of the road for Princess Anne or Mark Phillips. He in particular was anxious to get back into top-class competition to achieve that single championship that always seemed to elude him – an Olympic, European or World title as an individual. In 1981 he was to add a fourth Badminton win to his impressive list of victories while the Princess was to search in vain for another Doublet or Goodwill. The market in world-class event horses is very restricted and the schooling of novices takes years before they are ready to appear in first-class competition.

Since 1976 neither the Princess nor her husband have reached the same heights again. In her case there have been two children born and she has taken on an increasing number of public duties with rarely a day in the working year being free of at least one engagement.

Riding in three day events requires a single-mindedness and dedication that few other amateur sports demand. It also needs a choice of good horses. No matter how skilled and determined the jockey is, if the horse isn't up to it there is nothing you can do. Princess Anne has never had a wide choice of the best horses apart from Doublet and Goodwill, and she has also had to cope with the attention of the world's press wherever she has ridden. That's something that world-class sportsmen have to contend with in almost every sport, so she has rarely complained about the cameramen and photographers being present when she is actually competing. The problems have arisen immediately before or after an event, when one is either collecting one's thoughts and concentrating on the test to come, or afterwards, feeling at the very least 'hot and bothered'. This is not a time when any sportsman or woman wants to answer questions or pose for photographs, but for her it is where the additional, unwelcome attention comes in, which other competitors do not, in the main, have to contend with.

Together with Alison Oliver in the late 1960s and early 1970s she showed what a tough, uncompromising competitor she can be. Her courage is taken as read, her determination has been demonstrated many times. Still only in her mid-thirties she could go on competing for years if the right horse comes along. Both Alison Oliver and Bill Lithgow believe that she could represent Britain again if a horse can be found to match her ability – after all Derek Allhusen won his Olympic Gold Medal when he was fifty-three.

Chapter 7

THE ENGAGEMENT

During the Spring Bank Holiday of 1973 I was on duty as a reporter in the newsroom of B.B.C. Television in London. It was a quiet period as far as news was concerned and on the Whit Monday I was invited to lunch on board a houseboat moored alongside Cheyne Walk in Chelsea, the home of a colleague, Martin Bell, now B.B.C. Washington correspondent.

It was a brilliant spring day and we sat outside on deck watching the river traffic when, as nearly always happens on occasions like that, the telephone interrupted the peaceful interlude. I was needed back at base.

When I arrived in Shepherd's Bush I was told by the duty editor that something was happening up at Balmoral and that I should get up there as soon as possible and find out what was going on. Remember, there had been rumours and denials of a royal romance for months, so if it had not been a particularly quiet newsday we would not have pursued the story to that extent. However, off I went with my camera crew to fly to Aberdeen, the nearest airport to Balmoral, not quite knowing what I was going to do when I got there. We checked into a hotel in Ballater, the tiny market town alongside the royal estate, in which nearly every shop bears the distinction of being able to display the Royal Warrant, and then drove the six miles to Balmoral itself.

This part of Scotland was enjoying an unseasonably warm May and there were a number of holiday-makers around the gates to the estate hoping for a glimpse of a member of the Royal Family. I sent my name in via the lodgekeeper and eventually a member of the Household came out to talk to me. He asked what I wanted and I replied that there was a great deal of speculation about Princess Anne and Lieutenant Phillips and was there anything we could be told regarding an announcement of an engagement. After a great deal of hesitation and telephoning between the lodge and somewhere inside I was told to drive a few miles inside the estate, past Balmoral Castle itself, to Craigowan House, which was normally used by the Queen's Private Secretary when the Royal Family is in residence. (Now the Prince and Princess of Wales use it.) At the house I met Squadron Leader (now Sir) David Checketts, the Prince of Wales's Private

Secretary, who told me who was at the house at that time. The party included the Prince of Wales who had flown from the West Indies where his ship was based, on a flying, thirty-six hour visit, Captain Nicholas Soames, his Equerry, Princess Anne with her Lady-in-Waiting, Rowena Brassey, (who was to be present at the attempted kidnapping in the Mall a year later), and Lieutenant Phillips. The Queen and the Duke of Edinburgh were also staying on the estate but were not at Craigowan that afternoon.

David Checketts told me that there were no members of the Palace Press Office present and that if there were to be an announcement it would have to come from Buckingham Palace. I asked for permission to bring my cameraman inside the gates so that I could film a report about what I had just been told. This was granted and I was then told confidentially that there *would* be a betrothal, but the timing had not yet been decided.

I filmed two reports, one of which stated quite baldly the facts about who was at Balmoral, and the other said that an engagement would take place.

We rushed these reports to the B.B.C. studios in Aberdeen for transmission that evening on the national news, but I had spoken to the duty editor in London to warn him that only the first report should be used unless there was an announcement from Buckingham Palace in the meantime. Shortly before six o'clock that night the official announcement came and we were able to give the news exclusively from Balmoral. Then events moved with a speed that took the breath away. Princess Anne and her fiancé arrived at Aberdeen on board the Royal Train for the overnight journey to London. The announcement of the engagement was timed so that Mark could travel on the train with Princess Anne; prior to this the only commoners permitted to use this most exclusive mode of transport were Lords Lieutenant on official business for the Queen. The announcement came before Lieutenant Phillips set foot on the train. He had arrived at Balmoral from his regimental base in Germany driving his B.M.W. touring car, but the security problems which the police forces would have faced if he had driven back to London would have been insurmountable in the short time available, so perhaps the Palace was persuaded to make the official announcement sooner than they would have wished, in order to comply with this rather delicate matter of Court etiquette.

The Princess and her fiancé arrived at Aberdeen station to find that the news had spread like wildfire and there were hundreds of well-wishers waiting to offer congratulations to the young couple. The Princess was dressed in a tweed suit and she paused before getting on the train to show her engagement ring for the first time. It was a solitary sapphire set in diamonds on a band of Welsh gold. Meanwhile Prince Charles had also left Balmoral to return to his ship in the West Indies – in order to be present at the engagement he had made a weekend round trip of 16,000 miles.

I had been instructed by my editor to fly back to London as soon as possible because Princess Anne and Mark had agreed to be interviewed for television the following morning. After driving through the night from Aberdeen to Glasgow I caught an early flight to Heathrow and went straight to Buckingham Palace. There were dense crowds waiting outside the railings and as I drove to the Privy Purse entrance – the one on the right as you look at the Palace from the Mall – the Band of the Welsh Guards were playing on the forecourt one of the hit tunes of the day – 'Congratulations'.

The interview was to be filmed by both the B.B.C. and I.T.N. and Reginald Bosanquet and I were escorted to the rear terrace of the Palace by Ronald Allison, the Queen's Press Secretary. Once the cameras had been set up, Princess Anne and Lieutenant Phillips came out to join us and we began. It was Mark's first experience of television as far as I am aware and he was obviously a little hesitant over some of the questions. Princess Anne, though, was in great form and took control from the word go. She explained how difficult it had been to keep their relationship a secret for the six weeks since they decided to become engaged, at a party held at Windsor during the Easter weekend.

Lieutenant Phillips had flown from Germany and asked his future father-in-law formally for his daughter's hand. At the Palace we asked him how he felt when he spoke to the Duke of Edinburgh. He replied, 'Petrified – but he was very good to me.' Reginald Bosanquet asked if the Duke had enquired about his prospects. Mark got out of that one with a smile and a laugh.

Princess Anne said they hadn't finally decided when and where to get married but it would 'probably be sometime in mid-November'. When I asked where the ceremony would take place she said 'It's difficult, there are lots of things to be taken into account.' When we questioned her about when they realised their relationship was serious she replied 'I suppose after the Badminton Trials in April.' In fact, the couple confirmed some time later that Mark had proposed to Princess Anne on the final Sunday evening of Badminton. They had returned to his parents' home at Great Somerford and it was while they were out walking that he asked her to marry him.

When the television interview was over both sets of parents, the Queen and the Duke of Edinburgh and Major Peter Phillips and Mrs.

Phillips came out onto the Palace lawns to be photographed with the newly engaged couple, and afterwards we were invited back into the Palace to drink their health.

The speculation, rumours and denials which had been circulating for months were ended by the official Court Circular published on 30th May, 1973. It read:

It is with the greatest pleasure that the Queen and the Duke of Edinburgh announce the betrothal of their beloved daughter The Princess Anne to Lieutenant Mark Phillips The Queen's Dragoon Guards, son of Major and Mrs. Peter Phillips.

After a private family lunch at Buckingham Palace on the day of the engagement – it was Major and Mrs. Phillips's first introduction to their future daughter-in-law's parents – Princess Anne left by helicopter to fulfil a longstanding date at a Riding for the Disabled function in Buckinghamshire, and Mark returned to his unit at Bergen-Belsen in Germany before being posted later in the year as an instructor at Sandhurst.

For Princess Anne it meant an end to the non-stop worldwide interest in who she was going to marry. Even as a schoolgirl of fourteen her name had been linked with that of Prince Carl Gustav of Sweden who was four years her senior, merely on the strength of their meeting at the wedding of ex-King Constantine of Greece. It only needed the Princess to be seen with anybody in public for that person's name to be added to the list of prospective bridegrooms, and once she had left Benenden every eligible young man who escorted her became the focus of attention from an ever attentive press.

Prince Friedrich von Schwartenberg was an early contender – according to the press; another was Brian Alexander, son of one of Britain's most famous soldiers, Field Marshal Earl Alexander of Tunis. Then came David Penn, a former pageboy to the Queen, whose only claim to this sort of attention was the fact that he had spent a ten-day skiing holiday in the French Alps with the Princess and a group of her friends. Two polo players who were friends of Prince Charles also appeared on the list of would-be suitors, Sandy Harper and Captain Andrew Parker-Bowles, who as a member of the Household Cavalry was frequently invited to parties and functions at Buckingham Palace and Windsor. Andrew Parker-Bowles is now married and living in Gloucestershire within a few miles of both Princess Anne at Gatcombe and the Prince of Wales at Highgrove.

However, the one most fancied by the world's press as a prospective husband was Richard Meade. He had all the qualities Princess Anne admired in a man. First and foremost he was, and is, arguably the finest horseman Britain has ever produced. He has won every major title the equestrian world has to offer and as a double Olympic Gold Medallist, had reached the very pinnacle of his chosen sport when he met the young and at that time aspiring royal competitor. So there was an immediate affinity between two people who shared a passion for horses. In addition he was extremely good-looking, with impeccable manners and came from an excellent family with land in Monmouthshire. There was however one major obstacle, and that was the fact that Meade was twelve years older than the Princess. Many royal observers felt that the age gap was too wide for Richard Meade to be seriously considered as a prospective husband – something which eight years later was not even raised when Princess Anne's brother Charles took a bride exactly twelve years younger.

Anne and Mark were drawn together by their mutual love for horses and in fact they first met at a party in London given for the British equestrian team at the Olympic Games in Mexico in 1968. They met fairly frequently if spasmodically after that, usually at horse trials which were held up and down the country. It wasn't difficult to arrange meetings and to make sure that they were both included in the same house parties. On one occasion Princess Anne was staying with Lady Anne Fitzalan-Howard, eldest daughter of the Duke of Norfolk at her home in Yorkshire. By coincidence, a relative of the family who also had a house on the estate at Everingham had invited her nephew for a few days. His name? Mark Phillips.

This sort of 'coincidence' was to recur until 1971 when the press first began to notice that the couple were being seen together more and more. In April of that year they both competed at Badminton, Princess Anne coming fifth and Mark winning it for the first time, something which must have done his 'prospects' a power of good in Princess Anne's eyes. She is an intensely competitive rider and when someone beats her in fair contest she is full of admiration.

Later that same year in September, Mark was again to beat Princess Anne. It was at Tweseldown when he came third and she was one place behind. That was also the month when Princess Anne came into her own, winning the Raleigh Trophy and the individual gold medal at the European Three Day Event Championships at Burghley.

In October she went to Cirencester Horse Trials to watch Mark competing and it was while they were there that he was invited to Buckingham Palace to attend the Silver Wedding Anniversary celebrations of the Queen and the Duke of Edinburgh. By this time the Queen must have been aware that Lieutenant Phillips was not just another of her daughter's friends, but someone rather special. The following month Princess Anne made her first visit to the home of Mark's parents at Great Somerford in Wiltshire, a journey she would make with increasing frequency in the following months, driving herself down the M4 motorway, accompanied only by her detective. In the week before Christmas, when the Royal Family moves to Windsor, Princess Anne spent most of the time with Mark. They attended hunt dances together and she stayed the night on one occasion as a guest of the Phillips's at Great Somerford.

Christmas was spent with the family at Windsor, but as soon as they moved to Sandringham for the traditional New Year festivities, Mark was invited to join the house party. It was his first formal introduction to the Royal Family and he stayed at Sandringham for three days before leaving for Harwich to sail to the Hook of Holland *en route* to rejoin his regiment in Germany. Princess Anne drove him to the ship and it was on the quayside that the rumours which had been circulating for months were finally confirmed for the waiting press. She kissed him goodbye – for the first time in public – an eagle-eyed car park attendant saw them and told a number of reporters, and the royal watchers among the press said it confirmed what they had known all along: Anne and Mark were a pair.

The press interest, which had linked the two for nearly a year, intensified to near fever pitch. There was worldwide speculation about when the marriage would be announced; what sort of title would Mark be offered – it was then considered inconceivable that a husband to the Queen's only daughter should remain untitled, particularly as Princess Margaret's husband Anthony Armstrong-Jones had been created Earl of Snowdon following their marriage.

Both Princess Anne and Lieutenant Phillips insisted, however, in the face of all the publicity, that rumours of an engagement announcement were 'absolute nonsense'. The denials came fast and furious but their actions only served to add fuel to the fires. Princess Anne went to Ethiopia on public duties for The Save the Children Fund and when she returned in February she drove straight from the airport, ninety miles, to Great Somerford to be with Mark. A few days later Princess Anne herself denied there was any romance between them. She told a reporter: 'There is no romance. All we want to do is get on with training our horses in peace.'

The Palace Press Office also said it knew nothing of an engagement, but not in a deliberate attempt to mislead the press. It was simply that the family had decided it would be better not to inform the Press Office of their decision so that, at least for some weeks, the young couple could enjoy their happiness privately. Whether this was a valid reason for withholding information of vast public interest from senior members of the Household, depends on one's point of view. But one thing is perfectly clear: the Press Office could have been placed in an embarrassing position, while having to maintain a working relationship with those reporters and photographers whose job it was to keep their readers informed of royal events. As it was, Ronald Allison, who had been appointed Press Secretary to the Queen just three weeks before the engagement, did not issue any denials, but by then the damage had been done. The only 'official' denial ever actually given by Buckingham Palace came from the then Press Secretary, Robin Ludlow, at the end of January – some two and a half months before the actual engagement. Ludlow told John Knight of the *Sunday Mirror* that an engagement was not expected at that time, which was the literal truth. The journalist then wrote an article quoting this denial and was of course justifiably angry when the story eventually turned out to be wrong. The rest of Fleet Street continued to speculate about an engagement and did not follow up the 'denial' story.

There was one other reason why the engagement was kept secret for such a long time. Protocol demanded that before any public announcement was made Commonwealth Heads of State had to be informed officially as well as members of the British Government, the Archbishop of Canterbury and immediate relatives of Princess Anne and Lieutenant Phillips.

As soon as the announcement of the engagement became public, reactions poured in. Richard Meade, whose name had been linked with the Princess's some years earlier, said 'I am delighted for them both'; Mark's C.O., Lieutenant Colonel Maurice Johnston at the regimental depot in Germany was highly relieved that the secret was out. He had been one of the few 'outsiders' in the know from the beginning. As a subaltern, Mark had had formally to ask the permission of his Commanding Officer before he could get married. When Col. Johnston was asked for his reaction to the news he replied: 'I was completely in the picture from the beginning. It has certainly been a well-kept secret. Now it's official the regiment can share the joy and pride I have felt all these weeks.' The officers and men later toasted the happy couple in champagne and German beer and one of Mark's fellow subalterns joked 'Mark will be known from now on as The Princess's Own.'

From Paris, the Duchess of Windsor said that she had never met Mark but that she wished them 'all the happiness in the world'.

Mark's grandmother, Mrs. Evelyn Tiarks, said that she had not yet met the Princess but the family was very fond of her and 'it's quite a feather in the family's cap to have a member become engaged to a royal.'

Chapter 8

THE WEDDING

Mark Phillips was a very happy choice in every way. As the Queen's only daughter Princess Anne had had a great deal of attention focussed on her throughout her short lifetime and Mark, though totally unused to the sort of press coverage that he had attracted since his friendship and later courtship of Princess Anne, had remained level-headed. Even as a schoolgirl Princess Anne had declared that she would marry whoever she wanted and not simply someone who was regarded as 'suitable', which had been the lot of royal princesses for 900 years. As it happened love and acceptability came together in the person of Mark Phillips who was found to be eminently suitable by the Queen and the Duke of Edinburgh. So the stage was set for the wedding of the decade. Arrangements were to be the responsibility of the Lord Chamberlain, Lord Maclean, the former Chief Scout who is now Head of the Queen's Household. But grand though it was to be, the wedding was not a State occasion. This is reserved for events such as a Coronation or the funeral of the Sovereign – or on rare occasions, for example the funeral of Sir Winston Churchill, a State occasion is proclaimed by special decree.

Weddings of members of the Royal Family are usually regarded as personal family affairs. If it had been a State occasion the country would have paid for the wedding; as it was, the ceremony, the wedding breakfast and the reception that followed were all paid for by the Queen herself. The British taxpayer did foot the bill for over-time for the extra police who were drafted in to help cope with the security problem posed by thousands of onlookers from all over the world who flooded into London for the wedding.

They also paid for the cost of transporting soldiers into the area and for the building of the viewing stands along the route of the wedding procession, and for decorations in The Mall. For even if this was not going to be a State occasion, it was certainly going to be the most public of private affairs.

The date was set for Wednesday, November 14th – a date for double celebration in the Royal Family because this happened also to be Prince Charles's birthday. Between the engagement at the end of May and the wedding day, Mark Phillips was given what amounted to a crash course in royal duties. The army gave him a series of short lessons on how to conduct himself before the press and television cameras – when nearly fifty reporters and cameramen turned up to interview him in Germany shortly after the engagement, they found that on his own ground and in front of his own men, he wasn't nearly as shy and reserved as they had expected. He was thrust into a series of official engagements with his fiancée to give him a taste of what he could expect after the wedding, and it was noticeable that Princess Anne, who had been used to this sort of exposure all her life, made sure that he was never left with 'egg on his face' on these public occasions.

Genealogists delved deep into the family trees on both sides to see if they could establish a connection. They did! A joint ancestry with one of Henry VIII's soldiers, Sir William Griffith, means they are thirteenth cousins, three times removed.

It was decided that the wedding would take place in Westminster Abbey, the first royal wedding to be held there since Princess Alexandra had married Mr. Angus Ogilvy in 1963. Before the ceremony could take place, the Queen had to hold a special meeting of the Privy Council in order to give her formal consent. The Royal Marriage Act of 1772 does not allow a member of the Royal Family to be legally married without the consent of the Sovereign 'under the Great Seal declared in Council and entered into the Privy Council books'.

One of the biggest problems was how to restrict the guest list. Although it was, strictly speaking, a private function, there were certain people who had to be invited. Representatives of foreign governments, the Commonwealth, members of foreign royal families, the local authorities in Britain, the armed forces including those regiments associated with Princess Anne, the various organisations of which she is Patron or President, a multitude of official invitations before she and her fiancé could begin to ask their own friends.

Eventually the list was whittled down to 1,600 and this may well have been one of the reasons why nine years later Prince Charles decided that his marriage to Lady Diana Spencer would be in St. Paul's Cathedral where 2,500 guests could be accommodated. In addition it was to be the most televised event with an estimated audience on four continents numbering over 500 million, so the B.B.C. drafted in 300 engineers, producers and commentators from all over Britain to man the mobile control rooms and fifty cameras that would capture every moment from the time the bride left Buckingham Palace to the exchange of vows on the high altar in the Abbey.

As soon as the date of the wedding was announced governments, organisations and individuals throughout the world began choosing their wedding gifts. A palace official had said that Princess Anne and Lieutenant Phillips were 'starting from scratch and need everything'. Soon they would need nothing. The world and his wife sent presents which were so numerous that eventually they were shown in a special exhibition in St. James's Palace, in order to gratify public curiosity and incidentally to benefit a number of charities who received donations from the entrance money. The list runs to 101 pages and contains details of every single item that was accepted by the couple – 1524 in all, ranging from a wedding garter from Mrs. E. J. Dore to a Queen Anne chest of draws from the Army. The occupants of No. 10 Glamorgan Grove, Burnley, Lancs. sent a crocheted mat and the Chairman of the Revolutionary Council of the Union of Burma offered 'an important pair of drop cultured pearl earrings mounted with ruby and diamond and a pearl ruby and diamond sapphire brooch to match'. Show-jumper David Broome gave a Coalport strawberry set and Lord and Lady Fermoy, a cartoon by Thelwell: 'I'll be glad when she gets interested in boys.'

The royal presents were of course headed by those given by the Queen. A pair of aquamarine, diamond and baguette diamond flower-cluster earrings. A pair of diamond flower cluster earrings mounted in 18 carat gold. An 18 carat gold stalactite clip brooch set with brilliant cut diamonds. Two gold and enamel bell pushes, one enamelled pale blue with a cabochon amethyst push, the other in pink with chalcedony push, and a gold dress pocket watch by Patek Philippe on two coloured watch chains with an engraved inscription.

The Duke of Edinburgh gave the couple an eighteenth-century Chippendale period mahogny writing desk c. 1765. The Queen Mother gave a diamond tiara and the Prince of Wales sent a diamond brooch and two leather gun cases. Other members of the Royal Family gave more diamonds, jewellery, carpets, crystal, furniture, porcelain and china, with H.R.H. Princess Margaretha adding a practical touch: she sent eight dozen coat hangers. Extra staff had to be brought in to cope with the rash of presents and every donor received a personal letter of thanks within weeks of the wedding.

As the wedding day approached there were a million things to organise. The Lord Chamberlain and his staff of twenty-five were working non-stop to make sure that every eventuality was taken care of; there were matters of protocol, security and procedure which needed to be arranged down to the last detail. What was the order of seating for the guests in the Abbey? Who would line the route? Where would the honeymoon be spent? Which guests would be invited to the wedding breakfast and which to the reception? Who would be best man? How many bridesmaids would there be? Who would design and make the wedding dress? What about flower arrangements? Where should the television cameras be located to give the best pictures, while at the same time allowing the bride and groom a modicum of privacy during the sacred moments of the marriage ceremony? How many press representatives should be allowed into the Abbey and where should they be seated? Which members of the Royal Family should accompany the newly married couple into the anteroom behind the altar to sign the register? (Nearly every one of the family present did so and Princess Anne's marriage certificate must be the most signed document of its kind ever.)

These and hundreds of other details were all attended to by the relevant departments of the Royal Household under the supervision of Lord Maclean, who had had years of experience in dealing with functions of every size and description on behalf of the Royal Family. Every year there are more than eighty functions inside Buckingham Palace itself, ranging from investitures and State Banquets to the three annual Garden Parties, to each of which up to 9,000 guests are invited. So the prospect of organising the 'event of the decade' was not in the least daunting to this most urbane of courtiers.

First of all the media coverage. It seemed as if the whole world wanted to see the wedding pictures which were to be provided by the B.B.C. and I.T.V., listen to the radio commentaries and obtain copies of the hundreds of photographs taken.

The three major American television networks, A.B.C., C.B.S. and N.B.C., all sent their leading commentators and reporters to cover the event. The Australian Broadcasting Corporation and the Canadian Broadcasting Corporation both took the pictures live even though the time difference meant that people were staying up all night to see the wedding or getting up in the early hours of the morning. Ten countries throughout Europe, including some behind the Iron Curtain, also saw the event live. Even in Japan the entire ceremony was screened as it happened.

In Britain, colour television was in its infancy. The Royal Wedding was to do more for the sale of colour television sets than any other single occasion. Just as the Coronation of the Queen had done twenty years earlier, when there were comparatively few sets in Britain, Princess Anne's wedding was to prove a shot in the arm for British industry at a time when it was badly needed. Apart from the television sets which were sold or rented as quickly as they could be manufactured, there was also the birth of the souvenir industry to be reckoned with. Everything from flags to tea cloths began to appear in the shops all bearing a likeness – in some cases a little difficult to discern – of Anne and Mark.

There was Anne-and-Mark pottery, Anne-and-Mark writing paper, Anne-and-Mark bookmarks, Anne-and-Mark balloons, Anne-and-Mark games of every description. Some of the souvenirs were rather questionable in taste, particularly those made for next to nothing in the Far East and imported specially to cash in on the popular event. Everyone agreed that the wedding was a welcome oasis in the desert of austerity surrounding Britain at that time and the public determined to enjoy itself, either by being in London on the day or at least by sitting for hours watching it all on television.

It was a consumer bonanza with customers competing with each other to buy a limited edition of a pair of silver plaques bearing the bride and groom in profile for £1,250. A silver gilt Bride's Cup sold out at £125 and extra supplies of a two-handed loving cup at £50 had to be brought in when the first 500 sold in a few days. A bust of the Princess costing £100 went well and hundreds of crystal glasses with the initials of the couple engraved on them were sold at £35 each.

Not all the items were as expensive. It was possible to buy a bottle of beer specially brewed to mark the occasion for 16 pence and right at the bottom of the price scale was a box of matches wishing the bride and groom 'Health and Happiness' retailing at a half penny.

Just prior to the wedding Mark – who had by now been promoted to Captain in the normal progression any officer with his service would expect – and Princess Anne agreed to give a television interview. It was conducted jointly by Andrew Gardner and Alastair Burnet and consisted of a list of prepared questions which had been submitted to and approved by the Palace Press Office. Both the interviewers were experienced television journalists of many years' standing and the restrictions placed on them by the Palace coupled with the unnatural format of the interview made for an uncomfortable and at times embarrassing television programme. The idea of joint interviews, which is done simply to preserve impartiality on the part of the Palace, is unfortunate. Nobody gets any satisfaction out of it, neither the interviewees nor those asking the questions. It is impossible to hold a balanced conversation when each one is waiting for one of the others to say something, and the result is a stilted, untidy interview which leaves all those who take part feeling frustrated and unhappy.

It's a pity that lessons were not learned from this experience because nine years later exactly the same format was used in the pre-wedding interview with the Prince of Wales and Lady Diana Spencer, with almost exactly the same results.

The wedding day dawned bright and sunny, a good omen on this November morning. Hundreds of people had braved the cold and the severe rain storms of the bitter night of November 13th to make sure they would get a good vantage point for the wedding procession. Eventually as the day progressed 50,000 people would line the route, with a worldwide television audience of more than 580 million.

The B.B.C. opened up at 7.30 a.m. with the veteran broadcaster Fyfe Robertson giving news of royal arrivals, crowd scenes along the route and horoscopes for the couple about to be married.

There followed six hours of non-stop coverage of the morning's events followed by repeat programmes in the evening on both B.B.C. and I.T.V. The two television networks had brought in the resources of all their contributing regions, with the B.B.C. engaging a fashion commentator from the Royal College of Art to describe the dresses of the lady guests.

Cliff Michelmore was stationed with an outside broadcast unit at Great Somerford, the home village of the Phillips's, and Cliff Morgan had the company of some of Princess Anne's riding companions for the ceremony. Every aspect of the lives of bride and groom was examined in minute detail and paraded for public consumption. There were profiles of Princess Anne and Captain Phillips on both channels, a relay from an old people's home in Anglia and from a children's party in the East End of London.

Radio opened up even earlier than television. They began at 6.45 with a description of the pre-dawn preparations in Westminster Abbey, even talking to Mrs. Gwen Henderson, the lady who had the task of vacuum-cleaning the altar and the rose damask footstools, long before any of the principals arrived.

It was revealed that in order to cover their costs the Abbey had sold seats to reporters who were covering the event; £23 on the sanctuary stand, as opposed to £5 when Princess Alexandra had been married in 1963, though in all fairness it should be explained that the Abbey made no money itself – the charges were for special stands erected to accommodate the press. It was a profitable day for many of those taking part in the service. Members of the choir of the Abbey received royalties from the various recordings, film, radio and television to the tune of around £200 each, and Princess Anne herself had her allowance from the Civil List increased from £20,000 a year to £35,000. But again her Royal Highness did not see the extra money. It was needed for increases in salary for members of the Household.

The Abbey had been closed for nine days prior to the wedding so that all the preparations could be completed. Extra carpenters and electricians were brought in and spotlights were placed where they would give the kindest glow to the bride's hair and complexion.

Among the most delicate of the arrangements were those for the flowers. Mr. Harold Piercy of Constance Spry Ltd. was in overall charge of the operation and as the day of the wedding approached he had to alter his original plans quite drastically. He had intended to have four banks of flowers with the altar covered in a profusion of chrysanthemums and lilies. This was before he realised what the requirements of the producer in charge of the television coverage were going to be and how many of the Royal Family would be present.

Eventually Mr. Piercy had to settle for two banks of flowers and none at all on the altar as they would not only have prevented the cameras from seeing the couple but members of the Royal Family would have been hidden also. As Mr. Piercy said with a certain amount of sadness 'The Gentlemen at Arms were standing where we wanted flowers.'

Nevertheless, in spite of the restrictions the flower arrangements were a triumph of brilliant simplicity with each side of the sacrarium being guarded by an immaculate cone of chrysanthemums and lilies fully eight feet high.

The ceremony was due to start at 11.30, but for many of the participants it meant a start long before dawn. The horses and coachmen of the Royal Mews who were to form the wedding procession were up and about to exercise in the dark by 5 a.m. A few hours later the members of the armed forces who were to line the route, were ferried from their various barracks to their appointed places in The Mall, along Whitehall and outside the Abbey. Westminster Abbey opened its doors to the invited guests at 10 a.m. precisely so that they might be seated in proper order long before the royal guests would arrive.

It was symptomatic of the times that even at a royal wedding, lady guests were asked to open their handbags by the security officers on duty. With so many members of royal families from Britain and abroad expected and other important guests from governments and the diplomatic service no chances were being taken on any terrorists mingling with the crowds or slipping unnoticed into the Abbey.

Some of the earlier arrivals were to sit in the Abbey for an hour and a half before Princess Anne arrived, and a few had brought sandwiches and flasks which were to be consumed surreptitiously during the long wait. And although everyone knew that the event was to be televised, few realised just how bright – and hot – the heavy-duty arc lights would make the Abbey.

As the guests took their seats and prime ministers and presidents caught the eye, the choirmaster at the Chapels Royal, Mr. Harry

Gabb, sat at the great organ playing Handel's 'Water Music', Bach's 'Fantasia in G minor' and the music of Brahms, Mushel and Howells. Mr. Gabb had consulted with Douglas Guest, Director of Music at Westminster Abbey, about the selection of music and their choice had been submitted to Princess Anne and Captain Phillips for their approval. There was one slight problem: Captain Phillips wanted his regimental march played. It's a lively piece written by Johann Strauss called 'The Radetzky March' which is eminently suited to a cavalry regiment like the Queen's Dragoon Guards. The difficulty was in the tempo. Should it be slowed down to complement the solemnity of the occasion? After trying it at several speeds during rehearsals it was finally decided that the original version was more suited to the acoustics of the Abbey than any other, and Timothy Farrel who took over from Harry Gabb during the ceremony itself, managed to keep the tempo perfectly without forcing the Royal Family into the indignity of a gallop up the aisle.

The bridegroom had asked one of his fellow officers to act as his best man. He was Captain Eric Grounds, Adjutant of 1st The Queen's Dragoon Guards who had been one of Mark Phillips's closest friends ever since he had joined the regiment. An American-born athlete of international repute, Eric Grounds had distinguished himself as a member of the Army bobsleigh team, though at well over six feet he was considered too tall by most experts; something he took no notice of whatever, when he hurled himself at eighty miles an hour down the runs at St. Moritz and Igls.

Eric Grounds and Mark Phillips had spent the two nights before the wedding staying at The Cavalry Club, and it was from there that they were driven to a side entrance of the Abbey, where they were taken into a small room to change into their full dress uniforms of scarlet and gold with blue velvet collar and cuffs. One thing they didn't have to worry about was cleaning their buttons. A special anodized gilt had been used that did not require the usual 'spit and polish': just a rub over with a damp cloth.

Captain Grounds had been entrusted with the care of the wedding ring – made, as all royal wedding rings have been following the tradition started by the Queen Mother in 1923, from a supply of Welsh gold, mined in the hills around Dolgellau in Gwynedd. He claimed afterwards that it wasn't the thought of losing the ring that worried him. He said 'I'm never very good at standing up in public and speaking. The thought of doing it in front of the Queen terrified me.' As it happened his fears were unnecessary. He performed fault-lessly throughout the ceremony and, as it happened, he was not required to make a speech at the wedding breakfast.

Shortly before 11 a.m. the foreign royalty arrived at the Abbey, the most conspicuous being Princess Grace of Monaco, who caused a few eyebrows to be raised when she appeared dressed entirely in white, thereby breaching the age-old tradition that only the bride wears white at her wedding.

At 11 o'clock precisely the Queen's carriage procession left Buckingham Palace for the short journey to the Abbey, where they arrived exactly 12 minutes later, and as the six carriages of the Queen's procession were being brought to a halt in the forecourt of Westminster Abbey, the Glass Coach carrying the bride and the Duke of Edinburgh left the Palace and gave the watching crowds in The Mall and the millions on television their first glimpse of the wedding dress. Traditionally the design of the dress is kept secret until the day of the ceremony so that hundreds of copies are not rushed out. Nevertheless within hours of the dress being seen for the first time, seamstresses were busy duplicating the 'Princess line' with the high neckline and the distinctive sleeves which flared from the elbow. The copies were produced at £16 each; no one was telling how much the original, designed by Maureen Baker of Susan Small and made by a team of fifteen, all sworn to secrecy, had cost.

In the carriage behind the bride and her father were the attendants. Princess Anne had decided not to have any senior bridesmaids, but instead invited two nine year olds to be the only attendants: Prince Edward, her brother, and Lady Sarah Armstrong-Jones, daughter of Princess Margaret. The Prince wore a kilt and his cousin a pinafore dress and a jewelled Juliet cap.

As the bride's carriage arrived at the West Door to the Abbey, trumpeters of Captain Phillips's regiment, 1st The Queen's Dragoon Guards, played a fanfare specially composed for the occasion by Sir Arthur Bliss, Master of the Queen's Musick. Meanwhile the bridegroom and best man had slipped into place through an east cloister door and were waiting at the foot of the Sacrarium.

When the bride's procession reached the Sacrarium, Lady Sarah Armstrong-Jones took possession of the bouquet and then she and Prince Edward stood like statues for the remainder of the wedding service, something which perhaps only children with their background and training could manage.

The service was conducted by the Archbishop of Canterbury, Dr. Ramsey, who was also celebrating his birthday, assisted by the Dean of Westminster and the Rev. Andrew Elphinstone, the Queen's cousin and a godfather to Princess Anne. As the central sacrament of the service was being performed, only sixty people were able to see what was going on, those in the Sanctuary, both families, close friends and those taking part in the service. The Queen and Princess Anne had requested that television cameras should not be placed in front of the bridal couple, so that the actual moment of consecration when the ring is placed on the bride's finger, should be kept a strictly family affair.

Once the couple were pronounced man and wife they moved to the chapel of Edward the Confessor to sign the registers. There were three of them: one the Royal Marriage Register which is kept in the custody of the Lord Chamberlain and two Abbey registers, plus the Abbey's distinguished visitor's book.

At this point in the proceedings the young attendants were slightly uncertain of what they should do and where they should go, but an almost imperceptible nod from the Queen guided them in the right direction. The marriage registers were signed by the Queen, the Duke of Edinburgh, Prince Andrew and Prince Edward, the Queen Mother, Major and Mrs. Peter Phillips, Captain Eric Grounds, the Archbishop of Canterbury, the Dean of Westminster and Lady Sarah Armstrong-Jones. Mark was to say afterwards that he had to pinch himself when he saw his parents' signatures alongside those of the Royal Family.

As the couple walked back down the aisle, the great organ of Westminster Abbey thundered out Vidor's Toccata, perhaps the most stirring of all wedding music, which Princess Anne had heard at the wedding of the Duke and Duchess of Kent.

The *Daily Mail* reported that throughout the ceremony Princess Anne had been helping Mark to take the strain of the occasion. As they reached the West Door of the Abbey to give the crowds their first view she said to him 'be ready to acknowledge the crowds on the way back,' and later on the balcony of Buckingham Palace she told him 'wave, come on, wave'.

The wedding breakfast in the ballroom at the Palace was restricted to about 120 guests: visiting royalty, the families and close friends. By royal standards it was comparatively modest with the menu consisting of scrambled eggs, lobster, shrimps and tomato in mayonnaise to begin, followed by a main course of partridge with fresh mushrooms, peas, cauliflower and new potatoes, and to finish peppermint ice-cream filled with grated chocolate. Somewhat different from the royal breakfasts of earlier times when as many as fifteen courses would be eaten in a five-hour feast.

Although many thousands of people had been waiting in the streets since before dawn, there was no sign of any of them going home before one last look at the royal couple as they left to start their honeymoon. The Queen led the wedding guests into the forecourt of

Buckingham Palace to shower the bride and groom with confetti as they entered their open landau for the short drive to the Royal Chelsea Hospital, home of the famous 'pensioners'. There they were to transfer to an official car for the drive to Richmond Park where they had been offered the hospitality of the home of Princess Alexandra and Mr. Angus Ogilvy at Thatched House Lodge for their wedding night.

Celebrations continued at Buckingham Palace where the Queen gave a party and Prince Charles invited thirty of his friends to join him for his twenty-fifth birthday dinner. Mark's parents had driven to their home in Wiltshire where the village of Great Somerford was *en fête* throughout the day and night. Away from the formality of the royal festivities the Phillips's danced the night away with the rest of the villagers in a marquee with a special wooden floor hired for the occasion.

The following day the honeymoon proper was due to start as Anne and Mark left Heathrow Airport to fly to Barbados where the Royal Yacht *Britannia* had been placed at their disposal.

By a happy coincidence this did not involve a great deal of expense as the yacht was *en route* to New Zealand to make ready for a State Visit by the Queen and the Duke early in the new year so it did not even have to go very far out of its way.

A West Indies cruise aboard the world's finest private yacht may seem the perfect way to spend a honeymoon, and certainly the 21 officers and 256 ratings who made up the crew went out of their way to make sure the young newlyweds were not disturbed. But even a captain who is in reality a Rear Admiral cannot legislate against the weather, and for the main part of the first week it was stormy, to say the least, and both passengers suffered the agonies of *mal-de-mer*.

However, when the storms subsided the honeymoon progressed as planned, with *Britannia* island-hopping throughout the West Indies, playing a game of hide-and-seek with the hordes of pressmen and photographers who were following the yacht in a fleet of assorted craft.

It was not to be all play by any means. Buckingham Palace had arranged a crowded official programme to coincide with the honeymoon, and after two weeks on their own Princess Anne and Captain Phillips set out on an exhausting round of engagements which took them to Equador, Colombia, Antigua, Jamaica and Montserrat.

This was to be a testing time for the newest member of the Royal Family. Although as an Army officer he had received a certain amount of training that was to stand him in good stead during the build-up to the wedding and in the ceremony itself, there was no way he could be prepared for being a 'Royal', always on show, never allowed to show his real feelings, meeting hundreds of new faces every day, shaking hands with strangers and making small talk with people with whom one not only did not have a thing in common, but also when there was often a language barrier as well. If Mark felt any trepidation about his initiation into the world of royal duties it was not apparent at the time. Princess Anne, after a lifetime of training, bore the brunt of the pressure, making speeches, shaking hands, carrying on polite conversation, attending dinners and receptions and giving her husband invaluable advice on how to cope. For example, members of the Royal Family rarely eat much when they attend luncheons or dinners. They drink even less – if you see a picture of one of the Royals holding a glass at a cocktail party, you can be fairly sure it contains something innocuous or even if it is something a bit stronger, then the same glass is retained throughout the function, rarely being refilled.

All in all it was a successful introduction to the royal round of duties for Mark, but like so many others who are occasionally given a glimpse of life in the 'inner circle' he realised just how hard they work while appearing to be completely relaxed.

After the sunshine of South America and the warmth of the Caribbean, they returned to Britain on December 16th just in time to join the rest of the Royal Family for their traditional Christmas holiday at Windsor. Mark's parents and his sister Sarah had also been included in the guest list for Christmas and they joined in the usual festivities, including the Queen's favourite game, charades. Everyone who stays at Windsor is expected to take part in the family games and no one is excused, prime minister or president.

So for the Phillips family 1973 came to a close. A year that had seen their life alter beyond belief. At the beginning of the year they had been a quiet, country family living in the seclusion of rural Wiltshire with a son who was a Lieutenant in the Regular Army.

Now they had dined at Buckingham Palace, seen their only son marry the Sovereign's only daughter, the Queen was their relation by marriage, they had become public property through radio, television and press, and finally they were spending Christmas with the Royal Family at Windsor Castle. It really had been quite a year!

As for Mark, he had taken on a new wife and a new job. He was being posted from Germany to the Royal Military Academy at Sandhurst and was about to move with his wife, fourth in line of succession to the Throne, into married quarters provided by the Army.

Chapter 9

ROYAL HOMES
OAK GROVE HOUSE AND GATCOMBE PARK

The Royal Military Academy at Sandhurst is situated on the borders of Surrey and Berkshire and for nearly 200 years it has been the world's leading establishment for training Army officers. Cadets come from all over the world and in recent years more and more have come from the third-world countries of the British Commonwealth. Its reputation is pre-eminent in military circles and the standard of instruction is envied and emulated throughout the world.

Mark Phillips had been posted to Sandhurst as an instructor and promoted to the rank of Captain. Although his regiment, 1st The Queen's Dragoon Guards, based in Germany, was sorry to see him leave, it was realised that as a member of the Royal Family, it would have been impossible for him to remain as a squadron commander in his old unit and carry on with his normal duties. The attention of the world's press and other even more undesirable bodies, would have thrown an intolerable burden on the shoulders of his comrades. Also there was no way in which the Army authorities would have been able to provide Princess Anne with suitable accommodation, and as a leading member of the 'family firm' she would not have been able to continue to carry out her increasing number of public engagements from a base in Germany.

As Captain Phillips had no intention, at that time, of leaving the Army, the alternatives were few. He could have been given a staff position in London at the Ministry of Defence, but his temperament and obvious suitability to a more active life ruled out that possibility very quickly.

So the opportunity of becoming an instructor at Sandhurst appeared to be the ideal solution to the problem.

Before Captain Phillips took up his appointment, he and Princess Anne visited the Academy several times to inspect a number of properties which were thought to be suitable. Eventually they decided on Oak Grove House which was located in the grounds of the Sandhurst Estate about fifty yards from the main Sandhurst/Camberley Road.

Oak Grove had been the traditional home of the Director of Studies at the Academy but was vacant at the time because the previous

25. Lord Snowdon has always been one of Princess Anne's favourite photographers, and perhaps this portrait study taken on her nineteenth birthday explains why. It captured for the first time the awakening glamour of the emerging young woman.

26. (*Top*) Princess Anne was appointed Colonel-in-Chief of her first regiment, the 14th/20th King's Hussars, in 1969. When she visited them in Paderborn, West Germany, the Commanding Officer, Lt. Col. J. M. (Mike) Palmer, was delighted to let her drive a fifty-ton Chieftain tank.

27. When Princess Anne attended the Festival of London Stores Trades Fair in May, 1969 (*above*), she was accompanied by Lady Susan Hussey, one of the Queen's Ladies-in-Waiting. The angle of this photograph gives Royalty's view of the public.

28. The Australian visit in April, 1970, provided the Princess with an opportunity to see for herself a working sheep farm. Here she looks on as fleece is carried away at 'Talbarea' in Queensland.

29. (*Top*) Prince Charles and Princess Anne paid their first visit to the United States in July 1970, as guests of President Nixon.

30. (*Above*) The following year saw the Princess in East Africa, where she was amused to see President Kenyatta being tempted into a dance at a reception in Gatundu.

31. Princess Anne gives an affectionate pat on the nose to Derby XXI, mascot of the 1st Battalion, The Worcestershire and Sherwood Foresters Regiment (29th/45th Foot) before, as Colonel-in-Chief, she presented the Battalion with new colours at Battlesbury Barracks, Warminster.

32. When Princess Anne entered Badminton for the first time in April, 1971, no one really expected her to complete the tough cross-country course – it was her first major international competition. In partnership with Doublet she finished in fifth place overall – a remarkable result. Winner that year was Mark Phillips on Great Ovation.

33. A proud Queen presents her daughter with the Raleigh Trophy as the Individual Three-Day Event Winner at the European Championships at Burghley, Lincolnshire, in September, 1971.

34. (*Above*) The Princess, as Patron of the Riding for the Disabled Association, chats with some of the children at Coldwaltham House Riding School near Pulborough in Sussex during one of her visits in May, 1972. This is one of the charities for which she will 'go anywhere and meet anyone'.

35. (*Top*) September, 1973: Princess Anne receives help after Goodwill crashed at the notorious second fence at Kiev.

36. (*Above*) On another of the Queen's horses, Columbus.

tenant had left to take up another appointment elsewhere. Captain Phillips was not eligible to occupy Oak Grove House in his own right because, in the strict grading system the Army conforms to, it should have gone to an officer who was at least a Colonel. However, the circumstances in this case were unique and as the house was to become the official residence of Princess Anne, it would have been impracticable for the Queen's only daughter to have lived in the usual married quarters allocated to a Captain. Captain Phillips did, however, have to pay the same rent a Colonel would have paid: about £400 a year. For this he got a five-bedroomed Georgian house built in 1810 and standing in its own grounds of half an acre. The house is approached by a crescent-shaped drive and it is shielded from the rest of the Sandhurst Estate by mature beech and oak trees. It is convenient for the stables, being only 100 yards away and about a quarter of a mile from the parade-ground, so the noise of the shouting drill sergeants as they try to instil the mysteries of military discipline into raw recruits, does not disturb the peace and quiet of a rather pleasant, village-like atmosphere. The house was one of the original quarters built at the same time as Sandhurst was founded and there are still royal cyphers to be seen on the outside drainpipes. The interior accommodation is spacious but not lavish; apart from the five bedrooms there are two bathrooms and a dressing room while downstairs there is a drawing room, study, dining room and cloakroom, with wine cellars and storage room below ground level.

Previous occupants would have had servants provided by the Army, but by the time Captain Phillips and Princess Anne took up residence the practice had long since ended and they had to hire, and pay for, any domestic help they needed.

The presence of the young couple at Sandhurst posed one or two security problems for the Army authorities. Sandhurst had been a camp which normally allowed access to members of the public, and while they had no wish to deny people the privileges they had enjoyed for some years, there was the possibility that many more people than usual would find their way into the grounds, purely in an attempt to see where Princess Anne lived. Oak Grove House was not remote in any way and there would be nothing to prevent anyone from walking up to the front door if they wished. A comparatively low-key security system was employed which involved stationing a solitary policeman in a sentry box just outside the main entrance to the house, and floodlights were installed around Oak Grove, as they already were on all the main buildings of the Academy itself.

Before Princess Anne and Captain Phillips were able to move into Oak Grove House a certain amount of renovation and decoration had to be carried out. This was a normal practice carried out whenever a new tenant moved into new quarters and the cost was borne by the Ministry of Defence as a routine Army expense.

Princess Anne and her husband took a personal interest in the choice of decorations for their new home and their enthusiasm for horses was expressed in their selection of wallpaper in the dining room. It was grey and white with rural scenes of couples on horse-back used as a motif. When they came to furnish the house the large practical number of wedding gifts they had received came into use. The centrepiece in the dining room, the contemporary mahogany table and chairs, whose backs form the monogram A.M. were given to them by the Royal Warrant Holders' Association, the green and yellow striped seats harmonising with the green curtains. Another gift, a 200-year-old grandfather clock, was presented by the City of Westminster.

The drawing room contained at least two valuable and useful gifts in the furniture. The linen-covered sofa and patterned armchairs were given by the Lords Lieutenant of all the counties of England and Wales, while the Prime Minister of Iran, Mr. Hoveida, had sent a beautiful example of one of his country's most ancient crafts, in the form of a Persian rug, in which more horses were seen prancing around.

When the redecoration and repair work was complete Princess Anne and her husband moved in – this was in February, 1974, just a few weeks before the attempted kidnapping in the Mall, which was to have such profound and long-lasting effects on the future security of the Royal Family. The Army were slightly nervous about having a Royal in their midst, and while they had already instituted a system of checking all vehicles which entered the grounds – following a serious bombing incident at Aldershot the previous year – they still allowed members of the public to have free access at all times. There was one footpath which ran very close to Oak Grove House and this was closed, partly in the interests of security and partly because of the 'nuisance value' when pedestrians walked along it deliberately in the hope of seeing the new occupants of Oak Grove

Being one of the older military establishments, Sandhurst is particularly well off for stables and there were six allotted to Oak Grove House, so Princess Anne and her husband were able to take all their horses with them when they moved in, with the 'star performer' at that time, the Queen's horse Columbus, being quartered at Alison Oliver's stables nearby.

So the couple settled down to life in an Army camp for the next two years. They joined in the normal social life of the officers' mess as often as they could and the junior officers at least found both Princess Anne and her husband to be congenial companions who never expected to be treated differently from anybody else. A number of the senior officers at Sandhurst were die-hard traditionalists to whom it was unthinkable that a princess of the blood royal should be treated as just another captain's wife, and at first they tried to insist that protocol was observed in all its formality in the many functions that are mandatory in the calendar of large military establishments throughout the world. But Princess Anne, while never allowing anyone ever to forget for a single moment who she is, has a strictly 'no-nonsense' approach to most things in life, and she quickly let it be known that while she was living at Sandhurst as a serving officer's wife, that was exactly what she wanted to be treated as: no more, no less. It didn't take long for the message to sink in and within a comparatively short time life settled down to a very pleasant routine, with Captain Phillips working his horses early in the morning and occasionally at lunch-time, returning to his duties as an instructor during the working day, and Princess Anne also combining her equestrian pursuits with the increasing number of public duties she was taking on after her marriage.

Because Oak Grove House was now the official residence of Princess Anne payment for part of the upkeep of the property came from the Civil List, but Captain Phillips does not, and never has, received a single penny from the List, and at the time they lived at Sandhurst, his only source of income was his army pay, £4,500 a year, which included a marriage allowance paid to all servicemen.

Sandhurst was an ideal location for the young couple being only fifty-three miles from London, so if Princess Anne had an official engagement during the day in or around the capital, she was able to travel there and back in the course of the day. If it was necessary for her to stay in London overnight, she used her set of rooms at Buckingham Palace, which she retains up to the present time. The suite consists of a sitting room, dining room (which doubles as a meeting place when several members of her staff need to get together, e.g. for the twice-yearly programme conferences), and a bedroom. Princess Anne's rooms are situated on the second floor of the Palace facing out over the Mall.

From the moment Princess Anne and her husband moved into Oak Grove House, she spent as few nights as possible away from home. By a happy coincidence another young officer who was a friend of Princess Anne's had also been posted to Sandhurst at the same time. Malcolm McVittie, now a Major with the Argyll and Sutherland Highlanders, had been a junior officer on duty at

Balmoral during the summer of 1970, when he was invited to a drinks party at the Castle. The Queen usually invites officers who are mounting guard at royal residences, to attend a number of social gatherings during the year, and Malcolm McVittie found himself sitting between the Queen and Princess Anne on the first occasion he dined at Balmoral. The younger officers who were all around the same age as the Princess, decided to return the compliment and they asked her to join them for dinner in their mess at Ballater, the nearest town to Balmoral. Malcolm McVittie says that at first he was a bit worried about how to entertain the daughter of the Sovereign, but she was extremely easy to get along with and on that first date she joined in the fun of the evening as enthusiastically as all the other guests.

Life in 1970 was so much more relaxed than it is today that a brother officer, David Stewart, was able to send Princess Anne's chauffeur away saying he would drive her home himself. When the time came to leave it was the Princess who took the wheel of Stewart's brand new Reliant Scimitar sports car and by all accounts she frightened the life out of him in the short six-mile drive. There are no records to show if the Princess was impressed by David Stewart or not, but one thing is certain: she liked his car so much that even to this day she has retained a Reliant Scimitar as her personal form of transport.

The following year McVittie was invited to Princess Anne's twenty-first party on board *Britannia* which was berthed in the Naval Dockyard at Portsmouth, and they met several times during the next couple of years at various social functions. Meanwhile he had married, and he was able to present his wife Wendy when they were both invited to the Royal Wedding and the dance that preceded it at Buckingham Palace. This was also the first time for both to meet Mark Phillips.

So it meant that there was at least one familiar face to greet the Princess and her husband when they set up home at Sandhurst. Malcolm McVittie found himself in the unusual position of being the only personal friend of the Princess at Sandhurst, and he and his wife found that Princess Anne was the only other officer's wife they knew.

McVittie recalls that 'Princess Anne and Mark set out deliberately to join the normal mess life of the college and they refused point-blank to give dinner parties exclusively for the senior officers. When they entertained at home it was usually an informal gathering for the younger men and their wives or girlfriends, and when she dropped in to one of their homes she had no objection to sitting around the kitchen table. If we were getting together for a few drinks, or in her case the inevitable Coca-Cola, we found that one of her favourite places for sitting was on the floor.'

Mark Phillips designed a course for a special one-day event to be held at Sandhurst and just in case the whole thing should turn out to be a disaster, which it wasn't, the couple decided to hold the celebration party the night before the event, rather than afterwards. Princess Anne made all the arrangements and invited everyone who was involved in the preparations to a supper party at Oak Grove House. Everyone had a splendid time, mixing informally in the way that equestrians do regardless of rank or position.

Life at Sandhurst continued pleasantly but uneventfully for a number of years, apart from the horrendous happenings in The Mall, during the early months; with Princess Anne combining her public duties with increasing commitment to her riding career. She had been aiming at a place in the British Team for the 1976 Olympics which were held in Montreal and there were great celebrations at Sandhurst when she was chosen.

Just before she left to compete in Canada, Wendy McVittie gave birth to her first child, a daughter. Somewhat tentatively her husband asked Princess Anne if she would consider being godmother to the child. Without hesitation she replied that she would be delighted and the day after her return from the Olympics, feeling no doubt more than slightly 'jet-lagged', she turned up at Sandhurst Chapel to stand as godmother as the baby was christened Alice Louise.

The McVitties were thrilled and delighted at the honour the Princess had done them and their child. Alice Louise herself was to appreciate her special start in life as she grew older. Princess Anne accepted the role of godmother as she does everything else. She took it seriously, determined to fulfil her obligations. Every year since the christening she sends cards and presents at Christmas and on birthdays and she writes personally to her goddaughter every now and then to find out how she is progressing at school and if there is anything that she, Princess Anne, can do for her. Life in the British Army is such a transitory existence with postings rarely coinciding with one's personal preferences that solid friendships are difficult to maintain, but Malcolm McVittie says 'Ours if not a friendship that relies on seeing one another constantly. We may go a year or two without our two families meeting, but if we are ever in Gloucestershire and we know that they are at home we always call. Princess Anne leads such a busy life with so many calls on her time that it seems presumptuous to assume one would be welcome, but when she says "if you want to see me drop in" she means it – and we do.'

Immediately after the wedding, Eric Grounds had been posted to

Northern Ireland on undercover intelligence duties. There, in order to preserve his anonymity, he grew his hair long and rarely shaved. On a weekend pass to London, he was telephoned by Mark Phillips who invited him to Oak Grove House for a meal. 'Mark asked me if I had a dinner jacket with me,' Major Grounds, who has now left the Army, remembers. ''Hardly,' I replied. 'It's not the sort of thing I need in my job.'' However, he was told to come to dinner anyway. When he arrived he found that his fellow guests were the Queen, the Duke of Edinburgh, the Queen Mother and Lord Porchester, the Queen's Racing Manager. Both Prince Philip and Lord Porchester had changed out of their dinner jackets into sports jackets and flannel trousers. Eric Grounds recalls it as one more instance of the thoughtfulness of the Royal Family.

Within a year Princess Anne herself was to become pregnant and Captain Phillips was to leave the Army. He had completed his two-year posting as an instructor at Sandhurst and there was the problem of where to send him next. He wanted to return to his regiment as a company commander. They were on attachment in Northern Ireland before returning to their base in Germany. Captain Phillips was finding out that being married to the Queen's only daughter was going to prove a severe handicap to an ambitious cavalry officer. Before his marriage he could have expected to accompany the regiment wherever it was posted and possibly eventually end up as commanding officer. But it would be difficult to achieve the highest rank without seeing active service, and it was considered to be out of the question for a member of the Royal Family to serve in Northern Ireland.

Not only would he have become a prestigious target for terrorists but the problems posed by his presence would have added considerably to the heavy load being carried already by the military authorities in the Province. The alternative was a posting to the Ministry of Defence in London as an administrative officer in Army Training, and although he made the best of it, the desk-bound job came a poor second to a man who had joined the Army because he enjoyed the active, outdoor life of a mechanised cavalry regiment. Apart from anything else, being tied to a desk in Whitehall meant that there was little time during the day when he could get away to work his horses. At Sandhurst, the stables were practically adjacent to the working areas; in London it meant driving several miles through the time-consuming traffic jams of the West End.

As with most people who lead physically strenuous lives Captain Phillips felt a sense of frustration at the mountain of paperwork on his desk that never seemed to get any smaller, and he could see little future for himself as an Army officer who was never going to see active service, so he began to consider alternative careers. The problem was twofold: as an Army officer he had been trained for very little in civilian life, and once he had resigned his commission, he would automatically have to forfeit the tenancy of Oak Grove House.

The obvious solution to the first problem was to utilise his outstanding talent with horses and the only way to do that profitably was to relinquish his amateur status and become a professional trainer. He was fully supported in his resolve by Princess Anne who sympathised with his position. She knew that by marrying her he had virtually destroyed his own military career and she was as anxious as he was that he should find an outlet for his extraordinary energy and skill as a horseman. They began to look seriously for suitable houses, fitting in their house-hunting forays with Captain Phillips's work in Whitehall and her public commitments.

Then finally after viewing properties in almost every county surrounding London and even further afield, they found the house which was to become their new home.

It's very easy to miss Gatcombe Park. As you leave the village of Minchinhampton in Gloucestershire on the country road that runs due east, the entrance to the estate is on the right-hand side, about a mile from the village. But unless you know where you are going, or you are with someone who has been there before, you could quite easily drive past. There is no sign that indicates the name of the house, and Gatcombe itself is not visible from the road. What you will see, is a pair of gateposts leaning at an alarming angle until recently, and a wooden gate, left permanently open, simply because it won't shut. There is a lodge just inside the gates, and when you drive along the half-mile drive to the house you have to proceed with great care. It's deeply rutted, with large pot-holes, and the laurel bushes overhang the drive make motoring a fairly hazardous process.

Before you reach the house itself, you come upon a divide in the drive with a signpost directing all traffic to the right – this takes you around the back of the property, past a security post which has been skilfully designed to blend in with the woodland surrounding it, and which is permanently manned by officers of the Gloucestershire constabulary. If you are expected and are a welcome guest, you will be allowed to drive your car around to the front of the house, where you park on a thinly gravelled terrace, alongside Princess Anne's Scimitar or her husband's Range Rover.

The first impression you get when you face the house is that it's not nearly as big as it looks in photographs. It's beautifully proportioned, but the illusion of size comes about because of the magnificent conservatory which is attached to the house on the left side as you look at it. When Princess Anne and her husband decided that they needed somewhere other than the married quarters provided for them by the Army at Sandhurst they had no intention of buying anything as large as Gatcombe, or indeed anything so far away from London. Gatcombe is 112 miles from Buckingham Palace and Princess Anne felt at that time that a sixty-mile radius was about as far as they could go from London, if she was to be able to carry on her official duties without too much interference. The couple were actually looking for a small country house with perhaps 100 acres so that they could accommodate their horses and Mark could then leave the Army and use his expertise to set up as a professional trainer.

The trouble was that almost every house they looked at which at first seemed reasonable and suitable to their requirements, suddenly took a dramatic leap in price as soon as the vendors – or their agents – realized who the would-be purchasers were. So they were forced to travel further afield in their search and Gloucestershire came within their orbit mainly because they were used to being in the county for events like Badminton, and also because it wasn't too far from the home of Mark's parents in the adjoining county of Wiltshire. One of the first houses they considered was Highgrove near Tetbury, but this was rejected for a number of reasons including the price, and the fact that the house was so close to the main road might have created security problems for those officers whose job it is to guard Princess Anne and her family. Obviously these were not thought to be problems which could not be overcome in later years, when Prince Charles and the Princess of Wales made it their first home outside London.

Eventually it was the Master of Trinity College, Cambridge, Lord Butler who solved the problem for Princess Anne and Captain Phillips. He had heard that they were house-hunting in Gloucestershire and he wrote to them suggesting that they might like to look at his old family home, Gatcombe Park.

When the couple first went to view Gatcombe the house had not been lived in fully for more than ten years. It was damp and needed complete rewiring. There was an air of decayed elegance about the place which indicated how graceful a home it had once been, but in 1976 it must have taken tremendous imagination to visualise how the house could look when restored to its former glory.

However, the surroundings had lost none of their charm through the ravages of time, and the view from the front of the house is still truly magnificent, with rolling valleys and deep woodlands stretching away as far as the eye can see, and they even have a 'folly' built by a former owner, down in the dell just below the main house.

The estate included an arable farm of 500 acres and Princess Anne says that this meant they had to rethink their plans completely. They hadn't thought of a farm when they were looking for a home, but the estate at Gatcombe held great attractions for them even though it was obviously going to be beyond their price range. At that time Captain Phillips's Army pay was around £4,500 a year, just about enough to secure them a mortgage on the lodge at Gatcombe – if they were lucky!

It is now a matter of public record that the problem was solved by the Queen agreeing to buy the property for the young couple. There were many wildly inaccurate guesses in the press about the actual price they paid, but of course Buckingham Palace would not comment on what was a purely personal transaction. The probable price was slightly less than £500,000, and with agricultural land in the county at that time fetching around £1,000 an acre, it seems the Queen got a bargain. In fact at half a million pounds, it means the house was thrown in for nothing. Today the estate is worth well over a million pounds.

On the 29th September, 1976, Captain Phillips officially took over the tenancy of the house and became Master of Gatcombe, and then followed the nightmare of deciding the priorities needed to make the house habitable and where to start first.

There were major interior structural alterations that needed to be done, mainly to the rooms on the first floor of the eighteenth-century mansion, where the front of the house looking over the beautiful valley below it had been mainly taken up with bathrooms, and the bedrooms were all restricted to the dark, rear of the house, with no view and very little sun.

Downstairs the house was to be left very much as it had been since it was built, with the beautifully proportioned drawing room and dining room flanking the front hall. But at the back of the house there was a small pantry which served also as a control centre for all the electricity and plumbing connections in the house. Not only was it archaic, but in a highly volatile and potentially dangerous condition. Obviously much needed to be done and a great deal of money had to be spent; money which could not in any way come from Princess Anne's allocation from the Civil List because her official residence at that time was still Oak Grove at Sandhurst, and until they moved into Gatcombe the money for the renovations had to be found from other sources.

So Captain Phillips did what most other young people in his position would have done: he took out a mortgage. His credentials were impeccable, and he had good security to offer. Once again following the Royal Family custom of not discussing private financial affairs, we do not know the amount that was raised, or even whether it was from a building society or a bank, but there's little doubt that it was a substantial amount of money, and when later Captain Phillips said they were 'just like any other young couple with a mortgage', only to raise cries of derision from several quarters, he was actually speaking the truth. Maybe he did not have to pay interest on mortgage payments for buying the property, but the amount he borrowed to make the necessary alterations to the house is doubtless as much, if not more, than that which most couples would borrow to buy a house in the first place.

Anyway the money was forthcoming, and the builders moved in to gut the entire first floor. The house was rewired and replumbed throughout with the bathrooms being moved back to the rear of the house and the bedrooms returning to the front where their occupants could enjoy the magnificent view. There is a very large attic area at Gatcombe which had previously been a warren of small, dark rooms used only by the many servants who had worked in the house in the days gone by. On this floor a complete nursery suite was constructed, which is entirely self-contained, having its own bedrooms, bathrooms, sitting room and kitchen. But even though it is self-contained it does not follow that the children are restricted to this part of the house.

Indeed, no rooms are sacred at Gatcombe. The household is very much a modern edition of the English country home and nowhere is there any evidence of the sort of grandeur one might associate with the homes of other members of the Royal Family. From the first day when Princess Anne and her husband went to live there, the house has had a 'lived in' look. There's the strong impression of dogs around the place and if the children are free to roam through the house, so are the dogs. On my first visit I shared a sofa with an inquisitive Doberman, who looked much more fierce than she really was, and a frisky corgi who was a refugee from Buckingham Palace, where he had apparently upset the rest of the Queen's pack, being the only male among all the females.

As you enter the front door you are immediately in a stone-flagged hall at the rear of which stands an old-fashioned rocking-horse, the sort that collectors pay vast sums of money for these days but which, in the Phillips's home, is used very much as it was originally intended, as a plaything for two young, but very high-spirited, children.

Riding boots and Wellingtons litter one side of the hall underneath a long, ancient table on which copies of *Horse and Hound*, *The Field* and *Riding Monthly* are stacked, and a water-bowl is kept filled and waiting just inside the front door for whichever of the household animals is first in from the fields. When Princess Anne decided to live at Gatcombe, the Keeper of the Queen's Pictures sent a large selection of oil paintings and watercolours from the Queen's collection. The couple could choose whatever they wanted to adorn the walls of their new home. The paintings on offer were said to be worth over a million pounds; they were all politely sent back and the pictures one sees now at Gatcombe are nearly all sporting prints depicting some aspect of equestrian life. Similarly, the books which line the shelves in the library, though including many of the works of writers of the classics, also feature prominently a set of first editions of Princess Anne's favourite author, Dick Francis, that most successful writer of thrillers, all with a 'horsey' background. Mr. Francis has, of course, another older association with the Royal Family. He was for many years the Queen Mother's steeplechase jockey.

There is a formal drawing room immediately to the left of the hall and this is where official guests are entertained. Beyond this room is Princess Anne's sitting room, a comfortable room with an elegant bow window, where Princess Anne sits at her desk dealing with her correspondence and writing her speeches.

The estate at Gatcombe is now over 1,000 acres, much larger than was originally envisaged. The extra acreage came to be part of the estate because Captain Phillips had approached one of his neighbours with a view to buying 'a few fields'. The neighbour instead offered his entire 500-acre Aston Farm, which not only was completely beyond the pocket of the new master of Gatcombe, but also meant that if he were to acquire it he would have to become a full-time farmer.

Mark Phillips told Angela Rippon that he approached a number of institutions and insurance companies to see if they would buy the farm and lease it back to him, but there were no definite offers when he and Princess Anne mentioned it to the Queen. She immediately offered to 'become the institution' and that's what happened. Her Majesty bought Aston Farm, for an undisclosed amount, and Captain Phillips rents it from her. He also decided that modern-day farming needs a more professional management than he was able to bring to it at that time, so he enrolled at the Royal Agricultural College at nearby Cirencester where he learned how complicated are the techniques applied to farming in the latter half of the twentieth century.

This then is Gatcombe as it is today. A comfortable country home set in the rolling Gloucestershire countryside with a thousand acres of prime agricultural land surrounding it, providing full-time employment for a number of people and intended to produce a profit at the end of each year. – slightly different from the home Princess Anne and Mark Phillips set out to find when they decided to leave Sandhurst, and now of course they have been joined in their part of the Cotswolds by the Prince and Princess of Wales, and Prince and Princess Michael of Kent, all of whom live within a few miles.

Chapter 10

SECURITY

The 20th March, 1974, is the date from which all royal security was reviewed. On that day an attempt was made to kidnap the Queen's only daughter and hold her to ransom.

Princess Anne and Mark Phillips had been married for only five months and had recently taken up residence in married quarters provided for them by the Army, at Oak Grove House at Sandhurst.

Her Royal Highness had started to take a keen interest in a charity which was to become one of her favourites in a very short time, Riding for the Disabled, of which she became Patron after being introduced to the organisation by its President, the Duchess of Norfolk.

On Wednesday, 20th March, 1974, the Princess and her husband had agreed to attend a special showing of a short film entitled 'Riding Towards Freedom', which told the story of the Riding for the Disabled Association, and in which they both appeared in several sequences. The film was shown in the early evening at Sudbury House, Newgate Street, near Ludgate Circus, in the City of London. Shortly after seeing the film the couple left to be driven back to Buckingham Palace; the time was a little after 7.30 p.m.

The royal car, an Austin Princess limousine, was driven by fifty-five-year-old Mr. Alexander Callendar, a married man with two children who had been employed in the Royal Mews for twenty years. Sitting alongside him was a young policeman, Princess Anne's official bodyguard, thirty-year-old Detective Inspector James Beaton. In the rear of the car were Princess Anne and Captain Phillips together with Miss Rowena Brassey, the Lady-in-Waiting, who was sitting on the folding seat immediately behind the partition which separated the driver from the passengers.

The car had left Newgate Street, driven down Fleet Street, into The Strand and across Trafalgar Square. It turned into The Mall and a little over three-quarters of the way along, just after the turning for St. James's Palace on the darkest part of this famous thoroughfare, with less than a quarter of a mile to go to Buckingham Palace, a light-coloured Ford Escort saloon accelerated alongside the Austin Princess, swerved sharply in front of it and forced the royal car to stop.

A man leaped out of the Escort and fired a gun into the royal car, smashing one of the rear windows. Inspector Beaton had by this time got out of his side of the car and run around to the side where Princess Anne was sitting. There he found a young man trying to open the door, who, when he saw Inspector Beaton, shot him in the chest. Beaton fired back but missed due to his injury. He then attempted to fire again but his gun jammed. The gunman had meanwhile managed to open the rear door of the royal car and he grabbed hold of Princess Anne by the arm and said to her 'Please get out of the car.' Mark Phillips had hold of Princess Anne's other arm and a tug-of-war ensued, which he won. He pulled Princess Anne back to his side of the car and managed to slam the door shut.

Princess Anne's blue velvet dress, which she had worn when leaving on honeymoon after the wedding, was ripped and the sleeve was practically torn off. The Lady-in-Waiting had by this time opened the door on the other side and crawled out where she lay crouched along the near side of the car.

The man then threatened to shoot Princess Anne if Inspector Beaton didn't throw down his gun. As the weapon was jammed and useless anyway, Beaton did as he was told. The attacker produced a second gun and said he would shoot if the door was not opened. He raised the gun to carry out his threat and Beaton, although badly wounded, put his hand directly in front of the muzzle of the pistol, a .22 calibre hand-gun. The gun was fired and Beaton was hit in the hand. Princess Anne, although badly shaken, remained calm and asked the attacker what he wanted her for. He replied 'I'll get a couple of million.' Rowena Brassey says that the Princess remained completely calm throughout and spoke to the man in a quiet, low tone trying to keep his attention.

Inspector Beaton had been wounded twice, but he refused to give up. Instead he told Mark to release the door so that he, Beaton, could kick it open and hit the gunman with it. He did kick it open but failed to hit the man who fired again at Inspector Beaton, hitting him for the third time. The bullet went into his stomach, through the intestines and pelvis and eventually lodged in the tissues at the back. Beaton managed to stagger out of the car onto the pavement, where he lay until police reinforcements arrived to take him to hospital for an emergency operation. Mr. Callendar, the chauffeur, was still sitting in the driving seat with the engine running; this had all happened in a matter of seconds. He began to get out of the car but the gunman instructed him to remain where he was and turn off the engine. Mr. Callendar however disobeyed him and made to open the front door. He was immediately shot in the chest at point-blank range. Rowena Brassey said afterwards: 'The funny thing was it didn't sound like shooting. It wasn't a bit like the noise guns make when you hear them on television. When Mr. Callendar was shot he didn't realise it for a few seconds, then all of a sudden he said "Good God, I've been shot." '

A short distance away, twenty-two-year-old Police Constable Michael Hills was on duty outside St. James's Palace. He heard the shots and ran across The Mall to see what was happening. When he saw the royal car with its smashed rear window he summed up the situation in an instant and without thought for his own safety, grabbed the gunman by the elbow. The man turned and shot P.C. Hills in the stomach. Even though he was badly injured he managed to activate his personal radio and call for help saying 'There's a shooting, I've been shot.'

A number of police cars, summoned by the radio calls and by people who had heard the shots, sped to the area, but before they could arrive there was to be even more shooting and wounding. A taxi had been travelling behind the royal car along The Mall when the incident occurred. The passenger was a well-known Fleet Street journalist, Mr. Brian McConnell, who got out and approached the gunman. McConnell said 'Look, old man, these are friends of mine: give me the gun.' Instead, the gun was aimed, the trigger pulled and McConnell was shot in the chest.

By now The Mall was alive with police and the attacker ran into St. James's Park to make his escape. He was pursued by an unarmed detective, Peter Edwards, who chased him into the bushes, brought him down with a flying tackle and arrested him.

The attempted kidnapping had failed, the incident was over, four people had been wounded and the whole thing had taken less than ten minutes. Rowena Brassey was still crouching alongside the limousine and a young dancing instructress, Samantha Scott, went to her aid. She described to reporters afterwards what she saw. 'I stopped my Mini and ran to the royal car. We huddled on the ground. I could see Mark Phillips protecting Anne while the man tried to get them. They were huddled on the ground. I could see yellow roses scattered over the floor of the car. When the gunman had gone, I opened the door of the car and put my hand on Anne's shoulder. I said to her, 'Are you all right, love?' She replied sweetly, 'I'm all right, thank you.' I asked Mark Phillips if he was O.K. and he said 'I'm fine, thank you.'

Another witness to the attack was an actor Brian McDermott who was driving in The Mall at the time. He said: 'Suddenly, I found myself in the middle of chaos. Then I heard what sounded like a couple of backfires. Then I saw the windscreen of the maroon Rolls being shattered [it was a reasonable error, the actual car used on that occasion being a large Austin Princess], and I realised there was shooting going on. Suddenly, it looked like Northern Ireland. Then I saw this girl ducking from the gunfire. At the same time there was fighting going on on the pavement. Within no time there was a great action going on. There were sirens blaring and police all around The Mall.'

Looking back on the incident after ten years Rowena Fielden (as she now is) says that the biggest surprise of all was the fact that Mark Phillips wasn't shot. 'There were so many bullets flying around in such a confined space, it's amazing that he wasn't hurt.'

The injured men were taken to hospital for emergency operations and the royal couple were driven the short distance to Buckingham Palace where they spent half an hour describing the attack to Scotland Yard Deputy Assistant Commissioner John Gerrard. Though they were 'badly shaken' they were able to give a detailed account.

After giving her statement to the police, Princess Anne made a personal telephone call to Indonesia where her parents were on a State visit. She spoke to her father, the Duke of Edinburgh, to assure him that all was well with her and he woke the Queen to relay the story to her. The time in Indonesia was 5 a.m. Then a telephone call was made to San Diego, California, where the Prince of Wales was paying a courtesy call as part of his duties as communications officer on board H.M.S. *Jupiter*. Later that same evening Princess Anne and Captain Phillips returned to their home at Sandhurst, travelling in separate cars; Captain Phillips in his Rover 2000, closely followed by Princess Anne, apparently none the worse for her experience, driving herself as usual, at the wheel of her Reliant Scimitar sports saloon. There was one extra precaution taken, however: an escort of detectives from Scotland Yard's Special Branch accompanied them.

Alison and Alan Oliver were driving home from an evening engagement when they heard on the car radio that there had been shooting in The Mall and an attempt made to kidnap Princess Anne. As they pulled up in the driveway of their house they heard the telephone ringing. Alison rushed to answer and when she picked up the receiver the voice at the other end said, 'It's me, I'm all right.' In the midst of all the confusion Princess Anne had realised that her close friend and confidante would hear a perhaps garbled version of what happened on the news and she was anxious to reassure her that all was well. Alison Oliver remembers 'feeling weak at the knees when I heard the news flash and a tremendous feeling of relief when I heard her voice. It was typically thoughtful of her to think of others at such a moment of stress. I've never been so glad to get a telephone call in my life.'

Immediately security measures were increased at Sandhurst, with an armed cordon thrown around the Royal Military Academy and two companies of soldiers patrolling the grounds throughout the night. Floodlights, which had been installed when the Princess first took up residence, were switched on all buildings within the grounds, including those on Oak Grove House itself. Before leaving Buckingham Palace, Princess Anne had issued a brief statement in which she said: 'We are very thankful to be in one piece. But we are deeply disturbed and concerned about those who got injured, including our chauffeur Mr. Callendar and Inspector Beaton. Inspector Beaton acted particularly bravely and although shot he continued to protect us. We are extremely grateful to all those members of the police and public who tried to help us.' Princess Anne left for Sandhurst only after issuing instructions that she was to be kept fully informed on the conditions of those who were injured.

She still clearly remembers the event: 'My first reaction was anger. I was furious at this man who was having a tug-of-war with me. He ripped my dress which was a favourite blue velvet I had had made specially to wear away on honeymoon, but of course our main concern was for the people who had tried to save us and who had been shot. They were very brave and looking back on it now their actions seem even more courageous when you think about them in the cold light of day.'

Of the four men wounded in the incident, Inspector Beaton had the worst injuries, having been shot in the chest, stomach and hand. James Beaton had been bodyguard to Princess Anne for only five months, in fact he was appointed to the job on the day of the Royal Wedding, November 14th, 1973, when he was a sergeant. Mr. Beaton was promoted to Inspector within weeks of his appointment, having passed his promotion examination, after eleven years with the police. A married man with two children he still retained the native burr of Aberdeenshire where he had been born thirty years earlier.

News of the kidnapping attempt was flashed around the world within minutes. The Prime Ministers of all the Commonwealth countries were informed immediately and in the House of Commons a debate on Scottish devolution was interrupted so that the Home Secretary, Mr. Roy Jenkins, could make a statement. M.P.s of all parties crowded into the Chamber to hear Mr. Jenkins say: 'I regret to have to report that an attempt was made by an armed man to kidnap Princess Anne at 8 p.m. this evening when she was on her way to Buckingham Palace with her husband. The attempt did not succeed. Neither Princess Anne nor Captain Phillips was hurt. I much regret to say, however, that Princess Anne's protection officer sustained very severe injuries and her driver, a police constable, and a member of the public were also seriously hurt.'

Mr. Edward Heath, Leader of the Opposition, offered the sympathy of the whole House to those injured and to Princess Anne and Captain Phillips. He went on to suggest that the Home Secretary would want to consider what sort of inquiry should be made. One of the basic questions would be how knowledge of the movements of Princess Anne and Captain Phillips came to be known so that anybody could attempt an attack upon them. The Leader of the Liberal Party, Mr. Jeremy Thorpe, deplored any act of violence against any person in this country and Mr. Donald Stewart for the Scottish Nationalists, who had been debating a subject close to their hearts when the announcement was made, expressed abhorrence at the news given by Mr. Jenkins.

When he left Parliament, the Home Secretary drove to the scene of the incident, where police still swarmed all over the place looking for clues. They had already recovered two loaded pistols. The maroon and black Austin limousine still stood where it had been forced to stop. It was shattered by gunfire. The rear offside window and the front offside window were destroyed and the rear window had a star shaped bullet hole in it. Glass fragments were everywhere and there were bloodstains both inside the car and on the pavement alongside. The taxi in which Mr. Brian McConnell was travelling was also still there, raked by gunfire. Television and radio reporters rushed to the spot and programmes were interrupted to give the latest details. There was a great amount of speculation about who was behind the attempt and the I.R.A. issued a statement denying that they were involved in any way. The Prime Minister, Mr. Harold Wilson, ordered an immediate inquiry and Sir Robert Mark, Metropolitan Police Commissioner, assigned three Deputy Assistant Commissioners to head the investigation.

The injured men had been taken to two nearby hospitals: Inspector Beaton and Mr. Callendar to Westminster and P.C. Hills and Mr. McConnell to St. George's Hospital at Hyde Park Corner. Their injuries were serious and needed immediate surgery, but the following day they were all off the danger list. Princess Anne and Captain Phillips sent them flowers and 'get well' messages and they received personal visits from Lord Maclean, who as Lord Chamberlain is head of the Queen's Household. Later when they were well enough to receive more visitors, the royal couple went to see them to offer their personal thanks.

Within three days the Home Office announced that it was considering what medals should be awarded to those who tackled the gunman. The Queen had been consulted and had indicated that she did not want exceptionally important honours bestowed just because her daughter was involved.

Eventually the Queen recognised the bravery of the people involved and Inspector James Beaton received the highest award possible for gallantry in civilian life, the George Cross. Michael Hills, the police constable who had been on duty at St. James's Palace and Mr. Ronald Russel, a businessman who had also tackled the gunman, were awarded the George Medal. Three others involved in the incident, journalist Brian McConnell, chauffeur Alexander Callendar and policeman Peter Edwards, the man who had caught the gunman, were all given the Queen's Gallantry Medal. Edwards also earned himself a bonus by catching the attacker. As a result of his action he was promoted to the rank of Detective Constable.

On Princess Anne's twenty-fourth birthday, August 15th, 1974, the Queen created her a Dame Grand Cross of The Royal Victorian Order for her brave behaviour throughout the ordeal and her husband was made a Commander, while Lady-in-Waiting Rowena Brassey became a member of the Order. The Victorian awards are the Sovereign's personal prerogative and are given only for service considered to be of great value to the Queen herself.

Later that same year, in November, when the injured men had recovered, the Queen gave a special investiture which was followed by a reception to which all the men who had been involved in the operation were invited with their families. It was an opportunity for the Queen to thank them personally for saving her daughter's life, and for Princess Anne and Captain Phillips to add their own appreciation.

Sometime later Inspector Beaton left the Palace Protection Squad for a number of years. But in January 1983 he returned to royal service when he was appointed Personal Detective to Her Majesty the Queen.

Meanwhile the true story of the kidnapping attempt was being revealed in court. If an author had submitted the plot as a work of fiction, it would have been rejected as far too improbable.

The gunman had been identified as Ian Ball, an Englishman born in Watford, Hertfordshire, in 1947. In court it was revealed that he planned to hold Princess Anne for a ransom of £3 million and a free pardon for all his offences. The ransom note had been found on him when he was overpowered in St. James's Park. It was addressed to the Queen and read:

Your daughter has been kidnapped – the following conditions to be fulfilled for her release. A ransom of £3 million is to be paid in £5 notes. They are to be used, unmarked, not sprayed with any chemical substance and not consecutively numbered. The money is to be packed in 30 unlocked suitcases clearly marked on the outside. The following documents are to be prepared: a free pardon to cover the kidnapping, and anything connected with it, i.e. the possession of firearms or the murder of any police officer; a free pardon for any offences committed by myself from parking to murder. As the money is to be banked abroad, I shall be asking for a free pardon to run indefinitely for being in contravention of the Exchange Control Act. Documents are to be prepared for a civilian action to be taken against the police if they disclose my true identity with damages of not less than £1 million. A civilian action to be taken against you or your consorts if you reveal my true identity. No excuses will be accepted for failing to compile these documents. If they cannot be drawn up under existing laws, the laws must be changed.

Ball's letter then went on to describe how the ransom money was to be delivered to him personally on an aircraft waiting at London's Heathrow Airport, bound for Zurich. He wanted the transaction handled by one of his solicitors, a Mr. Clarke. The letter continued: 'No one else will be acceptable. If he is ill, I want him brought to me on a stretcher. If he is dead, I want his body dug up and brought to the plane.'

Ball then wrote that the Queen would have to come and see him herself and give a sample signature so that he could be sure she really was the Queen. Once he had flown to Switzerland, the plane would return and Princess Anne would be released.

A letter written by a madman? Certainly one of his solicitors had stated at a previous hearing on March 28th that 'It should be known in the interest of the defendant and the public generally that the defendant has a confirmed history of psychiatric illness. He was diagnosed in hospital in 1967 as a schizoid and he is being examined at the moment by eminent psychiatrists.'

At the age of twenty-six Ball described himself as a 'loner'. Throughout his life he had felt inadequate and unable to make friends. Even at school he had been such a nonentity that no one could even remember him. He lived with his parents until he was in his early twenties and had a number of jobs, none of any consequence, and again he was seen to be a misfit.

He hadn't worked for two years prior to the kidnap attempt, and four years before the event had slipped into a life of petty crime. He was arrested and convicted three times for receiving stolen property and obtaining goods by deception. It was while he was on probation for one of these offences that his mental state was noticed. He was found to be suffering from nervous debility and psychiatric depression and he attended St. Mary Abbott's Hospital, Kensington, as an outpatient after refusing to be admitted as an inpatient. One of the reasons he gave for the attempted kidnapping was to bring public attention to bear on the lack of facilities for the treatment of mental patients under the National Health Service. He could have been treated privately for his condition but in his confused state he preferred to spend his money, which he saved by living in cheap lodgings and eating only one meal a day, on flying lessons at the former Battle of Britain airfield at Biggin Hill in Kent.

Mentally disturbed he may have been, yet he laid his plans for the kidnap attempt with great care and attention to detail. Shortly before the attack, Ball withdrew all his savings from his bank account – when he was captured he had nearly £700 in notes on him. He also burned all his personal papers, including driving licence, passport and pilot's licence, as well as removing the labels from his clothes.

He rented a house in a quiet cul-de-sac in a residential area of Fleet, Hampshire, just a few miles from Oak Grove House at Sandhurst. The street where Ball went to stay was known locally as 'Brigadiers' Row' because so many army officers lived there. He kept himself very much to himself with the curtains tightly drawn and listening to classical music on records for much of the time.

The week before the attempt he hired a typewriter from a shop in Camberley, Surrey, and attracted attention from the assistant because he said he only needed it for one day, to type two letters. The letters turned out to be the ransom note and a letter to a firm of solicitors in Hounslow, Middlesex, whom he wanted to act as intermediaries in the ransom negotiations.

He hired a Ford Escort car and this was very nearly his undoing. On the very day of the attempted kidnapping, Ball was questioned by the police who were investigating a series of burglaries in the Camberley area. Ball had parked his hired car near the rear entrance of the Royal Military Academy, Sandhurst, so that he could observe Princess Anne's movements. A detective chief inspector noticed the car, asked to see Ball's driving licence, which was produced, presumably a forgery since he had already burnt the original licence with his other documents, searched the boot of the car and then allowed him to leave when nothing was found. This was less than eight hours before the incident in The Mall.

The house he had rented was ready to receive its royal guest and

Ball set off for London to commit the crime and earn himself a rather dubious place in history.

When he appeared before Lord Chief Justice Widgery at the Old Bailey on 22nd May, 1974, Ian Ball pleaded guilty to the kidnap attempt, the attempted murder of two police officers and wounding two civilians. He was ordered to be detained in a special hospital under the Mental Health Act without limit of time.

Two days after the attempted kidnapping, the Home Secretary announced that all royal security measures would be reviewed immediately. Among the subjects to be considered were the setting up of a special police squad to guard royal homes and the Royal Family; whether all royal cars should be fitted with bullet-proof glass; should there be a special communications centre established with two-way radios fitted to all vehicles used by the Royal Family; why the pistol carried by Princess Anne's protection officer jammed after firing only one shot; should advance publicity be given about the travel arrangements of the Royal Family and the routes they would use?

Mr. Jenkins said that he had discussed with the Metropolitan Police Commissioner such action as was seen to be sensible to increase the safeguards already taken against attacks of this kind. Of course the conclusions reached by any inquiry into security surrounding the Royal Family and other public figures must remain confidential if they are to be effective, and one of the other great problems was how to achieve the extra degree of security required without an unacceptable interference with the ability of those being guarded to lead lives as near normal as possible.

It was about this time that the Queen and other members of the Royal Family had started the practice of 'walkabouts' – mingling informally with crowds of onlookers, some of whom had waited hours for the opportunity of exchanging a few words with the royal personality. It was an innovation that pleased the Queen enormously and proved extremely popular with her subjects. Never before had there been such public access to the Monarch and her family and the Queen was known to favour the custom being continued, even after the incident in The Mall. The entire Royal Family hated the idea of any massive security net being thrown around Buckingham Palace and the other royal homes and the Palace Press Office said that the idea of 'bullet proof cages' was out!

There was concern in many quarters that the attack would spark off a series of similar incidents with other public figures. In the House of Commons Mr. John Lee, a Labour member representing the Handsworth constituency of Birmingham, said: 'There is always the danger when acts of this kind happen that disturbed persons might resort to imitative tactics.' The Home Secretary had already indicated that preliminary inquiries had shown that the attack was an isolated incident, carried out by a man with no terrorist connections.

It should be emphasized that even though Princess Anne had been travelling in an unescorted vehicle, she had been accompanied by an armed police officer, and there were already in existence a number of sophisticated arrangements to guard the Royal Family. For instance, radios at all royal homes were tuned to high frequency police wavelengths to make sure contact would not be lost even if the telephone lines were cut; panic buttons were installed at Buckingham Palace, Balmoral, Windsor and Sandringham, wired direct to the nearest police station so that help could be summoned within minutes. Bleepers were in use – electronic devices that enabled police to keep track of the movements of any royal car, so that if it deviated from its prescribed route, they would be aware immediately.

Nevertheless, police protection, though professional, was some-what casual. They deliberately kept a low profile and this is exactly what the Royal Family had wished until then.

In 1981 I spoke to Princess Anne about security in the early days when she was at school at Benenden in Kent. Talking about her detective she said: 'I didn't see much of him. You don't judge things as they are today, the detective was there really only for travelling purposes and he didn't live on the premises, he lived just out of the school grounds . . . he was seen occasionally wandering about, but nobody really bothered about him.'

Vastly different from the royal protection squad these days. Every member of the Royal Family has a number of police officers working a rota system, twenty-four hours a day, seven days a week. They are specially trained in unarmed combat and marksmanship and each has to adapt to the particular lifestyle of his royal 'charge'. Princess Anne's detectives spend more time with her than with their own families. They see her more frequently than her husband, and at Badminton and Burghley they can usually be seen dressed in casual country wear, holding the hand of one or other of the royal children. They live at Gatcombe Park with a very pleasant room inside the house and whenever Princess Anne leaves the grounds, the detective is the figure you see sitting beside her in her own car. Even if Captain Phillips is travelling with the Princess, he is usually required to sit in the back. Not because protocol demands it – security does.

The life of a royal protection officer is very demanding. They travel all over the world. If Princess Anne is going on a visit to Africa, Nepal, Japan or wherever, one of her policemen will have been over every step of the route months in advance, in company with her Private Secretary, to check that every eventuality regarding the safety and comfort of the Princess has been catered for. All the officers in the Royal Protection Squad are volunteers and many of them stay with the Royal Family for years. Superintendent John McLean has been with the Prince of Wales for more than ten years and has become a familiar figure at royal events. An expert wrestler, he swims, runs, skis and sails with his employer and has become a valued friend as well as a most efficient aide.

He and his colleagues have been called upon to come to the rescue of the Prince of Wales on a number of occasions, perhaps the most publicised being shortly after the kidnap attempt in 1974. The Prince was on an underwater warfare course at Portland in Dorset as part of his naval training. One night as Prince Charles lay sleeping, a brother officer, a lieutenant, became deranged and broke into the adjoining sitting room breaking up the furniture. Prince Charles went to investigate and narrowly missed being attacked with a chair. The detective sleeping nearby heard the commotion, and overpowered the man in time.

In 1979, there occurred the most horrific crime involving a member of the Royal Family. The Queen's 'uncle' Earl Mountbatten of Burma – Lord Louis – was murdered along with two members of his family and a young friend, when their boat was blown up by terrorists just off the coast of Ireland. It was a tragedy which affected everyone in this close-knit family, but in no way could this have been described as a breach of security. Lord Mountbatten had no reason to suppose a holiday in one of his favourite countries was going to end this way. He had retained a home in Ireland for over half a century and had many friends among the local populace. The senseless destruction of innocent people was just another example of the mindless violence of recent years which has seen attacks on world leaders.

In 1981 something happened which no one would have believed possible in Great Britain. Shots were fired at the Queen as she rode her horse along The Mall into Horseguards for the Trooping of the Colour ceremony at the annual Birthday Parade. As it happened the young man who fired the shots had loaded the gun with blank cartridges, and though the Queen was badly shaken, she recovered her composure immediately and carried on with the parade as if nothing had happened. Nevertheless the incident showed that if anyone wants to harm a public figure there is very little that can be done to prevent it, beyond taking reasonable precautions.

In 1982 an even more dramatic event occurred when an intruder, Michael Fagin, climbed over the railings around Buckingham Palace, scaled a drainpipe, entered the Palace through an open window and eventually, after wandering around the corridors on the first floor, managed to get into the Queen's bedroom. When she woke in the early morning, she found him sitting on her bed nursing a cut hand and dripping blood over the bedclothes. Her Majesty together with two of her personal domestic servants eventually managed to contain the man in a closet and thankfully the Queen was unharmed by the incident, apart from the traumatic experience of waking to find a stranger in the room which most people would regard as the safest in Britain.

Nearly every member of the Royal Family has at some time experienced an attempted assault on their person. Always without success, but even when such attempts are made with the best of intentions – for example by people who simply want to meet and touch the Royals – security has to be strict.

Some years ago Princess Anne was bothered for months by a man who was obsessed by her. He wanted to meet her desperately and made a number of determined efforts to get her to agree to see him. He used to hang around the Palace gates; he got to know the engagements she was undertaking and he would turn up at every one. In fact he made a thorough nuisance of himself to the Princess, her Household and the police. He would telephone the Palace at all hours asking to be put through to the Princess, and even on one occasion managed to find the address of a Lady-in-Waiting. He arrived on her doorstep one evening demanding to be allowed in to talk about Princess Anne. Finally he was persuaded that his persistance was going to get him nowhere and after a 'friendly but firm' talking to from the police he left the Princess alone. He may have been a harmless old man obsessed with a young princess, but who knows what might have happened if he had managed to get close to her. It's a sad commentary on the times we live in, but suspicion is the name of the game where security and public figures are concerned. If the Royal Family and other world leaders are to continue to be seen in the public eye and live what passes for a normal life, there are risks they are required to run. That they do so, and do so willingly, is in itself a tribute to their courage, determination and devotion to duty.

Chapter 11

PUBLIC LIFE – TODAY

Before one can begin to comprehend the full extent of the roles Princess Anne combines in her public life, it is perhaps helpful to examine the complete list of organisations, both military and civil, with which she is associated.

Within half an hour of her birth in August, 1950, she was enrolled as the millionth member of the Automobile Association, an honour she wasn't to appreciate for some years, but her earliest official civil appointment took place on 1st January, 1970, when she became President of The Save the Children Fund and later in the same year, Patron of the Riding for the Disabled Association. These are the two organisations which claim most of her time and for whom she will go anywhere and meet anyone, at home or abroad. In November, 1970, Princess Anne was installed as Commandant-in-Chief, St. John Ambulance and Nursing Cadets, while two years later in April 1972, she inherited the position of President of the British Academy of Film and Television Arts (BAFTA) from her uncle, the late Earl Mountbatten of Burma.

The Jersey (CI) Wildlife Fund approached her for support in 1972 and in September of that year she became its Patron. On 27th February, 1976, the Princess was made a Freeman of the City of London and in June the same year she became Visitor of Felixstowe College.

She is President, Windsor Horse Trials, President, the Hunters Improvement and Light Horse Breeding Society, and Honorary President, the Royal Caledonian Hunt. Her Royal Highness is Patron of: Gloucester and North Avon Federation of Young Farmers, Royal Port Moresby Society for the Prevention of Cruelty to Animals, the Horse of the Year Ball and the Benenden Ball. She is Vice-Patron of the British Show Jumping Association, Home Farm Trust and Bourne End Junior Sports and Recreation Club.

Among the clubs and associations of which she has become an Honorary Member are: the Island Sailing Club, the British Equine Veterinary Association, the Royal Yacht Squadron, Minchinhampton Golf Club, the Royal Thames Yacht Club, Sussex Agricultural Society and the Young Adventure Club. In March, 1972, the Princess was accorded life membership of the Flying Doctor Society of Africa and she has been a full Member of the Reliant Owners' Club since January, 1971. She is also a Member of the Beaufort Hunt.

Since 1971 Princess Anne has been honoured by six of the City of London Livery Companies, three of whom, the Farriers', Loriners' and Farmers', made her Honorary Freeman, while she is also a Yeoman of the Saddlers' Company, Freeman of the Fishmongers' Company and Honorary Liveryman of the Carmens' Company.

Between 1979 and 1983 Her Royal Highness accepted appointments with four widely differing organisations. She became Patron of Royal Lymington Yacht Squadron; Chancellor of London University; Patron of the National Union of Townswomen's Guilds in September, 1982; and President of the British Olympic Association in April, 1983. As a former competitor in the Olympic Games herself, this latest position is one to which she is able to bring a unique royal perspective.

Princess Anne shares with other members of the Royal Family close connections with the Services, both at home and throughout the Commonwealth. In 1969 she became Colonel-in-Chief of her first two regiments, the 14th/20th King's Hussars and the Worcestershire and Sherwood Foresters (29th/45th Foot). In 1972 her first overseas regiment, the 8th Canadian Hussars (Princess Louise's) was added to the list, and then in June, 1977, when the Princess was appointed Colonel-in-Chief of the Royal Corps of Signals, she also automatically attained the same rank with its sister regiments, the Canadian Forces Communications and Electronics Branch, the Royal Australian Corps of Signals, the Royal New Zealand Corps of Signals, The Royal New Zealand Nursing Corps and the Grey and Simcoe Foresters Militia – Canada, and became Patron of the Royal Corps of Signals Institution. In June 1983, Princess Anne succeeded her great aunt, the late Princess Royal, as Colonel-in-Chief, the Royal Scots (the Royal Regiment).

It was in July, 1974, that the Princess's association with the Senior Service began when she was appointed Chief Commandant of the Women's Royal Naval Service, WRNS; later that same year she became Patron of the Association of Wrens and President of the Women's Royal Naval Service Benevolent Trust. She is President of the Royal Navy and Royal Marines (Haslemere) and she has been elected to life membership of the Royal Naval Saddle Club and the R.N.V.R. Officers' Association.

Her Royal Highness has been associated with the equestrian side of the Services since 1974 when she agreed to become Patron of the Army and Royal Artillery Hunter Trials, and one of her most recent Service appointments took place in August, 1981, when she became Commandant-in-Chief of the Women's Transport Service (FANY).

Princess Anne is President of the Royal School for Daughters of Officers and Patron of the Royal Tournament. She is Honorary Air Commodore R.A.F. Lyneham in Wiltshire and a Life Member of the Royal British Legion Women's Section.

Her activities encompass almost every aspect of service and civilian life from the academic to the technical, from the sporting heights of the British Olympic Association to the caring work of The Save the Children Fund and the Riding for the Disabled Association. Altogether the Princess is involved with sixty-three different organisations and each one regards itself as having proprietorial rights to her attention and interest – and what's more, they seem to get them!

In 1970 Princess Anne accepted her first civil appointment when she agreed to become President of The Save the Children Fund. She was the Fund's sixth President, suceeding the late Viscount Boyd of Merton, and only its second lady President; her great-aunt, the late Countess Mountbatten of Burma, had held the job from 1949 to 1960.

From the very beginning Her Royal Highness was determined that she was not going to be just another royal figurehead. She began to involve herself in the activities of the Fund and her appointment coincided with a considerable expansion of its interests far beyond the borders of Britain and Europe, to the emerging nations of the Third World, in Africa, the Middle and Far East.

The Princess told the first Annual General Meeting she attended, that she was anxious to see a considerable growth in the support given to the Fund by young people. She went on: ' . . . I feel there is still a vast reservoir of youthful enthusiasm for helping good works that remains to be tapped. Young people of my own age group must see to it that The Save the Children Fund grows as successfully in the next fifty years as it did in its first half century.'

Princess Anne remained at the meeting for two days and she made it quite clear that she wasn't interested in meeting only the hierarchy of the Fund but the grass-roots workers who devote so much time and energy to alleviating the problems of the young throughout the world. So she spent a great deal of time talking with as many supporters as she could, asking questions, finding out what they were doing and what they felt she could do to help. There was no fuss and very little protocol, and it didn't take very long for the word to get around that the new President was an approachable young woman who didn't stand on ceremony and who was genuinely concerned with the aims of Save the Children.

Within a short time the Princess became involved in almost every aspect of the work of the Fund, travelling all over the country helping to raise funds and seeing for herself the ways in which the money was invested on behalf of the children. And even when she was carrying out other official duties she never missed an opportunity of pushing the Fund's interests. On a visit to Wolverhampton, the Princess gently turned down the offer of a present to mark her visit, suggesting instead a donation to S.C.F. When she visited Hong Kong as Colonel-in-Chief of the 14th/20th King's Hussars she combined the trip with visits to a number of S.C.F. projects in the colony. This visit also brought a great benefit to the entire population of a small remote village on the Sai Kung Peninsula. The community of Hang Hau had been trying for four years to get the village connected to the mains water supply. When it was discovered that Princess Anne was to visit them, the job was carried out immediately. Afterwards the local people christened their benefactor Princess Anne Water.

During her first year as President, Princess Anne appeared in two films on behalf of the Fund. The first was entitled 'The Princess and the Children' and won for the producer, Martin Benson, a silver award at the prestigious International Film and Television Festival in New York where it was entered in the Social Services category. The film showed the Princess's work as President of the Fund and one of the highlights was when she was interviewed by a number of boys and girls on various aspects of her personal life, including which football team she supported, what it was like to live in Buckingham Palace and what sort of things she liked to eat. It was shown at the 670 branches of the Fund in the United Kingdom and also on a number of television networks overseas. Unfortunately it did not receive a showing either on B.B.C. or I.T.V. in Britain, which is a pity, because if it had, it would have shown what a remarkable rapport the twenty-year-old Princess has with young children.

The second film was produced by the B.B.C. television children's programme 'Blue Peter' and was made during a two-week visit to Kenya, which the Princess made with Prince Charles in 1970. The experienced and popular television performer Valerie Singleton accompanied the Princess and together they were filmed touring some of the magnificent game parks of the country, and visiting Starehe Boys School in Nairobi, where over a thousand boys who are either orphaned or from poor families, are given an education to help them become teachers, doctors and engineers. This is one of the most successful S.C.F. projects in Africa and clearly Princess Anne had done her homework before the tour; the answers she gave to Miss Singleton's penetrating questions proved how knowledgeable she was about the work of the Fund in that part of the world. A certain amount of brusqueness in her comments during the film indicated her impatience with those who did not appear to realise that she was developing into a true professional who knew what she was talking about. The programme was an outstanding success and achieved for S.C.F. the sort of publicity money could not buy.

It soon became obvious that wherever the Princess travelled she was regarded as a roving ambassadress for Save the Children, whether she was on a royal visit or working purely for the Fund. In Australia, New Zealand, Hong Kong, Nepal, Thailand, the United States and Canada, she found time to visit the national headquarters and usually managed to interest her hosts in raising money for one of their projects.

Even when she visited the Channel Islands in a private capacity she managed to find time to meet local workers and encourage them in their efforts. Throughout the years she has been associated with Save the Children Princess Anne has demonstrated complete identification with its aims and a knowledgeable interest in its work. The Director General, John Cumber, says that she knows as much as anybody in S.C.F. about the extent of its activities, and more than most about its global involvement. He first met her when he was Field Director in the Sudan and the Princess made a short visit to Khartoum, on her return journey from Ethiopia, to get a first-hand account of the Fund's projects. Mr. Cumber remembers that his young President was curious to see how the Fund's money was being spent in these outlying areas. As she had not been in the least intimidated by the heat, the flies, the dust and the incredible squalor of Ethiopia, the intense heat of the Sudanese capital was not even mildly irritating.

In 1981 Princess Anne went to the Kingdom of Nepal where she was welcomed by Princess Sharada, the President of the Nepalese Children's Organisation. After a day spent at the Fund's headquarters in Patan she was hurled into the most arduous part of the tour – a steep four-hour climb through some of the world's most spectacular scenery from Tamur to Dhankuta to see the mother-and-child health clinic which had been built there. On this part of the journey the Princess showed how superbly fit she is, leaving several of her party gasping for breath in the rarified atmosphere.

But it was in 1982 that she undertook the most difficult, and at times dangerous, tour on behalf of the Fund. In October she set off to visit six African countries in a three-week spell that would cover some 14,000 miles. It was a semi-official tour which meant that the Princess not only worked for the Fund, but also carried out a number of royal engagements. The Princess's daily programme usually began at 7.30 a.m. and rarely did it end before midnight. John Cumber as Director General accompanied the Princess and remarked afterwards

'When the day's programme was delayed at any point, it was usually because our President would not be hurried away from our project but continued talking to the S.C.F. staff, expatriate and local, and their patients. The time we lost had to be made up on the road.' In Swaziland where the tour began the Princess saw the STOP polio immunisation programme in action, while in Zimbabwe she had to journey right into the bush to visit a village health centre. The President of Malawi, Dr. Hastings Banda, gave her party an official welcome to his country and in Kenya it was a return visit to Starehe School in Nairobi which she had first visited twelve years earlier. On that occasion she had been shown around by the Head Boy of the School. In 1982 he turned up again, this time complete with wife and children who were presented to the Princess.

Somalia was next on the list of countries, but it nearly did not get included because when the royal party were in Kenya they received messages from the Foreign Office at home advising them against the trip because of possible security risks; at that time Somalia and Ethiopia were engaged in a sporadic border war. The Princess insisted on sticking to the schedule and not letting down the staff and the patients at Boroma refugee camp where thousands of men, women and children had turned out to greet her. It took over five hours to drive over some of the most difficult roads in Africa, but the Somali authorities had taken every possible precaution to safeguard the Princess. The end result proved to be well worth the effort.

By now the press party which was attached to the Princess had begun to realise how hard she worked and the stories which appeared in newspapers back in Britain were amongst the most favourable the Princess had ever experienced. The reporters and photographers had expected the usual public relations exercise; instead they got a genuine newsworthy story and indeed, three of them were so impressed that they later became individual sponsors of children in Kenya.

The Princess has always been aware of her public image and there has always been an uneasy relationship with the press, so the about-turn by the journalists was duly noted.

Princess Anne's intelligent application to her role as President won over not only the members of the press, but the field workers of The Save the Children Fund, many of whom thought, until they met her, that her knowledge of what they were trying to achieve would be superficial and sketchy. 'Her commitment to her job sometimes comes as a surprise to people,' said John Cumber. 'Unless they've met her, our people don't know what to expect, and tend to pitch the explanations of their work at the sort of level any layman can understand. But she knows her stuff all right and they find they have to pitch it at a much higher level.' In fact her considerable knowledge of local diseases, and the treatment for them, surprised the S.C.F. doctors and nurses and this enabled them to be more frank when discussing their work with Princess Anne.

North Yemen was officially the final country on the itinerary in 1982 where the S.C.F. clinic was the destination, and from there it should have been home. Instead the Andover of the Queen's Flight made a long over-night haul, with three refuelling stops, *en route* for Beirut, where they landed in the early morning. For obvious reasons the visit had been kept secret until the last minute, but nevertheless hundreds of children lined the bomb-scarred approach road to the S.C.F. clinic where Princess Anne made history by being the first member of the Royal Family to visit Lebanon since the troubles began.

At the end of the three-week tour the Princess was disarmingly modest about the impact she had made. When it was suggested that in some of the more remote areas the people may not have known who she was, she replied: 'Quite possibly they didn't. It didn't worry me. I didn't stop to ask if they knew who I was.'

Other members of the Royal Family, knowing of Princess Anne's concern for underpriviledged children, report back to her on any needy cases. When the Queen visited a children's clinic in India in November, 1983, she was visibly distressed by what she saw and promised to tell Princess Anne about it on her return.

Princess Anne is realistic about her value as President. She summed up the tour in the following words: 'As President, quite apart from the fact that it helps to see what they are doing and how the thing is really working, one of the few things I suppose I can achieve is publicity, and that's not blatant in the sense that I'm going around banging the drum, but if it has that effect so much the better because that is something that I can do reasonably quietly and still bring people's attention to what's going on.'

The Director General of Save the Children is in no doubt about the value of the work done by the Princess. 'It's not just a question of publicity, important as that aspect is. But Princess Anne can get things done which would be difficult if not impossible for the rest of us. When she makes a request on our behalf it's very difficult for anyone to refuse her; she has such a discreet way of asking that sounds so reasonable – which of course it is, if ultimately the end result is of benefit to the Fund.'

If Save the Children was the first charity to which the Princess gave her support in a tangible form, Riding for the Disabled was not

37. Six-year-old Prince Edward being driven by his twenty-year-old sister at Windsor. The pony carriage is called a French Chaise and was given to the Princess of Wales (later Queen Alexandra) by the Prince of Wales (later King Edward VII) in 1875. It was driven by the Queen (as Princess Elizabeth) in the Windsor Horse Show in 1940 and today it is one of the favourite carriages in the Royal Mews, especially for giving rides to the younger members of the family.

38. (*Above*) A twenty-first birthday portrait by Norman Parkinson.

39. (*Opposite, top*) As Commandant-in-Chief, St. John Ambulance and Nursing Cadets.

40. (*Opposite, bottom*) Engagement day – 29th May, 1973.

41. By the time of the wedding in November, 1973, Mark Phillips
had been promoted to Captain and when he posed with Princess
Anne for this romantic photograph in the Long Gallery at Windsor
Castle, he was wearing the formal evening mess dress of his
regiment, 1st The Queen's Dragoon Guards.

42. The royal wedding in Westminster Abbey on November 14,
1973. Captain Phillips leads his bride back down the aisle, past
the Royal Family on the right of the picture and his own family
on the left.

43. (*Top*) The Royal Christmas at Windsor, 1975: the Royal Family leaves St. George's Chapel after morning service.

44. (*Above*) At the Commonwealth Games in Christchurch, New Zealand, in 1974, where they witnessed the Superheavyweight Class in the Weightlifting Contest.

45. (*Top*) This is the shot most photographers like to get.

46. (*Above*) 'If I wasn't who I am, I would like to be a lorry driver,' says Princess Anne. It's a job she enjoys frequently at the wheel of her horsebox.

47. Although he was selected as a member of the British Olympic Team for Montreal in 1976, Mark didn't get a ride. Instead he spent most of his time assisting his team-mates. Here he is helping Princess Anne and Goodwill get ready for the Dressage Phase at Bromont.

far behind. Lavinia, Duchess of Norfolk, is President of R.D.A. and it was she who first had the idea of inviting Princess Anne to become its Royal Patron, though, in retrospect, she thinks that perhaps she made a mistake in doing so. 'The Princess takes on so many jobs on our behalf, she should really be President, not I. If by Patron you mean someone who is simply a figurehead, then that is a complete misnomer for Princess Anne. She is much, much more than that.'

The Princess thought long and hard before accepting the invitation. 'Until then members of the Family had accepted almost everything they were offered, just because it was considered impolite not to. I decided right from the start that if I was going to become involved with an organisation, I was going to try and do something for them, apart from just lending my name.'

This was perfect as far as Riding for the Disabled was concerned. The Princess was right in the public eye at the time having recently won the European Three Day Event title on Doublet, and she was competing at horse trials throughout the country regularly, so she was an ideal choice as a focus of attention for a charity whose central theme was horses.

Riding for the Disabled consists of a large number of small groups of volunteers who provide facilities for people of all ages, both physically and mentally handicapped, to learn the basic skills of riding. Many thousands of disabled people have learnt to ride through the good offices of R.D.A. and the organisation has helped to add another dimension to their lives. Learning to ride is not easy for a disabled person, it requires courage, perseverance and equanimity, and for the helpers good humour is equally important.

Princess Anne says, 'The world is not designed for disabled people, and the sooner we come to terms with that fact, the better. The most valuable help we in R.D.A. can give, is to get our riders to achieve independence. That's the ultimate goal: to see them free from the need for help.'

Since the Princess became Patron of Riding for the Disabled in 1971 she has taken an active role in promoting the aims of the Association and one of the main benefits has been the fact that she is able to attract the sort of financial aid without which the Association would not be able to continue. The Hon. Verona Kitson was Chairman of R.D.A. for twelve years until her retirement in 1982 and she has no doubts about the value of Princess Anne's patronage. 'Most of the people involved with R.D.A. have something to do with the equestrian world outside, but they do not, of course, have the same clout as Her Royal Highness when it comes to asking favours of our potential benefactors. Princess Anne has a way of getting people to donate money and other gifts to charity which, in anyone else, would seem blatant. Apart from her fund-raising abilities, though, is the very real pleasure that riders and helpers alike get when she turns up at a meeting and spends much more time with them than was planned. She never turns anyone away and her patience with even the most severely disabled is an example to us all.'

Dick Moss, the Director of the Association, is responsible for keeping the Princess's office informed of all the activities of R.D.A., also for channelling all the requests for visits. His feelings about her are completely unequivocal: 'She's a marvellous Patron, always attending the Annual General Meeting and sitting through the business of Conference and contributing to all the discussions that go on about the various aspects of our work.'

Another of the unique benefits that accrue from having a member of the Royal Family as Patron came about in November, 1981. Just before the R.D.A.'s Annual Conference, Princess Anne invited 485 members to an evening reception in Buckingham Palace. She received personally every one of her guests and allowed them plenty of time to wander slowly through a number of the State Apartments so that they could enjoy the priceless collection of paintings and other works of art that are permanently on display. All her personal Household were there to help make it a friendly, informal party and one of the surprises of the evening was the sudden and unannounced arrival of the Duke of Edinburgh who dropped in to chat for a few minutes with several of the disabled guests. It's this sort of bonus that gives a tremendous boost to the helpers who work the rest of the year in small, out of the way groups, unselfishly helping others to help themselves.

Mrs. Marjorie Langford is the current Chairman of R.D.A. and she took over at a time when the number of groups in the country had grown to 545, providing riding facilities for some 14,000 disabled people throughout the British Isles. 'It's big business these days,' she says, 'with so many charities making constant demands on people's pockets you need to have a thoroughly professional approach, and perhaps even more important, is the way you spend the money that's donated.' Princess Anne gets reports from Mrs. Langford regularly and if she has a query about an item of expenditure, she is not in the least reticent about asking a number of pertinent questions. As Marjorie Langford says: 'The thing is she actually knows what she is talking about, and there is no one in R.D.A. who knows more than she does about what we do and how we do it.'

Disabled people are not always an attractive sight to the able-bodied and many people find it distasteful to be in close contact with someone with a severe handicap. I have been with Princess Anne on a number of occasions when I, personally, found it difficult not to show my feelings at some of the disabilities, but she has never flinched. She doesn't appear to mind how badly disfigured a person is or how many sticky hands grab at her dress. When I put it to her that this sort of thing did not seem to bother her, she did admit that perhaps that was part of her training, but she added 'It's not only important for the person concerned, but perhaps even more so for the parents who may be standing nearby. It would be terribly hurtful if one stepped backwards just to avoid someone dribbling over you.'

The Duchess of Norfolk has known the Princess for many years and has no hesitation about asking her to attend some function or other on behalf of the Association. She says: 'I've never known her turn us down, no matter where we ask her to go or how many times. She takes a personal interest in everything we do and if ever there was a working Patron, Princess Anne is it. The fact that she is also knowledgeable about horses is an added bonus of course, and a number of tips she has given have been incorporated into our standard procedure. We couldn't ask for a better leader than the one we've got.'

While a great deal of Princess Anne's time and energy is devoted to working for Save the Children and Riding for the Disabled, both very worthy causes, they could hardly be described as glamorous charities. Once a year, though, the Princess does have an opportunity for dressing up in her finest clothes, putting on her diamonds and meeting some of the most glamorous, talented and wealthy people in the glistening world of show business. The occasion is the annual presentation of awards to members of the British Academy of Film and Television Arts, of which Her Royal Highness became President in 1971. When I asked her how she became involved with the Academy her reply showed that like so many Royal duties it was a case of being gently coerced into volunteering. She said: 'Lord Mountbatten was involved with it from the start, and he bequeathed it to me, if that's the right word. Well, he made quite a good case out for it and he was a man it was quite impossible to say no to, so that's really how I got it.' But the Princess is a little sceptical about the so-called 'glamorous' side of the industry. 'BAFTA was formed in order to keep film and television on much the same side, especially as the British side of the industry seemed to be shrinking somewhat, and it was thought to be a good idea to get them together and to work in much the same direction. I'm constantly being told that British technicians are probably the best there are around, but it doesn't seem to encourage enough film-making in this country, which is a pity.'

Reginald Collin, the ebullient, gregarious Director of BAFTA has quite definite views on the value the industry places on having a member of the Royal Family as its President. 'Like so many other organisations these days we are constantly short of money, and whenever we ask Princess Anne to attend a fund-raising function on behalf of the Academy, we know that it's going to be a sell-out. There is more glamour surrounding the Royal Family than any of the stars who act in films or television, and it isn't only the big events that she comes to. In 1982, affairs of State prevented her from making the presentations at our annual awards ceremony, but she did turn up for the Craft Awards where the technicians are honoured. This is not televised and there are very few press representatives around, but the Princess spent the entire evening at the Academy making the awards and talking to the carpenters, electricians and lighting men who are rarely given the opportunity of being in the limelight themselves.'

Princess Anne herself admits that 'I get to see hardly any films and don't watch television all that much, but from my point of view it's an interesting profession. I perhaps have some experience of both sides of it from the little that I have done and I think I know what it's about.' She has in fact done a great deal more than 'just a little'. Since her first television programme with Valerie Singleton in Kenya in 1971, she has appeared on television as much as almost any other member of the Royal Family, and certainly in a wider variety of roles.

In 1981, she allowed a camera team from Thames Television to follow her for a year making a working profile. For this film she not only was filmed at home and abroad, in public and private, but she also saw the 'rushes' of the filming, made suggestions about the editing and recorded the final 'voice-over' commentary. For one particular segment of the programme she had to drive her car up and down the lanes around her home in Gloucestershire for several hours so the cameraman could get the right shots, while at the same time remembering where she was with her 'actuality' speech. It was a performance as professional as any of those for which she hands out awards every year, and the experienced film-makers in the crew were unanimous in their praise for her attitude to what can be a tiring and boring routine.

Reginald Collin is the first to acknowledge the debt BAFTA owes the Royal Family. He points out that it was a donation from the Queen and the Duke of Edinburgh which led to the formation of the Academy in the first place. In 1969 the B.B.C. had made a film about the Queen and her family, which was shown all over the world, and Her Majesty decided that part of the proceeds, around £60,000, should go towards establishing BAFTA, and it was from these beginnings that the present Academy grew to its present impressive headquarters in Piccadilly, London. This is the focal point for the film and television industries in Britain and contains the Princess Anne Theatre in which all the seats have been endowed by leading personalities from all over the world. So you could be sitting in a seat with Laurence Olivier's name on it, or that of Telly Savalas, Walt Disney, Julie Andrews or Richard Burton.

A further close working link between the Royal Family and the Academy has been established through Lord Brabourne, a cousin of the Queen. This very successful producer has long been associated with BAFTA and is now one of its Trustees, so there's no excuse for Princess Anne not being up to date with what's happening in the world of the cinema.

However, if there is one improvement the Princess would like to see at BAFTA, it concerns the 'bus lane' which runs immediately outside the building. Even Royal limousines have to stop beyond the lane and, as Princess Anne frequently tells Reginald Collin, 'Every time I come here I take my life in my hands.'

Another of Princess Anne's military units is the Royal Corps of Signals. This is a large organisation with more than 12,000 regular officers and men and some 5,000 part-time soldiers serving in the Territorial army. In all, the Royal Corps of Signals accounts for approximately nine per cent of the British Army.

For more than thirty years their Colonel-in-Chief had been the Princess Royal and since she died in 1965 they had been without a titular head until Princess Anne was appointed by the Queen in 1977.

Twelve years is perhaps a long time for a large Corps to be without a Colonel-in-Chief but whenever it was suggested that some other member of the Royal Family might be a suitable replacement, the Corps replied respectfully but firmly that they would prefer to wait until the person should become available whom they regarded as a natural successor to the Princess Royal. In the words of Major General Peter Bradley, the now retired Master of Signals, 'for us it was The Princess Anne or no one and we were prepared to await Her Majesty's pleasure'. On the 11th June, 1977, the Queen appointed Her Royal Highness to be Colonel-in-Chief, Royal Corps of Signals, and so began yet another of the remarkable parallels between her life and that of her great aunt, the late Princess Royal. General Bradley, as the then Master of Signals – who is the statutory head of the Corps and senior Colonel Commandant – acted as the main channel of communication between the Corps and the Colonel-in-Chief, so it was his responsibility to acquaint the Princess with the status and functions of her new position. He remembers calling on Princess Anne at Buckingham Palace for his first formal visit.

'She was expecting her first child, her hair was down on her shoulders and my first impressions were, how much prettier she was than she appeared in photographs. She may have been slightly apprehensive when she discovered the size of the Corps but she was clearly anxious to learn as much about her Corps and to meet as many people as possible as soon as she could.'

The Royal Corps of Signals is comprised of more than thirty regiments and it is allied to its counterparts in Australia, New Zealand and Canada, all of which have been visited by Princess Anne who is their Colonel-in-Chief also. She has likewise been to see the Queen's Gurkha Signals which is an affiliated regiment to whom she has granted the privilege of carrying her pipe banner.

In this context mention should also be made of the officers and women of the Women's Royal Army Corps, who serve with the Royal Signals in many places. During the period since she became Colonel-in-Chief, the Princess has acquired a great deal of knowledge of the work of the Corps in many parts of the world. She is allowed to see everything, even the most secret equipment, and once a quarter she is given a full report on the activities being carried out by her Corps. Any matters of immediate interest are passed on to her at once. Officers and men of the Royal Signals are included in every theatre of operations involving the British Army and they suffered a number of casualties during the Falklands campaign in 1982. After members of the Corps returned to their bases in the U.K. Princess Anne attended a reception in Blandford in Dorset where she met many of them and spent a considerable time talking to the relatives of those who had been killed or wounded. General Bradley cites this as one example of her compassion and fellow feeling for the members of her Corps and their families. It was also another of the occasions of which the national press took little note.

The Princess usually makes about four visits every year to the Corps and since she became Colonel-in-Chief she has met and spoken to at least 2,750 officers and men and more than 600 of their wives, not to mention hundreds of casual greetings and countless children. The Corps regards it as essential that the families should be included whenever the Princess is visiting, and contrary to the reports which sometimes appear in newspapers, they say she never passes anyone by. If a visit is taking longer than planned it is usually because Princess Anne is chatting with one of the families who have been waiting to see her. She is aware of the need for precise timing when official engagements are being prepared but if it's a choice between keeping to time or disappointing anybody, be it a soldier or his family, the timetable is the one to suffer. Her attitude is 'if they have taken the time and trouble to come and see me, the very least I can do is to spend a few moments with them, and what's more it's something I thoroughly enjoy anyway.'

The welfare of retired members of the Corps is also a matter of concern to the Colonel-in-Chief. She is patron of the Royal Signals Association, an organisation with 13,000 members at its sixty-two branches. In 1983 the Princess attended the Association's reunion at Catterick, where she had the opportunity to meet many of them.

By its very nature the Royal Corps of Signals is a highly technical Corps and Princess Anne would have been readily forgiven if she had shown only a perfunctory interest in the complicated equipment now used in modern communications; but all ranks have been amazed by her increasing grasp of electronics and detailed knowledge of the subject. They are advised not to try and impress her with technicalities. If they do try and dazzle her with science she is quite apt to turn the tables on them with a question even they cannot answer. It's all rather different from visits made by the last Colonel-in-Chief, in what perhaps were simpler times. When the Princess Royal, who was an extremely popular and much loved member of the Corps, made an official visit, the emphasis was different and the level of technical explanation restrained. The late Princess Royal occupied a very special place in the hearts of the Royal Signals and they still celebrate Princess Royal Day – 28th June, the anniversary of the formation of the Corps – every year by sending loyal greetings to Princess Anne, and obviously the comparison with her great aunt does not disconcert her at all as she is pleased to reply and quite content for the occasion to be marked in this manner.

General Bradley who admits to 'adoring her' pays the Princess, what in his opinion must be the ultimate compliment: 'If she wasn't who she is, she could have been a dedicated signals officer in her own right.'

The Senior Service provides Her Royal Highness with her only uniformed appointment. Princess Anne became Chief Commandant of the Women's Royal Naval Service (WRNS) on 1st July, 1974. (The post had remained vacant since the death of her great aunt Princess Marina, Duchess of Kent, the previous Chief Commandant, in 1968.)

The WRNS was formed originally in 1917 as a volunteer force but was disbanded shortly after the end of hostilities in 1919. It was reformed in preparation for the Second World War and by 1945 its strength had grown to 46,700. By the time Princess Anne joined the WRNS in 1974, the numbers had been stabilised to the present strength of 300 officers and a little over 2,700 ratings, who serve at naval establishments throughout the world.

During the first year of her association with the WRNS, Princess Anne paid visits to H.M.S. *Dauntless*, the initial training establishment, H.M.S. *Amazon* and H.M.S. *President*, where she was able to meet for the first time all the senior serving officers of the WRNS.

The following year she arranged for a reception to be held in St. James's Palace, for serving and retired members of the Service.

The Princess has always had a special affinity with the sea; with both her father and grandfather having served in the Royal Navy that is only to be expected, and she was particularly proud when the Queen appointed her to lead the WRNS. She accompanied her parents when they went to Portsmouth to welcome Prince Andrew on his return from active service in the Falklands in 1982.

Two of the previous Commandants of the WRNS, Miss Elizabeth Craig McFeeley and Miss Voula McBride, served under Princess Anne and they are in no doubt about what it means to have a royal princess as their Chief Commandant. Miss McBride says 'she took an active interest right from the start and we were kept on our toes from the moment she took command. It was not a case of just having a Royal name on the letterheading, but someone who really cared about the service and wanted to play her part in promoting its interests.' The Princess is also by virtue of her appointment, President of the Women's Royal Naval Service Benevolent Trust and Patron of the Association of Wrens. She attends the Annual General Meetings of the Trust which aims to provide relief in cases of necessity or distress to anyone of any rank who is serving or has served in the WRNS since the outbreak of the Second World War in 1939.

Miss Craig McFeeley recalls that 'Her Royal Highness has never been prepared to stand back and simply accept anything she is told. If she has a query about our work she will ask for specific answers and her knowledge of what goes on in the Navy comes as something of a surprise, when you realise the extent of her other activities. I think we were very lucky to get her because she exemplifies exactly the image we want the WRNS to have these days. She is modern, thoroughly professional, intelligent and as the first generation of the Royal Family to have a separate career – with her riding – she has brought a modern outlook to the position of Chief Commandant and that is so important in this day and age.'

The present generation of WRNS are able to identify with the Princess because she is the same age as many of them and with a husband who has served as a regular officer in the army, she knows at first hand some of the problems they have to cope with. In her mid-thirties now, Princess Anne could remain with the WRNS for the rest of this century; if she does they will be perfectly happy.

The Princess is also Commandant-in-Chief of the oldest voluntary organisation for women in Britain, The Women's Transport Service (FANY). Since 1907 they have been employed as ambulance drivers and interpreters in peacetime and in wartime. For forty-seven years The Women's Transport Service was led by the late Princess Alice, Countess of Athlone, until her death in January 1981. Seven months later Princess Anne took over, and the Corps Commandant, Sheila Parkinson, says that the Princess is carving a special niche for herself which they hope she will occupy for many years to come.

Every summer, usually in May or early June, around 30,000 people receive invitations to take tea with Her Majesty, the Queen, during the first two weeks of July.

The occasions are the annual Garden Parties which have now replaced the old style 'coming out' balls at which young debutantes were presented to the Sovereign. The Garden Parties, or to give them their correct title, Afternoon Parties, are held three times a year in the grounds of Buckingham Palace, with a further party being held in the gardens of the Palace of Holyroodhouse in Edinburgh. This is done so that Scottish guests of the Queen will not have the expense and inconvenience of having to travel to London in order to enjoy their brief moment of glory in the company of the Monarch.

It is usual for between 8,000 to 9,000 guests to turn up at Buckingham Palace and they will range from a council worker who has been invited as a reward for long service to the community, to the bishops and archbishops, diplomats and senior politicians who receive invitations every year.

The first indication one gets is when a large, white envelope with one's name handwritten and always addressed to the lady of the house, pops through the letter box. The envelope has not been stamped; there is simply a cypher containing the legend E II R in the lower left-hand corner.

When the guest lists were extended to include people from all walks of life the Queen was very anxious that no one should be put to the expense of hiring a morning suit if it was going to be a hardship, so she insisted that lounge suits were acceptable. Nevertheless, they are the exception, and the majority of male guests are attired in formal morning dress complete with top hat. Ladies almost invariably wear hats, and trouser suits are definitely frowned on.

Along with the invitation is a map showing the three entrances to the Palace and even pointing out the nearest underground railway station. And you also get a special car pass to be placed inside the windscreen so that on the day in question the police can identify your vehicle and allow you to park on one of the approach roads to the Palace.

The three entrances are at Constitution Hill Gate, Grosvenor Place Gate, and the Grand Entrance right at the front of the Palace. This is the one chosen by most guests because for most of them it may be the only opportunity they will have of actually going into Buckingham Palace itself and so queues start forming shortly after lunch to be in good time when the gates open at 3.15 p.m.

The 'crocodile' of guests enters via either the South Centre Gate or the North Centre Gate and is then guided across the inner courtyard to the Grand Entrance. The main staircase with its rich red carpet opens up before you as you pass through the Marble Hall and into the central Bow Room, having first delivered up any cameras you might be carrying to the courteous attendants who politely inform you that no photographs are allowed at any of the Garden Parties. Guests normally linger as long as they can in the Bow Room because it does give one a chance to see just a fraction of the treasures contained in the Palace. In recesses in the four corners are assembled the Mecklenburg-Strelitz table service of Chelsea porcelain, which was commissioned by King George III and Queen Charlotte and completed in 1763.

The Bow Room itself was redecorated in 1902 and the gold and white ceiling supported by columns of grey Carrara marble is softened by the deep red colours of the carpets and velvet curtains.

To get into the garden itself, guests pass through the glass doors onto the Terrace and descend the steps onto the most exclusive lawns in the world. There are forty acres of gardens containing lilies, delphiniums, rhododendrons, azaleas, camellias and three varieties of rose: 'Queen Elizabeth', 'Silver Lining' and 'Peace'.

On very hot afternoons some of the guests head for the lake at the West End of the garden where the elegant languor of the pink flamingoes has delighted the eye since 1959.

The tea tents are arranged along the southern wall of the Palace Gardens and old hands among the guests always make their way there as soon as they arrive; they know that most of the crowd will wait to see the Queen and then there is an enormous crush as thousands of people try to get served at the same time. The Queen and the Duke of Edinburgh attend all the Garden Parties with other senior members of the Royal Family going to at least one. Let us look at one occasion when Princess Anne joined her parents, her cousin Princess Alexandra and ex-King Constantine of the Hellenes.

At 4 p.m. precisely the Royal Party steps through an open glass door of the Bow Room onto the Terrace at the rear of the Palace. The Queen leads the way to the top of the steps leading down onto the Garden; as soon as she arrives at the top of the steps, one of the two military bands on duty plays the National Anthem.

The Queen is wearing a coral-coloured dress, with matching hat and carrying a black handbag. One pace behind her and to her left the Duke is attired in a grey morning suit, as is ex-King Constantine and the Hon. Angus Ogilvy who is accompanying his wife, Princess Alexandra.

Immediately in front of the Queen, at the foot of the steps, a line has been formed of those people who are to be presented before the Royal 'walkabout'. These are official guests such as incoming High Sheriffs, Lords Lieutenant and High Court judges. Meanwhile the other guests have arranged themselves into a number of lanes down which the Royal Party will walk – each member taking a separate lane. The Yeomen of the Guard form up lining the route the Queen will take, and this is always the most densely packed lane. Before the Royals emerge, a number of rather distinguished-looking gentlemen – all very tall with the immaculate bearing of former officers of the Household Brigade – have marshalled the guests and gone through the preliminary task of selecting those who will be honoured by being presented to Her Majesty. If a guest is wearing an unusual uniform, a particular decoration, or is perhaps handicapped in some way, there's a good chance that they will have something interesting to tell the Queen, so they are asked to stand a little in front of the lines of other guests. As the Queen walks slowly down the lanes acknowledging the applause of her guests, one of the courtiers will murmur that 'the gentleman you are about to meet, Ma'am, has worked for the Post Office for 47 years and never missed a day'. Then to the astonishment of the aforementioned guest, the Queen offers her hand and remarks how pleased she is to meet someone who has never had a day off in nearly half a century. And the truly astonishing part of the whole business is that the Queen makes one believe that she really means it.

Meanwhile Princess Anne has moved to her own lane on the Queen's immediate right. She is wearing a stunning outfit of an ivory-coloured dress with dark blue and red flowers patterned on it and an elegant, wide-brimmed, cream hat to match. The Princess is in good form and laughs and jokes a lot with a wide variety of people, none of whom she has met before, but everyone with a story they are anxious to tell the Princess, and she listens intently and asks intelligent questions with an air of someone who really does want to know.

One of Her Royal Highness's advance party is an old friend, Colonel 'Bill' Lithgow – for twelve years *chef d'équipe* to the British Equestrian Team at the time when she was in the forefront of international competition. He has just spied someone who looks familiar. It turns out to be the man who provided the commentary at the first cross-country event Colonel Lithgow attended many years ago, so he is brought forward to meet the Princess. They obviously have something in common and she spends quite some time talking to him and hearing about horse shows of days gone by.

One or two of the guests who are presented to the Princess are obviously nervous and a bit overcome at meeting her for the first time, but she has a remarkable capacity for putting people at ease, and in no time the atmosphere is relaxed and informal, with laughter being the most frequent sound to come from the groups surrounding the Princess.

Her party is made up of a Lady-in-Waiting, Mrs. Andrew Feilden, the former Rowena Brassey, her Private Secretary, Col. Peter Gibbs, another former member of the Household Brigade, and her personal detective, Inspector Philip Robinson. The other two police officers who share the duties of protecting Princess Anne, David Robinson (no relation to his namesake) and Colin Tebbutt, are also at the party together with their wives, and Princess Anne makes a point of talking to them all. She is all too aware of the disruptive effect on family life that being a member of the Royal Protection Squad can mean.

Occasionally a guest, either through nervousness or over-enthusiasm, will try to monopolise the Princess. When this is in danger of happening, the courtiers have a remarkable knack of being able to move the Princess on to the next group without appearing to be discourteous in any way and almost without the offending guest being aware that it is happening. The Princess herself, in common with the other Royals, never hurries. She progresses through the crowds who press forward eager to see her and hear what she has to say, stopping every now and then to exchange a word with someone who has caught her attention in the line.

The movement is towards the Royal Tea Tent where the diplomatic guests are taking their refreshment. This area is protected by more Gentlemen Ushers and you have to have a special invitation to be allowed in. There is, however, a line of chairs arranged in a semicircle in front of the tent and a number of ladies have laid claim to these seats so that they can watch, from a respectful distance, the Royal Party taking their tea.

Princess Anne has taken one hour and twenty-five minutes to walk the 200 yards from the Terrace to the Royal Enclosure. She has been on her feet all the time, leading the conversation with people from all walks of life, and in spite of it being a fiercely hot afternoon with temperatures in the upper eighties, she still manages to appear as cool and fresh at the end of the afternoon as she did when she first stepped through the glass doors of the Bow Room. While the rest of us were perspiring freely, she wasn't even 'glowing'.

Inside the Royal Tea Marquee there is more small talk to be made with diplomats of every race and creed and then at 5.50 p.m. the Royal Family leave the tent and walk slowly through the crowds back towards the Palace. The guests reluctantly start to go home, taking as long as possible over it; Princess Anne has completed another duty which she has made appear to be a pleasure, and for another year, the Garden Party is over.

On the 17th February, 1981, Princess Anne won an election, and in doing so became Chancellor of the biggest university in Britain. The University of London comprises over fifty separate institutions, which between them accommodate more than 42,000 students.

The Princess was asked by her grandmother, Queen Elizabeth, the Queen Mother, the retiring Chancellor, if she would allow the nomination and, after some consideration, she agreed, even though there was inevitably going to be criticism in the press, due mainly to the fact that she had not attended university herself.

Certain factions within the university decided to oppose the appointment of the Princess and two very important and prestigious candidates were found to fight the election. Jack Jones, the veteran trade union leader, was strongly supported and the imprisoned African leader, Nelson Mandela, who was unable to campaign for himself, received a great deal of sympathetic news coverage.

When the results of the election were announced, Princess Anne was an easy winner with 23,951 votes out of a total of 42,212, with Jack Jones coming second with 10,507 votes, and Nelson Mandela accounting for 7,199 votes. The remaining 555 votes were invalid.

Princess Anne regards the position of Chancellor as satisfactory from the university's point of view 'because it allows the Vice-Chancellor to get on with the business of running the University, while having someone else to do the formal public stuff'.

Her installation took place on 13th October, 1981, and although it was never made public she refused the offer of an honorary degree.

She declined politely, saying that she would prefer to wait until both she and the University felt that she was doing a worthwhile job and had earned the right to such an honour.

As Chancellor she is Head of the University and a member ex officio of the Court, the Senate and Convocation, and is elected for life, which means that if she follows the example of her grandmother she will probably be Chancellor for another thirty or forty years.

Although most of her duties within the University are purely ceremonial she does have the right, which she welcomes enthusiastically, to be kept informed of all major changes proposed throughout the University. There are now some 15,000 graduates of the University each year (the degrees are awarded by resolution of the Senate or by the Vice-Chancellor acting on its behalf) and are conferred at Presentation Ceremonies held, at the present time, three times a year in the Royal Albert Hall. Each year some 6,000 graduates are able to accept invitations to attend these Presentation Ceremonies.

Although the University is too large for the Chancellor to do other than formally acknowledge, on Presentation Day, every single graduate individually as he or she passes before her, those being awarded senior degrees such as Doctor of Science are individually 'hooded' by the Chancellor.

Princess Anne is determined to visit every institution in the University as soon as practicable and in her first two years as Chancellor she made twenty-six visits, including one to the University Marine Station at Millport in Scotland, the establishment furthest from the main University campus in London.

Academic staff and students alike have been greatly impressed at the depth of her knowledge and, in particular, when she went to the Royal Veterinary College in June, 1982, the hosts had very quickly to revise upwards the level of their explanations when they found out that she knew far more than they had anticipated about animal medicine.

Students are notoriously unimpressed by titles but Princess Anne has managed to convince them that she is anxious to do anything she can to improve conditions, where they need improving, and to help in any way she can. If she is succeeding it is because they have found her to be sincere, interested and, above all, not in the least bit arrogant or pompous. When she visited the Students' Union in March, 1983, they were delighted to find that not only did she seem to understand and appreciate their problems but that after the formal introductions had been completed she joined in the social activities and remained throughout the evening.

It is appropriate that London University should be another of

Princess Anne's 'firsts' because they have always been in the vanguard in promoting female interests. The University was the first in Britain to award degrees to female students; the first to appoint a woman as a professor, the first to elect a female Vice-Chancellor, Dame Lillian Penson, 1948–51; and when Queen Elizabeth became Chancellor in 1955 she was the first woman to hold this position in a British University.

In any one year members of the Royal Family will carry out nearly 2,000 engagements, with the largest portion accounted for by the Queen herself. Then come the Duke of Edinburgh, the Prince of Wales and Princess Anne who each attend some 200 functions in the working year. Because their commitments now take them the length and breadth of the country on an almost daily basis, and overseas perhaps two or three times a year, great use is made of air transport. In the United Kingdom it enables the Royals to undertake engagements in several different parts of the country on the same day and still return to their homes in the evening, thereby effecting tremendous savings in terms of money and manpower.

Whenever and wherever any member of the Royal Family travels by air, he or she is the responsibility of The Queen's Flight. Originally formed in 1936 by King Edward VIII as The King's Flight, it consisted in those days of a single aeroplane and the King's personal pilot. Nowadays the fleet has been enlarged to five aircraft: three Andovers and two Westland Wessex helicopters. The Flight is under the direct command of the Captain of The Queen's Flight, Air Vice Marshal John Severne, M.V.O., O.B.E., A.F.C., with two Deputy Captains, Group Captain Jeremy Jones and Group Captain Richard Duckett, and altogether there are now 180 men in The Queen's Flight, which operates from its headquarters at R.A.F. Benson in Oxfordshire.

Although they are located on the R.A.F. station, The Queen's Flight is maintained entirely separately, and their administrative offices, briefing rooms, workshops and stores are contained in the single hangar which also houses the aircraft. The three turbo-prop Andovers are now around twenty years old, but they are, without doubt, the finest aircraft of their type in the world, and in spite of their somewhat outdated appearance there are still years of service left in them yet. This is due in no small part to the maintenance which goes on around the clock. If an aircraft arrives back at Benson at six o'clock on a Saturday evening and it is not required until the following Wednesday, there is no question of leaving the servicing until after the weekend. Immediately the aircraft is wheeled into the hangar, work starts to check thoroughly every part, from propeller to tail, and the service crew does not go off duty until the aircraft is ready to fly. No aircraft of The Queen's Flight is allowed to remain unserviceable, weekends and public holidays notwithstanding. As Air Vice Marshal Severne comments: 'It's a matter of pride throughout the Flight and if anybody objected to giving up his Saturday or Sunday off, he wouldn't volunteer for the job.'

And it is significant that every member of The Queen's Flight, apart from the officers, is a volunteer. It would be considered presumptuous for an officer to offer his services to the Queen, and the way the system operates is that any officer who is recommended is interviewed by the Air Vice Marshal and if he is found to be acceptable, he is asked if he wants the job. He then has the option of joining this most exclusive body of airmen or returning to his unit; so while he is not a volunteer in the strict sense of the word, he does have the right to refuse the posting if he wishes; nobody serves in The Queen's Flight unless they want to.

As far as the Warrant Officers, Non-Commissioned Officers and airmen are concerned, they are allowed to volunteer and for each vacancy there are many applicants of which the best three are selected for interview. These are invited to spend a day at Benson: wandering freely around, getting the feel of the place and talking to the men they will work with if selected. At the end of the day they are interviewed by the Senior Engineering Officer who explains the requirements of The Flight and the working procedure. Then they are instructed to go away and think about it, before deciding. In this way there is no question of anyone being 'drafted' into The Queen's Flight, and although one or two change their minds after the first visit – Air Vice Marshal Severne said it can be quite a shock to the system to find that there *is* actually a hangar in the Air Force where even the floor is polished – most of those who are accepted stay for a long time. Postings in the R.A.F. are usually for three years, but in The Queen's Flight there is no fixed time limit, and one senior N.C.O. has recently retired after more than seventeen years.

Princess Anne is extremely popular with members of The Queen's Flight and she is one of the Royal Family's most frequent users of the aircraft. There is a helicopter landing pad on one of the fields just above Gatcombe Park, and this means that Her Royal Highness can travel to engagements within a radius of 200 miles from her Gloucestershire home. And when the Princess travels abroad on one of her tours she almost invariably uses one of the Andovers on all but the transoceanic routes.

Those permitted to use The Queen's Flight are members of the Royal Family, senior politicians on official business and the heads of the Armed Forces.

They do not use the Flight as a matter of right but only with the written permission of the Queen, which has to be sought for each and every journey. The system operates thus: if, for example, Princess Anne has an engagement that requires her to travel by air, her Private Secretary will telephone the Secretary to The Queen's Flight. This important position is held by Miss Brenda Matthews, a former member of the WRNS, who is the linchpin in the entire operation. Miss Matthews has been doing the job for two years and she is one of the two civilians who work in the The Queen's Flight, the other being Mrs. Anne Shuttleworth, the receptionist.

When Miss Matthews gets the telephone call she will look up the appropriate date in the advance diary that is regarded as the bible of the Flight, to see if there is an aircraft available. If there is, she will provisionally make the booking and start the planning; in the meantime the Private Secretary will write to Sir Philip Moore, the Queen's Private Secretary, asking for Her Majesty's permission for one of her aircraft to be used. This is no mere formality. The Queen sees every request herself and she has been known to refuse permission if she feels the occasion does not warrant the use of an official aircraft. Other members of the family know Her Majesty's feelings about the possible misuse of The Queen's Flight, so no one asks for an aircraft just to go to the races or to a similar private engagement.

Once permission has been received from Buckingham Palace, usually within forty-eight hours, the booking is confirmed and the wheels are put in motion. For every helicopter journey made by a member of the Royal Family, a proving flight is undertaken if it's a route that has not been flown before. If it's to be in Britain, the aircraft will go over the proposed route several weeks before the day of the engagement. The landing sites will be inspected, the security precautions tested and the anticipated weather will be checked as thoroughly as is humanly possible. For an overseas tour the aircraft may 'prove the route' months in advance.

There is a 'pecking order' even in the Royal Family, and if one of the junior members has booked an aircraft which is subsequently required for perhaps the Duke of Edinburgh or the Queen Mother, they will have to give way. If all the aircraft are in use and there is still a requirement to travel by air, The Queen's Flight will seek an aircraft from another branch of the R.A.F. or even make arrangements with commercial airlines if this is thought suitable.

The Queen's Flight is divided into two sections: the Captain and his two Deputies describing themselves as the 'travel agents' and the operational side being referred to as 'the airline'. The Air Vice Marshal is a member of the Royal Household and it is to him that the requirements of the Royal Family are made known. His job is to solve their transport problems and this he does by instructing the Flight to provide the service.

Altogether The Queen's Flight makes around sixty flights a month and though it may come as something of a surprise, Princess Anne is the second biggest user. In 1982 she made ninety-seven flights, a number exceeded only by the Duke of Edinburgh. Third place goes to the Duke of Gloucester, with the Prince of Wales, who is frequently photographed piloting one of the Andovers, coming a close fourth.

Whenever an aircraft carries a member of the Royal Family, other air traffic in the vicinity is warned to keep clear. A Purple Airway is designated which means that a corridor ten miles wide is reserved for the exclusive use of The Queen's Flight. Unless under strict radar control, no other aircraft may enter that airspace either at the same height or 1,000 feet above or below. Air traffic controllers along the route are warned well in advance and the Purple Airways come into operation fifteen minutes before the Royal flight takes off and lasts until thirty minutes after it has landed.

When Princess Anne undertook an eight country tour of Africa in 1982, Group Captain Jeremy Jones accompanied her as her Commodore. During the three-week visit they covered 14,000 miles in Swaziland, Zimbabwe, Malawi, Kenya, Somalia and North Yemen. Officially they were scheduled to return to Britain after North Yemen, but under cover of great secrecy the Andover made its long overnight flight to war-torn Beirut, having made three refuelling stops *en route*, in order that the Princess could visit children who were being cared for in a clinic sponsored by The Save the Children Fund.

The Andover had been flown to South Africa where Princess Anne joined the aircraft at Johannesburg Airport after flying from Britain on a commercial airliner. Wherever they travel, The Queen's Flight service their own aircraft. A large number of spares is carried on board because with such a small number of aircraft there is no back-up aeroplane. If anything goes wrong it is repaired on the spot.

Inside, the aircraft is divided into three compartments. The first, immediately behind the flight deck, is where the extra crew sit; in the centre are the seats for the members of the Household, while the rear compartment is reserved for the royal passengers. There are four very comfortable armchairs which are fully adjustable to a practically horizontal position so it is possible to sleep on the longer journeys, and there are two highly polished folding tables between each pair of chairs. The cabin is decorated in a subtle shade of blue, and while it is extremely comfortable, in no way would it be described as opulent. There is no public address system in the cabin and communication with the pilot is normally by means of a written note or personal message passed via the steward. Immediately behind the royal compartment is a small cloakroom, which again is functional rather than luxurious.

Because the Andovers are used mainly for short journeys, the food they serve is fairly simple but when, as on the Africa trip, these are flights of up to five hours duration, something a little more sophisticated is called for. Generally the standard is about equal to that served in the first-class section of a commercial airliner.

Princess Anne uses the time in the air to brief herself on the next engagement or to catch up with some of her mountain of paperwork or, on occasion, simply to sleep or relax with her personal stereo cassette player listening to some of her favourite music.

Because of the amount of time the Princess spends travelling with The Queen's Flight, either by helicopter from her home in Gloucestershire or by fixed wing aircraft from one of the nearby R.A.F. bases at Kemble or Lyneham, she has got to know various members of the aircrews quite well and it's an accepted custom that at the end of an overseas tour she will join them for a farewell dinner party.

This can take place either in the bush country of Somalia, a hotel in Kenya or, as was the case on a visit to Nepal in 1981, high in the mountains of northern India. On that particular tour the invitation from the crew was particularly welcome as the royal party had had an especially tiring visit, climbing mountains, walking miles along steep rocky tracks and living rough for much of the time. Meanwhile the crew of the Andover, back at their base in Katmandu, were living in comparative luxury at the local Everest Sheraton Hotel, complete with air-conditioned rooms and swimming pool, so when they issued their traditional invitation to the Princess and her Party, it was accepted with an alacrity and eagerness that took even these hardened world travellers slightly by surprise. At the end of an extended tour the Princess will always join the crew for a group photograph, personally signed copies of which are later given to and prized by every man on board.

Members of the Flight also take an intense interest in the projects which are supported by the Royal Family. When Group Captain Jones accompanied Princess Anne to Kenya in 1982 he was able to visit Starehe School in Nairobi where 1,400 boys from poverty-stricken homes receive an education through individual sponsorships. The Royal Air Force churchgoers back at Benson had sponsored James Mbugua, one of these children, for several years, and Jeremy Jones was able to meet the boy who hopes eventually to become a teacher.

Chapter 12

THE HOUSEHOLD

The public life of Princess Anne is organised by three highly efficient people working from an office situated on the second floor of Buckingham Palace looking out over The Mall, in what was previously the Palace schoolroom. It's easy to imagine when you see the Princess taking part in extensive overseas tours or completing a complicated series of engagements in Britain, that behind her is a large organisation, oiling the machinery of the royal progress, with banks of secretaries and clerks toiling away in the background. So it comes as something of a surprise to find that her staff consists of a Private Secretary, a Personal Secretary and a Secretary to the Office – plus a word processor and a computer.

If the office could be related to a similar organisation in commercial terms, Princess Anne would be the Chairman of the Board; the Private Secretary the Managing Director, and the Personal Secretary the Treasurer and Company Secretary. Lt. Col. Peter Gibbs has been Private Secretary to Her Royal Highness since 1982 when he joined her Household from the Ministry of Defence to which he had been posted from his regiment, the Coldstream Guards. Peter Gibbs is a large, friendly man who commutes from his home in Wiltshire to his office in Buckingham Palace and who has earned a reputation already in the comparatively short time he has been at the Palace, as someone with meticulous attention to detail, a characteristic he regards as vitally important in anyone doing his kind of job. In fact he says in all probability this is one of the reasons why so many Army officers have been invited to join the Royal Household. The Army trains its officers to pay close attention to detail in every respect and this is especially valuable when preparing a programme of events for Princess Anne, or indeed any other member of the Royal Family. Every item to do with the Princess's public life is channelled through the Private Secretary and he is responsible for seeing that requests for visits, overseas tours, presentations and speeches are brought to her attention. This is done at the twice-yearly programme meetings which take place in the Princess's dining room at the Palace in June and December.

Peter Gibbs will have collected all the available information about the proposed programme for the next six months and Princess Anne, with her own large diary in front of her, will listen to the invitations and decide which to accept and which to decline. She may ask for more information about a particular event or make a suggestion for combining two or three engagements in the same area on the same day. The Princess has a phenomenal memory and she will sometimes remark that a certain organisation received a visit not too long ago and perhaps it is a bit soon to be returning, or she may recall that a couple of years ago such and such a company did not put up a very good show. That doesn't happen very often, but when it does the Princess is not apt to forget!

Once the Princess has decided – and her decision is final – the Ladies-in-Waiting go off to another room where they spread their papers on the floor, have a cup of tea and parcel up the duties between them. Theirs is a flexible arrangement and when they are working out which of them is going to accompany the Princess there's quite a bit of 'give and take' on all sides. Some of them, for example, have children at school so during the holidays the others will normally take on the bulk of the duties so that they can spend time with their children. Princess Anne is perfectly content for the Ladies to arrange their own rota, as long as she is kept informed.

Meanwhile Peter Gibbs has started the ball rolling as far as the projected programme is concerned and letters confirming the visit are sent immediately to the appropriate people. Then follows a process which through practice has been refined to near perfection. The Private Secretary and/or one of the personal police officers will visit the proposed venue and go over every aspect of the programme. Col. Gibbs will inspect the areas the Princess is to see, find out if she is expected to make a speech, check the timing for various segments of the visit and suggest certain guidelines which should be followed whenever a Royal guest is to be entertained. The detective will want to meet the local police and check thoroughly all the security for the visit. If the Princess is to go on a 'walkabout' the buildings overlooking the area will be inspected; if machinery is being demonstrated, safety guards will be double checked; the suggested positions for radio, television and press have to be investigated. This 'recce' visit takes place weeks before the Princess is due and then a programme is worked out with specific timings for each part of the day.

With Princess Anne undertaking some 200 engagements each year, the amount of paperwork is prodigious, and when visits are in the planning stage the telephone is also in constant use. The office will receive queries on a wide variety of topics relating to the protocol, and numerous calls about the likes and dislikes of the Princess. How should she be addressed? Ma'am (rhymes with ham). Should a gift be presented to mark the occasion? Only if the office has been notified well in advance and agreed to it. What about presenting the Princess with a bouquet? It should be small, easy to handle and unwired. If she is to unveil a plaque, details of the inscription are needed. If there is to be a meal, the Princess prefers it to be simple and not last too long – an hour is generally sufficient for lunch. Hosts need to know which side of the car Her Royal Highness will sit if she is arriving by road. Unless she is driving herself, which she frequently does, she always sits on the off-side rear seat. Are there any particular dishes which the Princess refuses to eat? She does not care for shellfish or oysters but does not object to other people eating them. Her Royal Highness never drinks alcohol and usually only Coca-Cola with her meal. Mineral water should always be available and the Princess never smokes but, again, raises no serious objection to other guests doing so.

On the delicate subject of 'retiring rooms' hosts are advised to tell the accompanying Lady-in-Waiting the location, and of course retiring rooms are to be reserved for the exclusive use of H.R.H. during a visit.

On the question of dress and general behaviour, the advice is the simplest. Be comfortable and be yourself. A million and one items to be discussed and decided: all routine for the experienced team that surrounds the Princess but a once-in-a-lifetime occurrence for many of those who are being honoured with a visit, so each query is dealt with by a patient and understanding member of the Household whose innate good manners hide an efficiency which is envied throughout the world.

Mrs. David Hodgson is Personal Secretary to Princess Anne, but this is a title which disguises a far more important and complex position. Brenda Hodgson not only acts, as her title implies, as secretary to the Princess on personal matters, but is also responsible for all the accounts relating to the running of the office, the Household and Gatcombe Park. All financial matters which are concerned with the Princess's public and private lives are dealt with by Mrs. Hodgson, and if the three members of Princess Anne's staff regard themselves very much as a team, then Brenda Hodgson is the linchpin in that operation. She is the longest serving member by far, having been the first person to be employed by the Princess in 1969, when there was no Household, and she has been the constant factor in the office during a period which has seen three Private Secretaries. In 1969 Princess Anne was embarking on her first public engagements and it was felt necessary to engage someone to look after the administrative details. The Princess did not even have her own Lady-in-Waiting in those days; Lady Susan Hussey, one of the Queen's attendants, had been seconded to assist the Princess, and she discovered that Mrs. Hodgson might be available. At that time Mrs. Hodgson was working as assistant to a financial director of a successful commercial company, experience which was to prove invaluable in the years to come.

Brenda Hodgson recalls how she was invited to meet Lady Susan and then she was interviewed by Princess Anne before being offered the position. 'What we were doing,' she says, 'was starting absolutely from scratch. There wasn't even a typewriter or a desk in the office, just a table and chair.' There was no such thing as a job description – anything that needed to be done was attended to by Brenda and Lady Susan between them. Princess Anne had started her riding career by then and Brenda Hodgson reflects that 'there was a great deal of fan mail coming in at the time, especially from young girls who were also beginning to take up riding.' In a remarkably short time an office routine was evolved that has continued to the present day and by the time the Princess had won the European Champion-ships in 1971 it had become necessary to engage another young lady to help with the mountain of correspondence that arrived daily.

The engagement and wedding in 1973 was, without doubt, the busiest period for those in Princess Anne's employ with thousands of letters, telegrams, presents and even telephone calls coming in from all over the world. 'There was no way we could have coped alone,' says Mrs. Hodgson, 'so a number of temporary ladies were brought in to answer the letters and open the parcels containing gifts of every description.' It's a practice that had to be revived when the Princess's two children were born, and Princess Anne and her Personal Secretary have always been in total agreement on one issue at least: every letter, message and gift must be acknowledged with a personal letter. Even when the mailing list runs into thousands a day there is no question of a circular letter being sent. Brenda Hodgson explains, 'When people have been so kind and have taken such care in selecting or, in many cases, making a present for the Princess or her family, the very least we can do is reply personally and we are delighted to be able to do so.'

When Princess Anne and Captain Phillips moved to their first home at Sandhurst, it was Mrs. Hodgson's responsibility to help arrange the furniture and decoration, and when they considered buying Gatcombe she took over the massive task of finding out how much money was needed for repairs and renovations. All the household accounts are paid by her after each one has been seen and approved by the Princess and she administers the allocation from the Civil List, on Princess Anne's behalf; in 1983/84 this amounted to £116,200.

A part of her time is spent at Gatcombe, occasionally in the company of the architect trying to decide which piece of repair work should have priority. A house like Gatcombe needs constant attention and one of the biggest problems is to decide which projects are the most urgent. As the house is Princess Anne's official residence its upkeep comes from part of the Civil List, but anything to do with the farm or the stables has to be paid for by Princess Anne and Captain Phillips personally and the farm administration is carried out from a commercial office in Cambridge.

In 1980 it became obvious that Princess Anne's office was going to need to expand to cope with the additional commitments she was taking on, but the Treasury was unwilling for more staff to be engaged. Brenda Hodgson did some astute arithmetic and persuaded the authorities that an investment in a little hardware would pay dividends. She was given permission to lease a word processor and an Apple computer and it's a matter of some pride that Princess Anne's office was the first in the Palace to become automated.

The third and newest member of the team is Alison Bush, who joined them in 1982. She had been working for the Duke of Marlborough at Blenheim Palace when she received a telephone call asking if she was interested in replacing the young lady who was leaving to get married. She had already handed in her notice at Blenheim so there was no question of 'poaching', and after the usual sequence of interviews she moved into the second-floor offices. Alison is responsible for making sure that every piece of correspondence is perfect before it leaves the office and she also looks after the preparation of the official programmes which go out to the various organisations with which the Princess is associated.

When I asked her if there were any special 'perks' to working at Buckingham Palace she answered with refreshing candour: 'It's easy to park.' One considerable advantage in working for Princess Anne is that whenever the Princess travels abroad Alison Bush goes with her. There is always need for secretarial assistance on overseas tours and even though it's hard work, it does give a young lady an opportunity to see exotic places, in circumstances which would otherwise be impossible.

On the debit side, all three members of Princess Anne's staff work quite extraordinarily long hours. They are usually at their desks by 9 a.m. and they rarely get away before 6, or frequently 7 p.m. It sounds like an overworked cliché, but this really is a 'labour of love'.

They are devoted to the Princess and while they are adequately paid, they are certainly not over-rewarded in monetary terms. So their intense loyalty is not something that has been bought and paid for. The Princess is appreciative of their efforts on her behalf and aware of the disruptive effect working for her can mean to their social lives. She also demands complete efficiency and will not tolerate mistakes of any kind. They have learned to recognise her moods and preferences and they will only telephone her at Gatcombe when they have something to tell her that cannot wait. As Brenda Hodgson puts it: 'If I rang her with a question which could easily wait until the next time we met, she'd think I had taken leave of my senses.'

The Princess calls each of her Household by their Christian name but they are always fully aware of their employer's status and there is never any familiarity. It's a purely business relationship and if the Princess regards Brenda Hodgson in particular as her right hand, Brenda is the first to point out that it's because of the length of time they have worked together and obviously they do know each other very well.

Possibly another close link between them is the fact that Mrs. Hodgson has a son just two years older than Peter Phillips so inevitably they have that little extra something in common.

The Household at Gatcombe comes under the control of Mrs. Hodgson and she is responsible for the welfare of the butler who also doubles as Captain Phillips's valet, the cook, Princess Anne's dresser and the two ladies who come in daily to help with the cleaning. Contrary to popular belief there are no chauffeurs or gardeners employed at Gatcombe and the grooms who look after the horses work privately for the couple, as does the children's nanny!

Public interest in the Royal Family has grown to such an extent that members of the Royal Household sometimes work extremely long hours during the 'working year' coping with the flood of correspondence that rarely seems to dry up. For every invitation that is accepted there are many more which have to be declined, but in such a way that the would-be host is not offended.

It's a popular misconception that there is a general 'clearing house' in the Palace to which all requests for royal visits are sent. This is not so. If someone writes to Buckingham Palace asking for a member of the Royal Family to attend a particular function, they will receive a polite note informing them that it is necessary to state which particular Royal they would like to see and to write directly to that person. If Princess Anne is invited to open an exhibition or visit a new housing estate on a day which she finds impossible, the invitation is never passed to another member of the family. And neither is there a cross-reference system between the various Households to make sure that two members do not turn up at the same venue on the same day. The Private Secretaries do keep efficient records of all visits of course, so that their particular charge does not go over the same ground too often, but as far as duplication is concerned, the system does appear to be slightly haphazard. As Princess Anne herself has remarked, 'I have been known to share a helicopter with the Duke of Edinburgh on the odd occasion when we happened to be going in the same direction and only one helicopter was available that day.'

Apart from her three personal police officers, one of whom is always on duty, the Princess's closest companions are her Ladies-in-Waiting. There are six, of which two are designated Extra Ladies-in-Waiting, which means in theory that they do less duties than the others, but in practice they divide the work into fairly equal proportions.

The Ladies-in-Waiting are Rowena Feilden, Victoria Legge-Bourke, Shân Legge-Bourke and Celia Innes with Mary Carew Pole and the Countess of Lichfield acting as Extra Ladies-in-Waiting.

Mary Dawnay (now Mrs. Carew Pole) was the first Lady-in-Waiting to be appointed in 1970, after she had been included in the same theatre party as the Princess. She had no previous connections with the Princess but she knew the form, having two friends who were Ladies-in-Waiting to the Queen, and it was while she was in Kenya that she received an invitation from the then Lady Euston (now Duchess of Grafton), one of the Queen's closest companions, to join the Princess's Household. Within a few months she was joined by Rowena Brassey (now Mrs. Feilden), who had been working as a Lady-in-Waiting to the wife of the Governor General of New Zealand for two and a half years, and it was during Princess Anne's visit to that country that they first met. She returned to Britain, joined Princess Anne and together with Brenda Hodgson, the Princess's Personal Secretary, those three formed the entire Household. There was no Private Secretary in those days so the two Ladies-in-Waiting combined the role of acting as companion to the Princess on her official duties with that of being 'office manager'. They organised a rota system between them, working full time with a fortnight on and a fortnight off. Princess Anne didn't carry out as many engagements then as she does today, but it was a busy period in her life, and they both say that while the atmosphere in the office – in what is now Captain Phillips's bedroom – was somewhat chaotic, it was great fun and they both enjoyed themselves tremendously, even when Prince Andrew would rush into the office firing his water pistol. Princess

Anne's diary rapidly filled as she accepted more and more commitments and shortly after her marriage in 1973, Victoria Legge-Bourke was approached. Victoria is the only Lady-in-Waiting who is still single and she also has a full-time job in the residence of the American Ambassador in London, so she has to fit her engagements with the Princess into an already crowded schedule. Victoria Legge-Bourke and Princess Anne were at school together, but when they were at Benenden they were not particularly close friends as Victoria was a year ahead of the Princess. She had known a number of the Royal Household from childhood, her brother having acted as a page to the Queen, and as a teenager she was one of a small party invited to join a skiing party in France at which the Princess was also present.

Her sister-in-law, the Hon. Mrs. Legge-Bourke, lives in Powys in South Wales from where she allows herself an hour and twenty-five minutes to drive to Gatcombe when she is on duty with the Princess. She was not recruited by her husband's sister, strange as it may seem, but by the fourth Lady-in-Waiting to join the team, Celia Innes. Celia is now the mother of two small children and she came into the Princess's Household in the late 1970s 'quite out of the blue'. She was asked to attend a party at Windsor Castle without, she says, 'the faintest idea why'. She then made up the numbers at one or two other functions and eventually Victoria Legge-Bourke suggested that she might like to become a Lady-in-Waiting. Princess Anne never makes a direct approach herself for the obvious reason of wishing to spare any possible embarrassment if the person approached wants to say no.

When Celia Innes was formally invited to become a Lady-in-Waiting she wrote to Princess Anne explaining that she was married and had recently started her own business as a florist, 'did the Princess mind coming third in the order of priorities?' Princess Anne replied that she was quite willing to accept the situation and they have been together ever since.

Leonora, Countess of Lichfield, is the only Lady-in-Waiting who mixes socially with the Princess on a regular basis. Married to Patrick Lichfield, a cousin of the Queen, she has stayed as a guest at Sandringham and Balmoral and she and her husband frequently shoot with the Phillips's either at Gatcombe or on the Lichfield estate in Staffordshire. Leonora Lichfield has known the Princess for many years and she was a guest at the skiing party in Val d'Isère in France, after which Victoria Legge-Bourke was invited to become a Lady-in-Waiting. Like one or two of the other 'Ladies' she is an habitual smoker, something she certainly does not have in common with the Princess, who has never been known to even try a cigarette in her life. However, Princess Anne does not try to influence her staff or her friends one way or another. As she says, 'Smoking is a personal habit and who am I to object. As long as no one actually blows smoke directly into my face it doesn't bother me. I wouldn't dream of trying to make anyone give it up.'

Because the Countess has a large number of commitments of her own, particularly in Staffordshire, she too has to organise her life very carefully. As with the others she knows six months in advance when she is required by the Princess, but occasionally her husband, as a photographer of international repute, will have to travel abroad at short notice and she has to go with him. 'Then it's a question of ringing around and finding one of the others to stand in. But they are all very good and we try to help each other if we can.'

Mary Carew Pole is a magistrate living in Cornwall and accordingly she needs to organise her life around her family and public commitments. The fact that she lives so far from London also means that she tends to do more of the engagements that begin and end at Gatcombe; even so it can mean a 5 a.m. start to drive to Gloucestershire to meet the Princess and sometimes not getting back to Cornwall until the early hours of the following morning, if they have had a late engagement in the evening.

Rowena Feilden shared one of the most dramatic moments of the Princess's life when the car in which they were travelling from an engagement in the City of London, was attacked by an armed man, who was trying to kidnap the Princess and hold her to ransom. For her conduct in trying to save the Princess she was made a Member of the Royal Victorian Order by the Queen, though she is very quick to deprecate her own efforts on that occasion, saying she felt she should have done more. Although they have been together for more than ten years Mrs. Feilden still regards the Princess very much as her employer, in spite of the fact that Ladies-in-Waiting do not get paid a salary. They are, however, reimbursed for their expenses when they are on duty.

The one thing that each of the Ladies has in common is a highly protective attitude towards the Princess. They all think she is compassionate with a great sense of duty, and they get very annoyed when they read in the press that she has been sullen or uncooperative. Celia Innes says: 'Princess Anne has the greatest sense of fun and some of her comments, particularly when we are driving slowly somewhere with the car window open and she can hear what people are saying about her, should be written down for posterity.'

Mary Carew Pole has seen the Princess mature from a young, inexperienced teenager to the confident, self-assured woman she is today and is still amazed by her capacity for work. 'There are obviously some jobs which are less interesting than others but the Princess is never bored, and never appears tired; in fact we flag long before she gives the slightest hint of fatigue.'

The working day for a Lady-in-Waiting usually begins the afternoon before an engagement. If the day is to start at Buckingham Palace, the Lady on duty will go into the office to read the files and thoroughly familiarise herself with the programme ahead. There is a file for every single engagement, which will list the people to be presented; details of the venue – if it's a factory or other commercial undertaking, background material will have been gathered in advance; the seating plan if there is to be a meal; whether the Princess is expected to sign a visitors' book; how much time is allowed for each segment of the visit. The programme schedule is then photographically reduced to a convenient size for handbags and pockets and a copy is held by the Private Secretary, the Lady-in-Waiting, the detective and the Princess herself.

Before they arrive at the Palace on the day itself they may have spoken to the Princess's dresser to find out what she is wearing, not because they are particularly concerned about clashing, but usually to find out if hats are the order of the day.

Just before they are due to leave Buckingham Palace the Lady-in-Waiting will wait in the corridor just outside the Princess's sitting room. They never knock and rarely are they invited into the sitting room before an engagement. Once the Princess has joined her Lady-in-Waiting they move to the Quadrangle Entrance in the Inner Courtyard where one of the royal limousines is waiting. During the drive to wherever they are going, the Princess may go over certain aspects of the visit ahead, or, if she is to make a speech, she may read through it. Or, and this is even more probable, they will simply chat about inconsequentials. If they are using an aircraft of The Queen's Flight, they both use the time to read the morning's newspapers.

During the engagement the Lady-in-Waiting is never very far away from the Princess. If it's a civic visit Princess Anne will be accompanied by the Lord Mayor or Chairman of the Council; the Lady-in-Waiting will probably be paired off with the chief executive or town clerk. It's important that she is able to make her opposite number feel at ease because for many of them it's a once in a lifetime occasion and some of them do feel a little nervous at times.

Princess Anne has definite ideas about the value of a good Lady-in-Waiting. 'What they have to be good at is chatting to people and making them feel comfortable, because that helps me really. It's no good at all if you get somebody turning up in the morning looking like death and furious and ratty about life and un-communicative. And when they go out on a trip they're standing in a corner looking glum and bored. That's no help to anyone, least of all to the people at the other end, never mind to me. So it is important that they should be capable of being interested and mixing with the people we meet.'

The day following a visit is an important one for the Lady-in-Waiting. She always goes into Buckingham Palace and writes 'her letters'. A 'thank-you' note is invariably written after each engagement, and even though Princess Anne's office is equipped with a word processor which could reel off letters by the thousand, the thank-you letters are all written individually by the Ladies-in-Waiting within twenty-four hours.

The attitude of outsiders to the Ladies-in-Waiting varies considerably. Among the Princess's Service connections there is a very relaxed atmosphere; many of the officers of the regiments, ships and squadrons with which she is associated treat the Ladies-in-Waiting as old friends – and indeed, in several cases they are. But when one of them accompanies the Princess on a civic or commercial visit the attitude can vary, from obsequious servility to arrogant disregard.

The days when the Ladies-in-Waiting were always drawn from the aristocracy, from families with generations of service to the Crown, have long gone. In these days of instant communication and world-wide technological innovation, it's not enough to look pretty and speak with the right accent. The requirement in the latter half of the twentieth century is for well informed, gregarious companions who are at ease with people from all walks of life and who are prepared to put themselves out to accommodate a multitude of enquiries from anyone from a schoolgirl to a Lord Lieutenant.

The job carried out by the three personal police officers is one that for reasons of security cannot be described in too great detail. They are all volunteers, highly trained and when one of them is on duty with the Princess, the others are either carrying out 'recce' trips or undergoing refresher courses to keep them up to date with the latest developments in police work. They do not see as much of their own families as they would wish and if courage and loyalty can be taken for granted with these men, so too can discretion. They are with the Princess often more than with their own wives, and she sees more of them than she sometimes does her own family. Yet they are self-effacing to a fault and protective of her privacy to a man. None of them has ever spoken to a member of the press about their work or their boss and it isn't the threat of dismissal that keeps them silent. Their dedication to Princess Anne is remarkable in its intensity – and on occasion, frightening to an outsider. Ask one of them why they do it and he will reply 'Because no matter how hard we work, she works at least twice as hard.'

One other confidante of the Princess who is not a member of her Household, but who is in frequent contact with her is her dressmaker. With public attention being focussed constantly on the Royal Family, it's inevitable that the female members in particular come in for a certain amount of criticism with regard to the clothes they wear. When the Queen visited the United States in 1983 her outfits excited a great deal of comment, not all of it complimentary, and the Princess of Wales, who is regarded as having the most extensive wardrobe in the Royal Family, is seen as one of the most fashionable women in the world.

Princess Anne has never thought of herself as a trend-setter; on the contrary, she regards herself as being rather conservative in her dress. Nevertheless, as she admits, she is becoming a little more adventuresome as she gets older even if she does not follow fashion slavishly from year to year. Her clothes are designed and made for her by Maureen Baker in a tiny workroom just behind London's Oxford Street. They first met in 1968 when Princess Anne was about to leave Benenden and start her role in public life. Maureen Baker had been making clothes for Princess Alexandra for some years and it was she who introduced Princess Anne to the designer. At that time Mrs. Baker was working for Susan Small. Since then she has branched out on her own, and retained all her royal clients. Apart from Princess Anne Maureen Baker also makes clothes for other members of the Royal Family as well as for Mrs. Margaret Thatcher and television personalities such as Judith Chalmers. In the early days Princess Anne had little idea of fashion and she was prepared to be guided totally by Maureen Baker as she took her first tentative steps in the public eye as an adult. It was the era of the mini-skirt, a style which the designer felt was eminently suitable for the young Princess.

Another asset as far as Maureen Baker is concerned is the Princess's 'long, beautiful neck' which she feels makes her particularly satisfying to make for. At 5'7" she is the sort of height fashion designers have in mind when they show their dresses on their leading models, and according to Maureen Baker her measurements today are exactly what they were on the day she was married: which means she takes a size 8/10.

Most of her clothes are meant to last and Princess Anne doesn't mind in the least wearing something that is many years old. If she likes an article she will continue to wear it, and one of Maureen

Baker's tasks is periodically to alter the length of a coat or dress so that at least it doesn't become too unfashionable.

Today the Princess has very definite ideas about what she wants to wear and sometimes she will sketch something herself and hand it to Maureen Baker with the words 'This is roughly what I have in mind.'

Alternatively Mrs. Baker will make sketches which she takes to Buckingham Palace where she frequently arranges fittings while the Princess is between engagements. Maureen Baker has a pretty good idea of the sort of clothes the Princess likes and the type of dress which suits her, but even so she has been known to present a drawing which she regards as 'just the thing' to be told: 'I'm not wearing that,' and that's the end of it.

The Princess's favourite colours are greens and blues and occasionally she will return from a trip abroad with a bolt of silk or other material which has taken her fancy, which Maureen Baker will then make up in whatever style Princess Anne decides. Otherwise materials are chosen which will travel well.

Because much of Princess Anne's wardrobe is designed to be seen by the public it's important that when she arrives at a venue for an engagement her clothes are not creased. When an outfit is being planned, sketches will be sent by Maureen Baker to John Boyd at his studio in Knightsbridge. Mr. Boyd is milliner to the Princess and the unique style of many of the hats she wears is due almost entirely to his creative ability. If her dress designer has any criticism at all about her royal client, it's in the choice of shoes. 'Princess Anne spends so much time on her feet, her shoes are made for comfort,' and that's as far as Maureen Baker is prepared to go in commenting on the style of the Princess's shoes. The Princess laughingly agrees with this saying: 'I hate spending money on expensive shoes.'

The highlight of Maureen Baker's career was of course when she was invited to design Princess Anne's wedding dress. She remembers 1973 very well. She was in constant touch with the Princess making a complete wardrobe for a tour of Australia. At one of the fittings Princess Anne turned to her and said quite casually: 'You had better start thinking about the wedding dress.' Mrs. Baker wasn't sure she had heard correctly at first, but it was no joke. She was to be entrusted with the biggest commission of the year. She and the Princess had clear ideas of the sort of dress they wanted and once they had decided on the material – which didn't crease, even after the carriage ride to Westminster Abbey – the biggest problem was how to keep the design a secret. The press would have paid a fortune if they could have copied it. But with a staff intensely loyal and

48. (*Top*) Her Majesty the Queen at the Windsor Horse Trials with
Mark Phillips, Princess Anne, Lt. Col. Sir John Miller, The Crown
Equerry, and Alison Oliver, Princess Anne's trainer. The young
lady nearest the camera is Lady Sarah Armstrong-Jones.

49 (*Above*) The marriage certificate.

50 (*Overleaf*) The official wedding photograph taken in the Throne
Room at Buckingham Palace. Best man, Eric Grounds, stands
immediately behind the bride and groom.

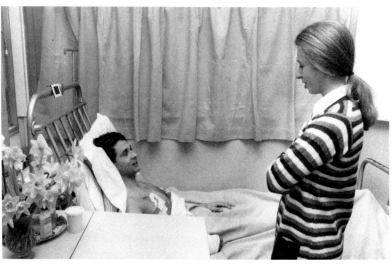

51 (*Opposite, top*) As Chief Commandant of the WRNS, Princess Anne takes the salute at H.M.S. *Dauntless* wearing, for the first time in public, the star insignia of Dame Grand Cross of the Royal Victorian Order.

52. (*Opposite, bottom*) Visiting her personal police officer, Inspector James Beaton, in Westminster Hospital after he had been shot.

53 (*Left*) In the stable yard at Gatcombe.

54 (*Below, left*) The day after arriving home from the Montreal Olympics the Princess acted as godmother to Alice Louise, daughter of Malcolm and Wendy McVittie at Sandhurst.

55 (*Below, right*) The author interviewing Princess Anne and Mark Phillips in 1975 for BBC TV at the Army Horse Trials, Tidworth.

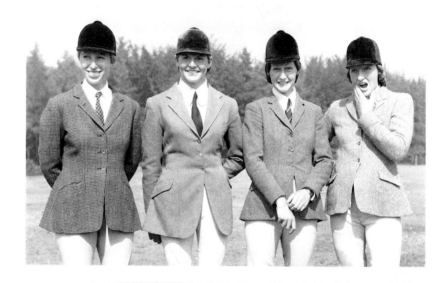

56 Britain's first all-female team for the European Championships at Lumuhlen, West Germany: Princess Anne, Sue Hatherly, Janet Hodgson and Lucinda Prior-Palmer who won the Gold medal with Princess Anne taking the Silver.

57 (*Above*) The five riders selected to represent Great Britain in the Olympic Games in Canada in 1976: Lucinda Prior-Palmer, Princess Anne, Richard Meade, Hugh Thomas and Mark Phillips. Mark was relegated to reserve position. Only Richard Meade and Princess Anne finished the event.

58. The christening of Princess Anne's son Peter took place in the
Music Room at Buckingham Palace and the baby wore the gown
of Honiton Lace which has been worn by all royal children since
Queen Victoria's time, including both the Queen and Princess
Anne. The gown is kept in a special room at Windsor Castle
between christenings.

59. (*Top*) Monty-Python actor, John Cleese, receiving an award as outstanding personality of 1982 from Princess Anne, President of the British Academy of Film and Television Arts.

60. (*Above*) Olympic Champions, Jayne Torvill and Christopher Dean, being greeted by Princess Anne, President of the British Olympic Association after their Gold-Medal-winning performance in the 1984 Winter Olympics in Sarajevo, Yugoslavia.

hardworking, not a word leaked out and the fittings were all organised to take place at Buckingham Palace itself. Maureen Baker recalls one occasion when the dress was almost, but not quite complete. Princess Anne suddenly said: 'I want my mother to see this.' Mrs. Baker was stunned to see Her Majesty walk into the room. It was a quite extraordinary moment, says Maureen Baker, 'Princess Anne was anxious for the Queen to approve and when she did, after one look, it was sheer magic.'

She was simply a girl who desperately wanted her mother to like what she had chosen and the smile which lit up the Princess's face when that approval was forthcoming was, according to Maureen Baker, 'a joy to behold.'

On the wedding day itself Mrs. Baker was inside the Palace making sure everything was perfect with the dress and when the guests returned to Buckingham Palace, both the Queen and Queen Elizabeth, the Queen Mother, came and spoke to her, complimenting her on the dress. She says: 'It was just like any other family wedding and, for a few moments one could almost forget where you were and who the other people were.'

When Princess Anne is at home at Gatcombe and no guests are expected she normally wears jeans and sweaters around the place. She's a very active person and she finds them comfortable and convenient. She has an enormous cap which she wears in the country to cover her long hair and when she wears it in the rain together with an ancient, waterproof jacket, she has an 'Oliver Twist' look about her which makes her look much younger than she is. For formal occasions Maureen Baker has made a number of full-length evening gowns, one of the most distinctive being in vivid coral; this is a particular favourite of one of Her Royal Highness's regiments, and they are always delighted if she chooses to wear it to one of their Service functions.

Perhaps the biggest single theme in Princess Anne's wardrobe is economy. She was brought up to believe that things were not to be wasted and there is no sign of frivolity in her choice of clothes. She says: 'A good suit goes on forever. If it's made properly in the first place and has a sort of classic look about it, you can go on wearing it ad infinitum. Those are the clothes I like, and there's no question about it, I expect my clothes to last me a long time.'

Chapter 13

PRIVATE LIFE

Princess Anne's private life is concentrated on her family and a few close friends. It's a close-knit circle and her idea of perfect relaxation is to spend a couple of weeks with the rest of the Royal Family at Balmoral, where there is little possibility of their recreation being disturbed; or inviting a couple of people to stay at Gatcombe to enjoy the sort of country pursuits that she and her husband relish.

The Princess made several friendships at Benenden which have lasted and a number of acquaintanceships from the equestrian world have developed into closer relationships. Three day eventing is the sort of sport where you keep running into the same people week after week, and inevitably, there are social gatherings where riders with similar interests are invited and friendships are formed.

Princess Anne is very much a country person. She freely admits that she spends as little time as possible in the city and only goes to Buckingham Palace when it is necessary as part of her public duties. Gatcombe is her home and it is where she spends most of her time. Because of the life styles they enjoy, the Royal Family tends to stick together more than most families and even though during the working year their paths rarely cross, at Christmas and during the summer they all join up at one of the royal residences, and these are occasions when outsiders are strictly excluded.

If Princess Anne is going to take part in a fancy-dress party at Windsor she wants to be assured that there isn't someone present who might be tempted to 'reveal all' to the press the following day, so it's really only with members of the immediate family that they can all truly relax.

Those few people who are admitted to royal circles as friends, observe an unwritten but rigid code of conduct. They have to remember that friendship can be conferred only by a member of the Royal Family and never sought from outside. It is imperative to keep in mind that there is always a dividing line between royalty and anyone else and even though friendship can be warm and informal, the curtain can come down at any time. And the final and most important of all rules is, no talking. Whatever goes on at a dinner party or dance must never be repeated. A number of people have found themselves suddenly, and without warning, cut off from royal society because of an incautious word in the wrong ear.

As far as Princess Anne is concerned, her friends come from all walks of life and a wide variety of interests. Her main rule seems to be that people act naturally. She doesn't care if they are the offspring of an earl or a carpenter, just as long as they do not try to be anything other than what they are.

The Princess admires excellence in others so she is attracted by people who have achieved success in their chosen field, no matter what that might be. One of her closest friends comes from a back-ground far removed from her own, but they have known each other for more than ten years, and he and his family are regular guests at Gatcombe Park.

Jackie Stewart certainly fills the role of someone who has achieved excellence in his chosen field. He was the most successful motor racing driver Britain had ever produced when he retired in 1973. World champion three times and still the holder of the record for the most Grand Prix wins with twenty-seven victories to his credit, Jackie is the younger son of a Scottish garage owner and even though his parents were comfortably off, he would not regard himself as coming from anything like the sort of background one would expect of those who become close friends of the Royal Family.

In 1971 Jackie Stewart was honoured by a variety of organisations, having won the first of his world championships, and he and Princess Anne, who was being similarly honoured because of her European title, attended a number of lunches and dinners in connection with being voted 'Sportsman and Sportswoman of the year'.

'I remember the *Daily Express* Sports Lunch in particular,' says Stewart. 'We sat beside each other at lunch and I remember the conversation being for me at least interesting, amusing and informative. Apart from her very down-to-earth attitude towards her success and her commitment to her sport, what impressed me most was her no-nonsense attitude to what she was doing. She had had a pretty rushed morning having exercised her horses before she had to be on parade at the Savoy, but she made it a very enjoyable occasion.' Another thing about the Princess which attracted Stewart's attention was her hands. 'They were not what I would have expected of a Princess. Princess Anne's hand had been well used in that, with riding, it was obvious it was not only a question of holding the reins. It seemed almost that they were working hands, and again it pleased me to think that someone who could have sat back and let others toil, so obviously took part in the sport to the fullest.'

Whatever it was there was an immediate chemistry between the two champions and throughout that year they met frequently at public functions. The friendship blossomed to include Stewart's delightful wife, Helen, his childhood sweetheart, and later, after the Royal Wedding in 1973, Mark Phillips who found that he too had a great deal in common with the Scottish world champion. Before he entered the world of motor racing Jackie Stewart had achieved international honours as a marksman, shooting for Scotland in their clay-pigeon team when he was just sixteen, so he and Mark Phillips, who had also been keen on shooting since childhood, struck up an immediate rapport. Since then the friendship has developed into a close relationship between the two families and the Princess and her husband usually try to spend at least one week every year with the Stewarts at their beautiful home on the shores of Lake Geneva in Switzerland.

Jackie and Helen Stewart are very anxious that the Princess and Captain Phillips should be left alone when they visit them, so they rarely invite other guests at the same time. As Jackie explains, 'Any friends we might invite may never have met Mark and the Princess, therefore conversation has to be made, which again would create an unnecessary element in an otherwise at-ease atmosphere.' And when the Princess stays with the Stewarts they make no special preparations. 'They have always stayed in the same guest accomodation at our home,' says Jackie. 'The only person who really knows they are coming is my secretary, and the Palace.'

To an outsider the idea of entertaining a royal princess in one's home might prove rather daunting, but apparently Princess Anne is not a demanding guest. 'Usually both Mark and the Princess want to totally relax when they come to stay with us, and I think this is something they have now found they can do easily,' explained Jackie Stewart. 'Basically it's just a question of enjoying the sunshine by the pool, reading, listening to music, occasionally playing a game of tennis and swimming of course. We seldom leave the house, but if we do it might only be to go out on the lake in the small power boat we have.' When the Phillips's return the compliment of inviting the Stewarts to stay at Gatcombe, the hospitality is equally warm and relaxed, even to the extent of including the couple's two sons in the party. Jackie Stewart says the royal couple have gone out of their way to be complete hosts, and to make them feel at home. 'When Paul and Mark, my two sons, have been with us they have laid on some riding for the boys, and this is something they had never done before going to Gatcombe, and they know the boys like clay pigeon shooting, so this is arranged also.'

Because Jackie Stewart is a former world champion racing driver who is still heavily involved in the world of motor sport, he has access to the latest cars as soon as they are introduced and spends a great deal of his time testing engines and tyres at race tracks throughout the world. On occasion he has sat alongside Princess Anne when she has been at the wheel. 'I have driven with her in one of her very large horse boxes; she was extremely efficient and confident, while at the same time recognising that from such a vehicle you get a wholly different perspective on how other people use the roads. As a driver Princess Anne is very competent. I have driven with her also on race tracks and had she wanted to drive racing cars I am sure she would have achieved a high degree of success. She has a tremendous feel for a vehicle – I suppose it comes from being such a good horsewoman. This is something I have recognised in Mark Phillips and a number of other equestrians. They are good drivers because they have good hands and good "seat of the pants" reactions. They are well co-ordinated; have good hand-eye-foot co-ordination, all of which are essential, in my view, on a horse and certainly in a car.'

Helen Stewart has been alongside her husband since the days when he was a Grand Prix driver, but in 1981 she was catapulted into the limelight in her own right when she was invited to become godmother to Princess Anne's daughter, Zara.

Although she had known, and been friends with, the Princess for ten years she was 'most surprised, slightly bewildered, but thrilled and proud to be asked.' It was a delightful gesture on the part of the Princess and this time it was the former world champion who had to take a back seat to his wife; a role he was delighted to assume when they went to the christening ceremony at Windsor Castle. All the immediate members of the Royal Family were present and even though it was an historic and formal occasion, the Stewarts were made to feel at ease immediately and they found the Queen and her family, all of whom they had met several times before, to be relaxed, friendly and very excited about baby Zara, the newest member of the most prestigious family in the world.

The Princess and Captain Phillips had been married four years when their first child was born, on 15th November, 1977, just one day after their wedding anniversary. The Princess had broken with tradition by deciding to have her baby in hospital, the Lindo Wing of St. Mary's Hospital, Paddington, London, and when the Queen's first grandchild arrived, weighing 7 lbs. 9 oz., he was the first royal baby to be born a commoner for 500 years.

The baby was born at precisely 10.46 a.m. and minutes later Captain Phillips, who had been present at the birth, telephoned Buckingham Palace to inform the Queen. Her Majesty had been about to hold an investiture which was delayed for ten minutes while she was given the news. When she arrived she said: 'I apologise for being late but I have just had a message from the hospital. My daughter has just given birth to a son.' A loud cheer went up from the investiture guests and an obviously delighted Monarch continued with the ceremony.

Because of the baby's place in the line of succession – he was fifth – it was necessary to inform members of the government at home and throughout the Commonwealth. After the Duke of Edinburgh, who was in Germany, had been telephoned, the Queen Mother was told of her first great grandson and the Prince of Wales, who was hunting in Yorkshire, received the news via short-wave radio. The Home Secretary, Mr. Merlin Rees, was the first government official to be informed, followed by Governors General across the world. Finally, Princes Andrew and Edward, at school at Gordonstoun, learned that they were uncles.

Captain Phillips had telephoned his parents at their home in Wiltshire where the local vicar ordered a special peal of bells to be rung in celebration. Mr. James Callaghan, the Prime Minister, sent a telegram to the Princess expressing 'warmest congratulations', the first of thousands which flooded into St. Mary's and Buckingham Palace.

The Professional Guild of Toastmasters held a special champagne celebration on the steps of the hospital and then presented the Queen with a bottle standing three feet high.

There was only one sour note in the entire proceedings, and it came, somewhat predictably, from the anti-royalist M.P. Mr. Willie Hamilton who said: 'How charming – another one on the payroll!'

Within a few days Mark went to St. Mary's Hospital to collect his wife and son and straight away they ran into trouble. When Princess Anne, carrying the baby, climbed into the car she sat in the front seat, immediately arousing the wrath of the car-safety lobbyists who felt that the royal couple were setting a bad example by not placing the baby in the rear of the vehicle. This was, of course, in the days before seat-belt legislation was introduced and even though they were correct in the criticism, it was the only unpleasant note in an otherwise happy event.

Mark drove his family from London back to Gloucestershire to their new home where Princess Anne had to cope with the dual problem of moving into her new house and nursing her infant son.

One of the first tasks facing the parents of the new baby was what to name him. Over the years the Royal Family has devised a formula for naming children by which the parents choose the first name with the second Christian name usually being that of one of the parents themselves. Then, if other names are to be used, these will come from other members of the family, cousins, aunts, uncles or grandparents.

Finally, it was decided that the names would be Peter Mark Andrew. The first two names were Mark's in reverse order while Andrew was, of course, a tribute to Princess Anne's brother who was absolutely delighted at the compliment. The christening took place in the Music Room at Buckingham Palace with the new baby dressed in the traditional gown of Honiton lace used for all royal christenings.

Master Peter was the Queen's first grandchild and the first royal grandchild in 500 years to be born a commoner. His parents had declined to accept hereditary titles and the Princess had made it known that she did not wish her son to be granted one in his own right. Looking back it seems probable that Princess Anne realised that with three brothers, all of whom would eventually marry and have children, her own children's place in the line of succession would diminish as the years went on, and she saw no reason why they should be given titles if they were not to carry out royal duties later in life. So Master Peter Phillips was installed in the nursery which had been created out of the attic rooms at Gatcombe, to be brought up as a normal child, enjoying the countryside and its attractions first and foremost, with his royal connections kept firmly in the background. He sees more of his parents than most other youngsters in a similar position might have done some years ago, but nevertheless from the earliest age he has got used to the idea that his mother has to go away for long periods occasionally and his time will be spent with his nanny or one of the police officers.

Peter was introduced to riding when he was three years old and obviously if he shows any talent for competition his parents will be on hand to give the best possible advice and encouragement. He attends the local village school in Minchinhampton with the Princess driving him to and from his lessons whenever she is at home, which is much more frequently than is imagined. It is an understatement to say that the Princess's son is energetic! He gallops about the place and visitors to Gatcombe are grabbed by him when they arrive and urged to 'hurry up, I've got something to show you.' His natural ebullience carries him away sometimes and when it does his mother, who is fairly relaxed most of the time, will give him a warning or two and then if Peter still doesn't behave Princess Anne will have him banished upstairs to give him time to cool down and calm himself.

There is obviously a great affection between father and son, and at weekends and during school holidays it is very rare to see Mark around the estate without Peter in tow. Peter loves the farm and during the summer he, together with Princess Anne and anyone else who happens to be around, will pitch in and help with the harvest. Even his royal uncles, Edward and Andrew, have been known to join in.

There is no doubt about the place that Peter occupies in the Queen's affections. He is, after all, the first grandchild and the Queen sees him in much the same way as her mother sees Prince Charles. Whenever the Phillips's visit Windsor, Peter insists that his royal grandmother takes him to play in the miniature Welsh cottage that was presented by the people of Wales when the Queen herself was a young girl, and whatever the demands on the Queen's time, she will always find a few minutes to spend with her first grandson.

Peter was four years old when his mother found that she was expecting another baby. Mark was delighted with the news and immediately before the confinement Princess Anne moved to Windsor which was convenient for the short drive to London for the birth. Mark remained at Gatcombe working on the farm until he was told that the Princess had been taken to hospital. Having been present at the birth of his son, he wasn't all that keen to repeat the exercise but he was prepared to be there if the Princess wanted it. As it happened, more by chance than intent, he arrived at St. Mary's in plenty of time to stay with his wife during the birth and afterwards announced that all was well and he was pleased that he had been present.

Princess Anne's daughter was born on 15th May, 1981, in the Lindo Wing of St. Mary's Hospital, Paddington, London. She was born at 8.15 a.m. and weighed 8 lbs. 1 oz. The baby was the Queen's first granddaughter and, like her brother Peter born in 1977, she is a commoner even though she is eighth in line to the Throne.

Immediately after the birth the baby's father rang Windsor Castle to tell the Queen and the Duke of Edinburgh that they had a grand-daughter. Princess Anne had wanted to have her second baby at home but the royal gynaecologist, Mr. George Pinker, insisted that the delivery should be in hospital where, if there were to be any complications, all the modern facilities were available. As it happened it was a normal birth with the Princess attended by four doctors: Sir Richard Baylis, the Queen's Physician, Mr. Clive Roberts, Consultant Gynaecologist, Mr. David Harvey, Anaesthetist, and Mr. Pinker.

The Queen saw her granddaughter for the first time when she visited the hospital on the evening following the birth, and Prince Andrew arrived shortly afterwards carrying a large bouquet of carnations.

Princess Anne remained in hospital for only four days before being driven to her home in Gloucestershire by her husband. It was three weeks before the name of the baby was announced and when it became known that Zara had been chosen there was a great deal of surprise that Princess Anne had swept aside royal tradition in the choice of the name. Zara is a Greek biblical name meaning 'bright as the dawn' and the royal couple chose it simply because they liked it. They had not decided on the unusual name because of a past association or friendship. It was just a personal preference and took the Royal Family as much by surprise as the rest of the world.

Princess Anne told me that, in fact, it was the Prince of Wales who chose the name. 'The baby had made a somewhat positive arrival and my brother thought that Zara was an appropriate name.' The name may well be unique in Royal Family circles but according to the Princess 'I heard from just about every Zara in Britain at the time and I promise you there are quite a few.' Zara is also the name of one of the daughters of Shân Legge-Bourke who is, of course, a Lady-in-Waiting to the Princess, so in all probability she had heard the name mentioned in conversation, even if it had not registered. Her full names are Zara Anne Elizabeth Phillips and while Princess Anne had never claimed to be a particularly maternal person, it soon became evident that she was besotted with her daughter. Shortly after the birth I was visiting the Princess at Gatcombe on a matter concerning a television programme in which she was involved. Before I left she invited me to a walk through the conservatory to the front terrace where baby Zara was sleeping peacefully in her pram. So I was privileged to be one of the first outsiders to see the child and there was no doubt in my mind about the pleasure and pride of her mother.

Zara has developed into as lively a child as her brother, and she is never far behind when he appears at horse trials or some other public function. The children dress in dungarees and Wellingtons at home and if Peter is growing into another version of his father, you only have to look at photographs of Princess Anne at the same age to realise who Zara takes after. She too was a child born to the saddle, and one of her presents from her parents for Christmas 1983 was a Shetland pony on which the two and a half year old was seen being led around the grounds at Sandringham. They both play with children from the surrounding area and as Peter's circle of friends has widened with his progress through school they are frequently invited to birthday parties and outings with other children of their own ages. And like all the other parents Princess Anne acts as hostess when it's her turn to give a party for Peter or Zara. Even though in the past she has admitted that she is not particularly maternal, she enjoys the fun and games that youngsters can only play with the maximum amount of noise, much more than she is prepared to own up to.

Close friends are few and far between and entertaining at Gatcombe is usually informal. The Princess doesn't mind in the least any of her friends proposing themselves for lunch if they know that she is around. As she says: 'It's easier for them to know when I'm here than the other way around. They know they are welcome and I like people to ring up or simply drop in if they are in the vicinity.'

Princess Anne enjoys her food but on the whole it has to be 'plain and wholesome'. Cooks come and go at Gatcombe at fairly rapid intervals and staff at any of the royal homes know that with a reference from the Royal Family they can usually get much better paid employment elsewhere fairly easily. If, however, a cook wants to try something new and out of the ordinary, the Princess and her husband are willing at least to give it a try. As she says: 'As I get older I'm becoming more adventuresome not only in my clothes but also with what I eat.'

There is no doubt that the Princess's closest friends are her family. Apart from her husband and children, the people she is closest to are the Queen, the Duke of Edinburgh, her three brothers and Queen Elizabeth, the Queen Mother. How difficult is it for an only daughter to maintain a close relationship with her mother when that person is also the Queen? When I put this question to Princess Anne there was no hesitation in her reply. 'I think you've got the question the wrong way round. It's much more difficult to remember that she's Queen than a mother. After all, I've known her longer as a mother than as a Queen, if you see what I mean. She has been Queen most of my life but that's not how I think of her – it's the other way around really.'

The Princess has always been closer to her mother than to any other member of the Royal Family, and if she has inherited any of the Queen's characteristics, courage and determination are the two which first spring to mind. When Princess Anne survived the kidnap attempt in 1974 it was due in no small part to the fact that she kept her head and didn't panic; exactly the qualities the Queen displayed in 1982 when an intruder got into her bedroom and was alone with her for some time before help arrived. Since that incident the Princess has been even closer to her mother and there is nothing the Queen could ask Princess Anne to do that she would not immediately and willingly do. The Queen is the biggest single influence on all her family and if there is a special affinity between mother and daughter perhaps it's because the Queen sympathises with the problems Princess Anne has had to cope with all her life. Always in second place behind her elder brother, who, since the day he was born, has been prepared to be King, and always having to prove that what she has attained she has done by her own ability, Princess Anne has watched her mother all her life. Her extreme sense of duty is due entirely to the example she has been set.

Nevertheless since she was a young girl, people have said that Princess Anne is her father's girl. She has the same attitude to life, the same forthright opinions. She loves sport and until recently they have shared a distrust of the press. When she was growing up she was constantly with Prince Philip at polo matches and sailing his yacht and he was responsible for directing her enthusiasms towards sporting rather than academic achievement. As a voluntary number two himself, the Duke helped his daughter come to terms with the situation in which she found herself, and though the encouragement she received from both parents, when she started her equestrian career, was perhaps rather half-hearted at first, nobody was prouder or more pleased than Prince Philip when Princess Anne won her European title in 1971.

Prince Philip may have to accept the position of second place to his wife on all public occasions but there is no doubt in anyone's mind who is the head of the family at home. He was the only one who was able to control Princess Anne in the days when she was experiencing the frustrations and tribulations of the Palace schoolroom before she went to Benenden, and it was largely due to his influence that she accepted her position and realised that through no fault of her own she would have to adopt a secondary position.

Today father and daughter share the same sense of humour, the same inability to suffer fools and the same impatience with those who do not grasp things as quickly as they do themselves. From him she has inherited her total honesty and unwillingness to compromise on things she believes in. As they both grow older they each have become less abrasive – and more popular.

In the early days of their childhood the Prince of Wales was obviously the apple of Miss Peebles' eye in the schoolroom and when he left to go to school, Princess Anne had many of the frustrations of Miss Peebles worked out on her. But apart from the fact that their temperaments are, and always have been, completely opposite, there has never been any more than the usual brother–sister rivalry. When Prince Charles left the Palace for Cheam, Princess Anne missed him dreadfully, and she couldn't wait for him to return at the end of term.

The Princess's mercurial temperament was always in complete contrast to the more sedate attitude of her brother and if her teasing began to wear thin after a while, he rarely retaliated, choosing instead to effect an air of benevolent tolerance towards his younger sister.

As they both grew older they grew closer, and it was Princess Anne who suggested that the Prince and Princess of Wales should look in the vicinity of their house when they were looking for a home away from London. Because Prince Charles and Princess Anne are closer in age than they are to Andrew and Edward, it is inevitable that they should share certain bonds. No one in or around the Royal Household doubts the mutual affection and respect felt by them.

Princess Anne was eleven when her brother, Andrew, was born and the atmosphere at Buckingham Palace had already started to change from the severe formality of earlier days. The Princess pushed Andrew in his pram around the Palace gardens and through several of the London parks when she could, often trying to do his nurse out of a job. They have always been good friends and if Prince Andrew has received more than his fair share of publicity because of the company he keeps, he has a champion in his older sister, and he is always welcome at Gatcombe – especially at harvest-time when he works off his surplus energy in the fields.

Prince Edward is a much more gentle creature who, in his early childhood, showed many of the traits of Prince Charles. As the Queen's youngest child he will always be regarded as the baby of the family and Princess Anne has a special affection for him. They share a love of country pursuits and he is a great supporter when she is competing. He spends a lot of time at Gatcombe when he is able and is regarded by Peter in particular as a favourite uncle.

Queen Elizabeth, the Queen Mother, has been described as the 'world's favourite grandmother', and she obviously occupies a very special place not only in the hearts of the general public but in the affection of her many relatives. Prince Charles has developed a singular closeness with his grandmother and while Princess Anne shares a similar affection she admits that 'grandmothers have a feeling for grandsons that is unique'.

The Princess has been close to Queen Elizabeth for as long as she can remember and she has always been able to take any personal problems to her knowing that she will receive a sympathetic hearing. In turn the Queen Mother relies on Princess Anne's support for a great number of her causes and as the Princess says, 'Nobody can refuse her anything so she recruits most of us at some time or another.'

Princess Margaret took an early interest in her niece and when

Princess Anne was about to embark on her public duties for the first time in the late sixties, Princess Margaret, who was at that time considered to be one of the most glamorous women in the world, helped considerably in the choice of clothes and make-up. She was a superb example of sophistication for a young girl to follow and the friendship which transcends the normal family relationships has continued. Whenever Princess Margaret has been criticised for her behaviour or indiscreet relationships, Princess Anne has stood by her and today she feels a sympathy for her aunt that is enduring and steadfast.

If Princess Anne has to be very selective with her personal friends at times to the extent of appearing to be somewhat aloof, she has been extraordinarily fortunate in her immediate family. Her generation of Royals has received more freedom than any before, but instead of this driving them apart, as might have been expected, it has brought them even closer. Their paths rarely cross in the line of duty, but they are all aware that should the need arise, each and every one is ready to help any of the others. And this is where they draw their strength – from the family. In the final analysis they all prefer to seek other members of the family if they want to exchange confidences or ask advice, rather than approach any outsiders.

Chapter 14

THE PRINCESS AND THE PRESS

When Princess Anne visited the U.S.A. in 1982 one reporter named her as 'the person I would least like to interview'. A few months later, at the end of a 14,000 mile, eight-country tour of Africa, three newsmen were so impressed by her conduct that they became sponsors for The Save the Children Fund.

The press expected that particular trip to provide stories of a possible break-up in the Princess's marriage. When it became obvious that there was no substance to the rumours that had been circulating prior to Her Royal Highness's departure, the reporters concentrated on the real reason for the tour – and found even better news stories than they had hoped for. At the end of the trip, Princess Anne was heard to remark drily 'I did notice my miraculous transformation.'

Like her father, the Duke of Edinburgh, the Princess has carried on a series of running battles with the media almost since she first came into the public eye. She has rarely been prepared to put herself out to accomodate reporters and photographers, unlike the Queen Mother who always pauses when entering or leaving a building so that the waiting photographers can get their pictures. As Princess Anne puts it: 'I don't do stunts.'

There has never been a time when she has not been of interest to the media and, particularly when she is competing at horse trials, the press attends in force. She regards her equestrian pursuits as being part of her 'private life' and feels that the press has no right to encroach. In much the same way that the rest of the Royal Family like to preserve their privacy when they are not on public duties, she believes she has a right to a private life.

Perhaps this is being a little naive, because human curiosity being what it is, there is no way the press is going to ignore members of the Royal Family simply because they feel they are 'off duty'. In point of fact, many of the best stories and photographs occur when the subjects are relaxing and 'off guard' and editors are only too well aware of this. 'Royal watching' is a growth industry in journalism just about everywhere in the world. There has never been greater interest in the Royal Family than at present and a photograph of the Queen or, more recently, the Princess of Wales, on the cover of a magazine, is said to guarantee an increase in sales, though one foreign periodical claimed, somewhat unchivalrously, that the reverse happened when they published pictures of Princess Anne or Princess Margaret.

Princess Anne is a naturally suspicious woman: she has to be. There are those who try to cultivate members of the Royal Family for their own ends so she has had to erect barriers between herself and all but a few close friends. She is also totally honest, so much so that she will not smile for photographers simply because they want her to if she doesn't feel like it. She has not achieved the artfulness necessary for a permanent 'love affair' with the press. If she has just had an exhausting round at Badminton or Burghley, the last thing she wants is to answer questions from a reporter and smile prettily into the bargain. Her 'naff off' remarks have become part of Fleet Street folklore and those who have got to know her over the years grudgingly admit that at times 'she's got a point.' She knows that they have a job to do, and when she is involved in an engagement as part of her royal duties, she is perfectly happy for photographers to be around, 'except when it is a Riding for the Disabled show and they keep getting in the way of the ponies'. The problem arises when the press, who quite understandably are looking for an off-beat story or out of the ordinary picture, ask her to do something that is out of character. This is when life becomes difficult for all concerned, including, occasionally, the Press Secretary who may be accompanying her. Princess Anne professes not to care about her image saying, 'it's too late, there's nothing I can do about it now anyway,' but she is honest enough to admit, 'it's nice when one reads something pleasant.'

The attitude of the press towards the Princess varies considerably. Local newspapers and televison in the areas she visits are nearly always full of praise, reporting her activities in full and quoting at length the speeches she makes and the reaction of those she has met. Of course they do not have the selection of stories to choose from that the nationals have and consequently they are not nearly so selective about the way they cover events. Fleet Street, on the other hand, needs more than just the average story or picture to sell its papers and they are constantly looking for the scoop that will beat the competition. 'Princess Anne ignores orphan waif' is a much better headline than 'Princess Anne charms children', and in any lineup of a couple of hundred people it's not difficult to find the ones who claim to have been overlooked.

The public's obsession with royalty is not new. In the latter part of the nineteenth century the everyday comings and goings of Queen Victoria and her family were reported regularly in the national press, and read just as avidly by a nation which was as fascinated with the mundane details of Royal Family life as we are today with the escapades of Prince Andrew, or the Princess of Wales's clothes.

In the days before radio and television the public satisified its appetite for news of the Royal Family through newspapers and periodicals. It has always been the case that a good royal story boosts circulation figures, and if these days members of the Royal Family become irritated by inaccurate Palace reporting they might reflect on the attitude of King George III who, because he was annoyed 'at the inaccuracies in the papers as to the Royal movements, took the advice of the Chief Metropolitan Magistrate and appointed a Court Newsman'. This was the forerunner of the Court Circular as we know it today and the sole task of the Court Newsman was to distribute daily a document supplied from the Court. For this he was paid an annual salary in 1866 of £45 and even today the Court Circular is, to the surprise of some readers, supplied not by the Palace Press Office, but by the office of the Master of the Household.

When Princess Anne holds her twice-yearly programme meetings at Buckingham Palace she is attended not only by the immediate members of her own Household but also by a Press Secretary, who will advise on the media coverage expected for the various engagements. The Press Secretary does not work exclusively for her; indeed the only person in the Royal Family who employs a Press Secretary is the Queen herself. Her Majesty's Press Secretary is Michael Shea, an ex-diplomat who combines his Royal duties with that of being a prolific author. In 1981, while masterminding the extensive coverage for the biggest media event ever, the wedding of the Prince of Wales, he still managed to publish three books under his own name. Michael Shea has total responsibility for all news emanating from Buckingham Palace. There are two Assistant Press Secretaries: Victor Chapman, a Canadian who previously worked for Prime Minister Trudeau, and John Haslam, a former B.B.C. Radio executive.

Victor Chapman works practically full time looking after the Prince and Princess of Wales, with John Haslam spending part of his time with Princess Anne, and the remainder looking after the press relations of the Duke of Edinburgh, Prince Andrew and Prince Edward. But these are first and foremost Assistant Press Secretaries to the Queen, and their ultimate responsibility is to her.

The Queen Mother and Princess Margaret have their own Press Secretary who is based at Clarence House.

For many years Princess Anne's press relations were handled by Mrs. Michael Wall who was Assistant Press Secretary to the Queen for more than twenty years until her retirement in 1982. A niece of

Princess Alice, Duchess of Gloucester, Anne Wall established an excellent working relationship with Fleet Street and both the B.B.C. and I.T.V., in a period during which she saw more changes in the attitude by and to the press than had taken place at any other time in the Palace's history. When she started in the Press Office almost the sole task was to tell the newspapers who was going where and what they were wearing. These days the Palace Press Office is on twenty-four-hour call handling queries from all over the world ranging from the subject of the Civil List to the state of the Prince and Princess of Wales's marriage.

Princess Anne has had to contend with years of adverse press comment and it is only in the last couple of years, since the Save the Children tour of Africa in 1982, that she has been getting anywhere near the friendly coverage enjoyed by most of the other members of her family. There is no doubt that favourable publicity is a great help to the Royals when they are carrying out public duties, and inevitably helps them to do their jobs. In the current state of near hysteria which surrounds almost everything that the Princess of Wales does and says, it's easy to forget that in the late 1960s when Princess Anne started her public career, she was subjected to much the same treatment. When she first appeared wearing a mini-skirt, pictures appeared in newspapers throughout the world and her flamboyant taste in hats was enough to start a fashion, with magazines devoting pages every week to her style of clothes.

When she first started going out with Mark Phillips, their friendship was dogged every step of the way by photographers and reporters and when she was stopped by the police for speeding, it made national headlines. So there's nothing new about the so-called 'press harassment' of the Royal Family.

On occasion the Princess has given interviews to a number of journalists about various aspects of her life, usually in connection with one of the charities she works for, but inevitably questions about her life style and attitudes are included by interviewers who wouldn't be doing their jobs properly if they didn't take the opportunities presented. Most reporters who have met Princess Anne in person come away with a totally changed view about her.

There may be strict lines of questioning laid down before the interview, but rarely does she refuse to answer any extra questions which may be put, and frequently she will raise other subjects and neatly turn the tables on the reporters by asking questions of her own. When Kenneth Harris of the *Observer* went to Gatcombe to interview her in 1981, he told her that she was not what he had expected. She then asked him to describe how he thought she would be. He did so, and his explanation broke the ice completely and paved the way for an exceptionally frank and informal conversation.

It doesn't always work out that way. In 1982 when she was on a tour of the U.S.A. Princess Anne was given incorrect news about the birth of Prince William of Wales and when she was asked to comment by American press men who were covering her tour, she asked them for more information. This was taken as a lack of interest on her part and reported as such. The truth of the matter was that as soon as official news of the birth was given to her – by her office in Buckingham Palace in the early hours of the morning – she said how delighted she was; and she meant it. It was another example of Her Royal Highness not wanting to be caught out and of the press looking for an instant headline, which she was not willing to provide.

Princess Anne has wide experience of television and radio. She has appeared in special films made for Save the Children and Riding for the Disabled in 1970 and she went to Kenya with the successful B.B.C. children's programme 'Blue Peter' to make a film with Valerie Singleton, one of television's most experienced and popular presenters. It was an honest and forthright film about the problems facing welfare workers trying to cope with disease among children, but even here the Princess was unwilling to compromise for the sake of her image. If there were unpalatable facts that had to be mentioned she was prepared to say them, even if it meant that she was criticized.

In 1981 she was the subject of a major television documentary based on her working life. The author had made the suggestion to Buckingham Palace, but the Princess was at first unenthusiastic, feeling that there would not be great public interest in her public duties. Eventually she was persuaded that it was important and interesting for a senior member of the Royal Family to demonstrate the amount of work they get through in any year. Thames Television were given the opportunity of producing the film and we were allowed almost unlimited access to the Princess and her Household for more than a year.

Once she had agreed to co-operate in the making of the film, Princess Anne involved herself in every aspect. She even allowed a special radio microphone to be placed inside one of her handbags so that conversation between herself and others could be recorded without the intrusion of large, hand-held equipment. Her Royal Highness invited the programme's producer and myself to Gatcombe and Buckingham Palace a number of times to discuss the project, when there would be just the three of us sitting around the fire with the Princess pouring coffee, and frequently 'half-hour' talks would go on for two hours or more.

Her then Private Secretary, Major Nicholas Lawson, was involved from the early stages and the entire project was overseen by the Queen's Press Secretary, Michael Shea, who not only gave tremendous encouragement when things were not going as smoothly as we wished, but also a great deal of advice on the ways to deal with members of the Royal Household. There was no part of Princess Anne's working life from which we were barred and for the first time television cameras were allowed to film one of the 'programme meetings' in the Princess's dining room at Buckingham Palace, where the schedule for the following six months is agreed to.

On one occasion I was due to film an interview with her at Gatcombe and while the camera team were setting up their equipment, I walked outside, up and down the drive. Princess Anne asked me how long they would be and when I said about an hour she drove out of the grounds saying she would be back in plenty of time. When she returned, we filmed the interview in a perfectly relaxed manner, and she remained afterwards to chat for a few minutes before leaving for an engagement. Later we learned that when she left Gatcombe in the morning she had gone to have two inoculations in preparation for her forthcoming trip to Nepal. She gave no sign of any discomfort throughout the interview.

There was one unfortunate occurrence during the filming. A member of the crew sold an 'inside story' to a national newspaper, claiming that Princess Anne was 'uncooperative and arrogant'. He apparently thought that she needed 'to be shown up'. The Princess and her husband were upset at the story, not because of the content particularly – they were used to this sort of treatment from a certain section of the press – but because it had come from someone to whom they had opened up their home. The fact that the story was totally untrue and the correspondent preferred to remain 'anonymous' added to the distress, and for a while it seemed that filming might have to be halted. But Ronald Allison, Head of Outside Broadcasts for Thames Television, and the man who liaises with the Palace on behalf of Independent Television, used his good offices to reassure the Princess's Personal Secretary, Brenda Hodgson, that great care would be taken in future, and we were allowed to proceed.

Eventually the film was shown on the I.T.V. network on December 23rd, 1981, and lasted a total of an hour and a quarter. If there was any criticism of the final product it wasn't directed at the Princess, who was shown as a hardworking, professional, and possibly undervalued member of the Royal Family. The final version did not show enough of the other facets of her life, but this was due entirely to the editing. With more than fifty hours of film to choose from and the Princess's complete co-operation – she even re-recorded part of her commentary to accommodate the producer – a more complete picture of Princess Anne should have been possible.

As far as Princess Anne's relations with the press these days are concerned, she is going through a peaceful period which has lasted since the Africa tour in 1982. No member of the Royal Family has been able to compete with the Princess of Wales since the Royal Wedding, in terms of press coverage, and while she is unable to take a bad photograph, Princess Anne is rarely pictured in flattering terms. Photographs never do her justice; indeed when you first meet her in the flesh it comes as an agreeable surprise to find out how stunningly beautiful she is. As she gets older she is becoming more gracious, increasingly elegant, and even if she still does not suffer fools gladly, she is far more tolerant now than at any time before.

Perhaps her battles with the press are over. Maybe we shall see the sort of coverage in the British national press that she has always attracted overseas in the African countries when she goes on behalf of Save the Children. On Tuesday, October 26th, 1982, the *Times* of Swaziland reported on the front page that 'A radiant Princess Anne yesterday met the children of Swaziland . . . and they loved her.' James Dlamini went on to describe her tour of the country as 'a smiling safari'. The people closest to her, the Ladies-in-Waiting and other members of the Household, say she is just the same as she has always been. She is not doing anything today that she has not done in the past and they get very angry when reports appear in the newspapers that the Princess is 'sour-faced' or 'sullen'. Shân Legge-Bourke defends her stoutly: 'She has a tremendous sense of fun and a quick humour. If only the reporters could hear some of the cracks she makes about them, they would soon revise their opinions.'

Certainly the Princess's happiest experience with the Press came about through a television interview with Michael Parkinson recorded in November, 1983, when she and Captain Phillips were on a private visit to Australia. Parkinson had agreed to pay £6,000 to The Save The Children Fund in order to get the interview and Princess Anne certainly gave him his money's worth. The Princess appeared relaxed, good-humoured and determined to enjoy herself. Afterwards Michael Parkinson went on record as saying 'I found her to be thoroughly pleasant, tough-minded, wry and, above all, humorous – in fact a strong-minded and intelligent woman.'

Princess Anne feels that the reason she has received a bad press for years is that she didn't fit the image the press thought she should have in the first place. 'I never was a fairy tale Princess – and I never will be.'

Chapter 15

THE PRINCESSES ROYAL

On Saturday, 26th July, 1958, His Royal Highness, Prince Charles heir to the Throne, was proclaimed Prince of Wales in a tape-recorded message played to the crowds who had gathered in Cardiff Arms Park to witness the closing ceremony of the Empire and Commonwealth Games. On that day the Queen's eldest son became the twenty-first holder of the style and title Prince of Wales.

On Thursday, 29th July, 1981, on the occasion of her marriage to Prince Charles, Lady Diana Spencer became only the ninth person to be known as Princess of Wales.

Yet of all the titles which are held by the Sovereign's closest relatives, the rarest is that of Princess Royal. Only six have been created in the three and a half centuries since Charles I decided to make his daughter, Mary, The Princess Royal in 1642. At that time she was just eleven years old, so the myth that the conferring of the title is only done when the recipient has reached mature age, is just that – a myth. Indeed, in more recent times, Queen Victoria insisted that her own daughter Victoria should be known as Princess Royal within two months of her birth in 1840.

There was another Anne who was known as Princess Royal. This was the daughter of George II who was crowned in 1727. One of his first acts as King was to issue a Royal Proclamation naming his seventeen-year-old daughter Princess Royal. She was only the second woman to bear the title, bridging a gap of nearly seventy years since the death of Princess Mary in 1660.

There is nothing automatic about the eldest daughter of the Monarch being created Princess Royal. In fact, there is no reason why the bearer of the title has to be a daughter of the Sovereign. As the title is the personal gift of the Monarch and can be bestowed without reference to Parliament, the Prime Minister, the Archbishop of Canterbury or anyone else for that matter, it might just as easily be given to any other female relative. If the Queen wishes the title to be reactivated during her reign, she might even decide to make her younger sister Margaret, Princess Royal. There is no precedent for this, as all previous holders of the title have been daughters of the Monarch, but there is nothing to stop the Queen doing it if she so wishes. Like the other honours which lie solely within the Queen's personal prerogative – The Order of Merit, The Orders of the Garter and Thistle, and most widely used, The Royal Victorian Order – the title of Princess Royal is given for life. It can be withdrawn, again only at the command of the Monarch, but in the case of a Princess Royal this has never been known to happen.

The style of Princess Royal carries with it no other benefits. Unlike the Prince of Wales, the Princess Royal does not inherit great estates along with the title. There is no tradition of a ceremonial investiture such as those accorded Prince Charles at Caernarvon in 1969, or Prince Edward in 1911. Similarly, the Princess Royal is not required to make any solemn vows before the Sovereign and in fact apart from the publication in the Honours List there is no official presentation, simply a Royal Warrant. The only record of the creation of the last Princess Royal is the announcement by King George V in his New Year Honours List of 1932, when he conferred the title on his daughter, Princess Mary, Countess of Harewood, who retained the title until her death in 1965. At that time Princess Anne was a fifteen-year-old schoolgirl who had not yet commenced her public duties so obviously it was considered inappropriate to consider making her Princess Royal at such an early age, in these modern times.

Of the six bearers of the title Princess Royal, none has been more widely respected or better loved than the last incumbent, Princess Mary. From the day she first received the honour from her father, King George V, on January 1st, 1932, until the day she died suddenly in 1965 she was known as Her Royal Highness, The Princess Royal. She was a woman with tremendous enthusiasms. She enjoyed to the full every aspect of her life, both personal and public, and saw more changes in the world in the first half of this century than almost any other member of the Royal Family, with the exception today, of course, of the Queen Mother.

In the latter half of the 1950s and in the early 1960s she played an increasingly prominent role overseas, acting as the Queen's representative in Nigeria, Zambia, the West Indies, Gibraltar, Cyprus, North Africa, Canada and the United States, making her first transatlantic crossing in 1953.

She was born in 1897, the year of her great-grandmother Queen Victoria's Diamond Jubilee. She was christened Victoria Alexandra Alice Mary and it wasn't until her father succeeded to the Throne that she became known as Princess Mary. She lived in the reigns of six kings and queens – Victoria, Edward VII, George V, Edward VIII, George VI and Elizabeth II. Two of her brothers became King; the eldest, born three years earlier than she, was Edward VIII, the King who was never crowned, and Bertie, born in 1895, became George

VI on the abdication of his elder brother. It was she more than any other who brought to the role of Princess Royal the affection and dignity with which we think of it today.

The parallels between The Princess Royal and Princess Anne are quite extraordinary. Apart from the obvious physical resemblance, they appear to share many other characteristics. When Princess Mary was growing up she was regarded as a tomboy, indeed her mother the Queen treated her in exactly the same way as she treated her sons and she was expected to share their games and pastimes irrespective of the fact that she was the only girl. She would challenge her brothers to bicycle races, join them in football matches and she was fearless when riding her pony. As her elder brother David, later Duke of Windsor said, 'Mary was our close companion . . . loving horses, she rode better than Bertie or I.' Half a century later similar sentiments would be expressed by Prince Charles about his 'tomboy' sister.

Another similarity between the two royal princesses was their reaction to their early lessons. Princess Mary shared a schoolroom with her brothers at York Cottage in the grounds of Sandringham Park. One of her tutors found her to be a disruptive influence on the boys and difficult to discipline because of her habit of answering long before the others had solved the problems. She overshadowed the other members of the small classes and her quick wit and mercurial temperament made concentration an impossible task. Fifty years later in the private schoolroom at Buckingham Palace Princess Anne would be blamed by her governess whenever her lively spirit swamped the more leisurely pace of her brother Charles.

There are no specific duties allocated to a Princess Royal, or if there are there is no record of them defined as such. Indeed, it wasn't until Princess Louise, daughter of Edward VII, became Princess Royal in 1905 that a Princess Royal took any part in public life in her own right. Her immediate predecessor, Princess Victoria, later to become Empress of Prussia, had held the title for more than sixty years, since shortly after her birth in 1840 until the day she died in August, 1901. She found the constrictions of court life in Germany even more stifling than the etiquette demanded of our own Victorian establishments. She had been trained to make the occasional visit to certain schools and hospitals, all of which were carefully selected to make sure that nothing offensive to the royal eyes and ears should ever be presented. However, when she married Prince Frederick William of Prussia and returned with him to spend the next thirty years of her life outside her native England, she found even this denied her, and the rules of the German court meant that she was to be relegated to a position that had been unchanged for centuries: that of a dutiful daughter-in-law whose only role was to attend to the wants of her husband's mother, the Empress. But if life for a royal princess in the nineteenth century was considered dull and boring, what would Princess Anne have made of her lot if she had been born 250 years earlier, as was her namesake, the other Princess Anne? The daughter of George II was born in 1709 and created Princess Royal in 1727 on the death of her grandfather, George I, and the accession of her father to the Throne. The family were German and did not move to Britain until Princess Anne's parents had been married for nine years. Until then it had been a life of unremitting boredom for a young child in the gloom and forbidding chill of the Palace of Hanover. England in the eighteenth century was a place of change, and when George I was crowned in 1714 both Princess Anne and her brother, who was to become Prince of Wales, were allowed to witness the Coronation and the festivities that followed, including The Lord Mayor of London's Show.

But after the initial excitement of those early days it was back to the routine of domestic life at Kensington Palace, in those days far re-moved from the warren of royal apartments in the residential area it has become today. Helen Cathcart in her book *Anne and The Princesses Royal* (W. H. Allen & Co.) gives an insight into a typical day for the Princess. 'She would rise at seven, pray, "coiffe" and breakfast, walk from eight till nine, read and then commence lessons, dining at one and then playing shuttlecock, but first walking or talking "of sensible things".' She also had shown some skill as a musician and as befitted someone of her rank, when a music master was appointed, the job was given to Handel – at a salary of £200 a year.

The present-day Princess Anne has a passion for horses and has reached the pinnacle of her chosen sport. The eighteenth-century Princess Anne also chose riding as her own emotional 'safety valve', hunting as frequently as possible during the season and often being the first over many of the fences and walls along the way. Sometimes she hunted so vigorously that she would return to the palace with her face covered in scratches and bruises from the overhanging trees and branches. But unlike our Princess Anne, she had no interest in carrying out duties of a social nature. There is no evidence that she visited the poor or infirm or indulged in any philanthropic gestures even after her marriage, when she was allotted £80,000 by Parliament from what was then the equivalent of the Civil List. The only record we have that tells us that she had any charitable feelings at all relates to her old music master, Handel. When he fell ill in 1737 it was Princess Anne who arranged that he travel to France to recover.

The friendship between master and pupil continued throughout the Princess Royal's life and they were both to die in the same year, Princess Anne on January 12th and Handel on 14 April, 1759.

Until comparatively recently royal daughters were not considered to be of any importance in their own right. The only value placed upon the birth of a female child to a sovereign, was in her usefulness as a future royal bride, in order to cement relationships between the ruling families of Europe and strengthen the ties of blood which linked all the royal houses.

The future was not all that far away for many of the infant daughters. Almost as soon as they could walk they were betrothed to the filial offspring of the neighbouring monarch, so that an alliance could be formed between the two countries – usually against a third. Another advantage to the father of a princess was the fact that he was getting her off his hands and so would not be responsible for her upkeep once she was married. Because even though female children were regarded as insignificant, and indeed until the seventeenth century most were denied even the title of Princess, nevertheless they were accorded the privileges, comforts and expenses of a royal household. Princess Mary, daughter of Charles I, was given an establishment consisting of a lady-in-waiting, a gentleman usher, a nurse, a governess, two pages, four footmen, five kitchen servants, a coachman, a groom, a seamstress, and a laundress, in addition to occasional visits by physicians and others required to administer to her well-being.

Compare this with the present-day household of Princess Anne. At Buckingham Palace the Princess has a Private Secretary, a Personal Secretary, and a Secretary to the Office, while at home in Gloucester she is attended by a butler, a cook, a dresser, two cleaning ladies who come in every day, and there is also a nanny for the two children.

So it was with a certain amount of relief and dedication that England's kings set about their royal match-making in the seventeenth and eighteenth centuries. Princess Mary, daughter of Charles I, was married to Prince William of Orange when she was just nine years old and he was only five years older.

Her father had inherited great debts from his father and the marriage settlement which guaranteed his daughter an annual income of £11,500 was not the least attractive part of the bargain. It was unusual in those days for the bridegroom to bring money into a marriage. Normally the bride's father would have to provide a handsome dowry to entice an eligible suitor for his daughter's hand. In this case the Prince and Princess of Orange were so anxious to enhance their social standing by marrying into the English Royal Family, that no price was considered too high.

From the moment Princess Mary entered the Court of her father-in-law, Henry Frederick of Orange, she was addressed as 'Princesse Royale'. So the title as we know it today actually originated as a courtesy title bestowed by a doting and somewhat snobbish father-in-law, in his unrelenting quest to elevate his own family's social standing to that of his contemporaries in the other royal houses in Europe. At that time a princess of the Royal House of Orange was known only as Highness, without the 'Royal' prefix.

So 1642 is acknowledged as the date from which the distinction and title of Princess Royal was originally used to describe the first-born female child of an English monarch.

If the later Princess Mary could be said to have witnessed in the first half of the twentieth century more changes in the world than many of her royal relatives, then the Princess Mary of the seventeenth century was also to see considerable transformations which came about during her lifetime. She was to witness the execution of her father, Charles I; then from her exile in The Netherlands wait throughout eleven long years of republican rule in Britain under Oliver Cromwell, until the Monarchy was restored and her brother called to the Throne as Charles II. It was at her palace in The Hague that Charles heard that he was to be recalled to the English Throne and the event held a particular significance for the Princess Royal, for her son William saw his rightful claim in the line of succession also recognised.

The Restoration was a period of English history when a Princess Royal should have enjoyed all the gaiety and splendour of which a Stuart Court was capable. There was public rejoicing in the streets at the end of the puritanical reign of the Cromwellians and for a princess who had returned to her native England after an absence of eighteen years, it should have meant a triumphant reversion to the pomp and lustre of a land anxious to make up for the sombre days of the Lord Protector. But Princess Mary had been in Holland for too long. Although she delighted with her brother in his acclaim, she found life at the Palace of Whitehall too frivolous after the ascetism she had been used to in The Hague. She had no inclination to satisfy the public's appetite to see her and in the winter of 1660 she withdrew completely into the privacy of her apartments, taking no part in the celebrations which continued throughout the rest of the palace.

Princess Mary died on Christmas Eve, 1660, when she was twenty-nine years old and she was buried five days later in Westminster

Abbey, whose records for December 29th, 1660, show that on this day took place 'the burial of The Princess Royal Mary, the King's eldest sister, mother to the Prince of Orange.'

As we have already noted, it was to be sixty-seven years before the title of Princess Royal was to be conferred on a Monarch's daughter. Princess Anne, whose life spanned the half century between 1709 and 1759, was created Princess Royal by her father, George II, in 1727 and she retained the title for the remaining thirty years of her life. Indeed, for yet another thirty years there was no Princess Royal, at least, not by Royal Proclamation. However, this did not mean the title fell into disuse, merely that the Sovereign, George III, did not officially create his eldest daughter Princess Royal until she was twenty-three years old.

Princess Charlotte Augusta Matilda was the fourth child born to King George III and Queen Charlotte. Altogether they had thirteen children who survived infancy – seven boys and six girls. George III has been maligned frequently as the Monarch who gave away the American colonies. His place in history is assured because the revolution in America took place during his reign, but according to the present Prince of Wales the friction which had been apparent between the two countries for many years was bound to flare up into an open break at some time; it was George III's misfortune to be on the Throne when it happened.

He was also thought to be insane in the later years of his life; a condition which has also been questioned by Prince Charles. In 1976, the Prince of Wales gave a television interview to Alistair Cooke, a British-born journalist who has lived in the United States for most of his life and whose 'Letter from America' has been broadcast by the B.B.C. for more than thirty years. During the interview Prince Charles defended his ancestor vigorously, claiming that his so-called madness was in all probability a disease of the blood which modern science has defined as porphyria, an illness among whose symptoms are depression and severe hallucinations.

The King and Queen had been married for more than five years and already had three sons when Princess Charlotte was born on September 24th, 1766. If her father has secured a place in history for the somewhat dubious distinction of having been accused of giving away a country, then his eldest daughter's niche is guaranteed for more pleasant reasons. She bears the distinction of having been the first royal princess to be born in Buckingham Palace – or, to give it the name which it was known at that time, Buckingham House.

Just a little more than a month later the infant princess was christened by the Archbishop of Canterbury and the Annual Register records that 'H.R.H. The Princess Royal was christened' on October 27th, 1766. This is the first indication we have that Princess Charlotte was to be known as Princess Royal, but it was probably simply a question of courtesy on the part of those who had been used to calling the first-born daughter of the Sovereign Princess Royal. There had not been the long gap which had passed between Princess Mary and the first Princess Anne; in fact Princess Anne had been dead for only seven years, so the title and its usage were still familiar to many in and around the Court. Nevertheless it was to be more than twenty years before Princess Charlotte was officially created Princess Royal, and then only because of fears that the King's illness would make it necessary for the Queen and her elder children to assume some of the duties of government requiring royal attention.

Just as today members of the Royal Family act as Counsellors of State when the Queen is abroad, so too in the eighteenth century there were legal definitions which enabled other relatives of the Monarch to help govern the country, in the event of indisposition or absence abroad.

In the case of George III, his son had been officially and legally proclaimed Prince of Wales shortly after his birth, so there was no problem about his position, but Princess Charlotte, although known as the Princess Royal since her christening, had no legal right to the title. As soon as this was discovered and it was realised that in reality she was no different in rank from any of her five sisters, the King, by then temporarily recovered from his sickness, resolved the problem by officially conferring the title of Princess Royal on his eldest daughter Charlotte on June 22nd, 1789, three months short of her twenty-third birthday. So it is quite possible that if it had not been for the mental state of George III in the latter part of the eighteenth century, there might well not have been a Princess Royal until the mid-nineteenth century.

The life of the Princess Royal changed dramatically between child-hood and adolescence. She had been the favourite child of her father and accompanied him on visits throughout the country and abroad. She could twist him around her finger and she occupied a special place in the heirarchy of the Court far beyond the normal position enjoyed by a royal daughter. Every member of the Court, including her brothers and sisters, addressed her as 'Royal', only the King himself using her Christian name. It was the custom of the time for the Royal Family regularly to put itself on show to members of the public. The King believed that all his people, of whatever rank, should be given the opportunity of seeing himself, the Queen and the royal princes and princesses. So once a week at an appointed time the Royal Family walked in the grounds of Kew or Richmond, and any member of the public was admitted to see the procession which lasted a little over an hour. Although Princess Charlotte would do anything to please her father, she found it an ordeal being submitted to the public gaze in this manner, unlike her brothers and sisters who seemed to take great pleasure in being the centre of attention.

It was a period of great enjoyment generally for the young Princess Royal, and the carefree lifestyle continued for many years until the King's illness forced the Queen to assume more and more responsibility for the affairs of State. The Prince of Wales had earned a reputation for extravagant high living and because of his father's refusal to confer the status of Prince Regent upon him, he enjoyed to the full a life of gambling and debauchery, away from the rigours of the Court and George III. So it was left to the Queen to instil a sense of responsibility into her eldest daughter so that she could take on the role her brother so obviously did not care for.

Princess Charlotte became secretary to the Queen, which meant acting not only as a conduit between Her Majesty and members of the government, but also as a constant personal companion, assuming the character of a senior lady-in-waiting. She was allowed almost no time to herself, and as in those days there was no provision by Parliament to make her financially independent she relied completely on her mother to pay her household expenses. As the excesses of the Prince of Wales and his brothers became even more shocking, the constraints of life for those around the Queen at home became even more oppressive. Fearful that the exploits of her sons should come to the ears of her daughters, Her Majesty banned all newspapers from the palace. Letters between the Prince of Wales and the Princess Royal were intercepted lest she should be corrupted by even a written contact with her brother. After a gay, carefree life growing up, as Princess Charlotte entered womanhood her daily routine took on the sort of drudgery usually seen only in the confines of a closed order of contemplative nuns.

For holidays there was just an annual visit to Weymouth, this being long before the days of Balmoral which were to come in Queen Victoria's time. The Princess Royal undertook no public duties on her own, but as secretary to the Queen she did accompany her mother when she went to visit charitable institutions which cared for the poor and infirm. On a number of occasions they visited commercial organisations, and the results of their visits inevitably meant an increase in prestige – and business – for the company concerned, a forerunner perhaps to these days when a royal opening or unveiling is a most highly sought after prize by firms with an eye to free publicity.

Princess Charlotte was to suffer the boredom and drudgery of this life until she was thirty, an age when most women would have given up all hope of marriage and a family of their own.

The King, unlike most of his contemporaries in the royal houses of Europe, not only had not sought a husband for his daughter, but had actively discouraged those suitors who had come seeking her hand in marriage. Eventually, Prince Frederick William of Württemberg, a widower with three children, was to send an emissary to the Court, to ask the King to consider allowing the Princess Royal to become his bride. The Prince's man was to be kept waiting for several months before he was even admitted to present his master's request. The King was not attracted to the idea, but after many weeks deliberating he decided that if Princess Charlotte was in favour he would not stand in her way.

The Princess, who would have accepted a two-headed man with a squint, if only to get away from the slavery of her life at Court, agreed to become betrothed to the Prince with an alacrity which even in those days was considered to be slightly indelicate. And at this time she had never seen her husband-to-be, had no idea what he looked like or even how old he was.

It was to be nearly a year before she met him; the King had insisted that Prince Frederick William should come to England, rather than have the bride travel to Württemberg. When eventually they did meet, she was pleasantly surprised at her fiancé's appearance and they were married within two weeks at the Chapel Royal.

After a short honeymoon spent at Windsor the couple left for the Continent and Princess Charlotte was never to see her mother and father again. Indeed it was to be thirty years before she returned to England. By this time she had become Queen of Württemberg, through the courtesy of Napoleon, who had restored the Kingdom to her husband. Her father George III had died and her brother was on the Throne of England as William IV, when she finally came back to her homeland for a visit in 1827.

She had changed beyond recognition but she was greeted with acclaim and affection by all who saw her. It was fortuitous that she should go to Windsor at that time for within the year she was to die at the age of sixty-three – contented and happy as the Princess Royal Charlotte, Queen of Württemberg.

There was a twelve-year gap before the next Princess Royal was created. Victoria was on the Throne and her daughter and namesake, Victoria Adelaide Mary Louise, was born on November 21st, 1840.

The Princess's birth was in the same year as her parents had married.

Although the country had hoped for a male heir to the Throne, Princess Victoria was loved and cherished from the moment of her birth and almost from the very beginning she was referred to as 'Princess Royal'. Her father Prince Albert made sure that the title was conferred on her formally at the earliest possible moment and within two months of her birth on January 19th, 1841, the Royal Warrant was issued stating that she would be known henceforth 'by the style and title of Her Royal Highness, The Princess Royal'. Princess Victoria was heir to the Throne for slightly less than a year. In November of 1841, her brother Bertie was born, created Prince of Wales, and remained so for longer than anyone before him, or since; sixty years as Prince of Wales until he succeeded to the Throne as Edward VII in 1901.

Princess Victoria was the apple of her father's eye and he took a special personal interest in her education. There was never any question of her going to school, that kind of decision wouldn't even be discussed for at least another hundred years. Prince Albert decided she should learn Latin, French and German of course, the latter language being the Prince's mother tongue and the one used more than any other in the family. In addition, she was taught by her father the politics of the time, or at least given an edited version, thought suitable for the ears of a young royal of the day.

At the great Exhibition of 1851 in Crystal Palace, Princess Victoria met for the first time the man she was eventually to marry. She was ten; he was exactly twice her age: Prince Frederick William of Prussia, the Emperor's heir.

It was to be seven more years before they were married, but they were eventually betrothed for two years in secret. Again the marriage came about in part through the desirability of an alliance between the British and Prussian Empires, even though the Prince and Princess had been attracted to one another from the first time they met. Prince Albert and Queen Victoria were delighted that their daughter had made such a fortunate choice and Prince Albert at least felt that the marriage would strengthen the ties between two of Europe's greatest families and provide a binding and peaceful relationship between the two countries.

Princess Victoria and Prince Frederick William were married in the Chapel Royal at St. James's Palace in 1858 and, like her ancestor Princess Mary, the first Princess Royal, she too left her homeland for a life of exile. Berlin was to be her home initially and she was thankful that her father had forced her to speak German for the language was all she had in common with her new relatives.

Court etiquette was far more formal than she had been used to in England and her husband was allowed to make no decision without the permission of his uncle the King – even when it came to alterations and decorations at their new home in Potsdam, the King had to be consulted on every detail. Once when the young bride sneezed during a reception she was informed that 'sneezing is not permitted in the presence of the Sovereign'.

In 1861 the King of Prussia died, making Vicky's husband the Crown Prince, and she assumed the title of Crown Princess of Prussia. But instead of her new rank giving her more freedom and authority within the confines of the Court, it simply meant that she was nearer the Queen, her mother-in-law, and constantly at her beck and call. Even when Prince Albert, Queen Victoria's Consort died, the Crown Princess was refused permission to travel to England to comfort her mother. As she was pregnant, it was felt that it was more important to protect the possible future successor to the Throne than for the Princess to attend her mother. Nevertheless she did insist on being allowed to travel to Windsor and she returned to Berlin in time to give birth to her second son Henry.

Princess Victoria lived through one of the most turbulent periods of Prussian history, and it was only when it was realised that when her husband succeeded to the Throne his wife would be Empress of Prussia, that in England steps were taken to create Queen Victoria Empress of India. It would never have done for the Princess Royal to have succeeded to a title superior to that held by her mother, Queen Victoria.

Princess Victoria eventually gave birth to eight children, the youngest of whom, Princess Margaret of Hesse, would live through two World Wars before she died in 1954. If Princess Victoria's brother Edward was to wait for sixty years as Prince of Wales before succeeding to the Throne as Edward VII, his sister was to wait for nearly the same period before her husband became Emperor of Prussia. So she had enjoyed the title and distinction of Princess Royal all her life when she eventually became Empress in 1888, but it was a title that she carried for less than one hundred days. Her husband died three months after he succeeded to the Throne and his widow became Dowager Empress. She died in 1901, the same year as her mother who had occupied the English Throne for longer than any other Monarch before or since. She had spent most of her life in Germany but until the day she died she regarded herself as English and frequently wrote to her mother reaffirming her love of her mother country.

Queen Victoria and her two eldest children are still the holders of

61. Princess Anne photographed in the grounds of Gatcombe Park with her son, Peter, who was born on November 15, 1977, the day after his parents' fourth wedding anniversary. Much has been made of the fact that Peter, the Queen's first grandson, was the first royal baby to be born a commoner in 500 years, but his mother felt there was no need for him to be given a title, even though at the time of his birth he was fifth in line of Succession to the Throne.

62. (*Above*) The year 1981 was one of double celebration for the
Royal Family. On May 15th Princess Anne's daughter, Zara, was
born at 8.15 in the evening, giving the Queen her first granddaughter. Baby Zara (the name means bright as the dawn) made
a 'somewhat positive appearance', according to her mother, and
has continued to make her presence felt. After the christening in
Buckingham Palace, the Queen's cousin Lord Lichfield captured
this charming study of Princess Anne with her two children in the
Music Room.

63. (*Opposite, top*) Later in the year the wedding of the Prince of
Wales to Lady Diana Spencer brought most of Europe's remaining
Royalty to London. Princess Anne rode in an open carriage to St.
Paul's Cathedral together with her husband and her aunt, Princess
Margaret, who was accompanied by her son, Viscount Linley.

64. (*Opposite, bottom*) In 1980 attention focussed on Queen Elizabeth, the Queen Mother, as she celebrated her eightieth birthday.
At Her Majesty's request a photograph was taken of her
surrounded by her family – even here one of the royal corgis could
not be kept out of the picture!

Five faces of Royalty

65 (*Above left*)
As Chancellor of the
University of London
she performs the ceremony
of the 'hooding of a
Higher Doctor'.

66. A night out with the
stars (*left*) means a rare
chance to chat with show-
business personalities such
as Petula Clark.

67. While in Somalia
(*above*), it is back to
working clothes at a Save-
the-Children-Fund refugee
camp in 1982.

68. (*Opposite, top*) Riding
for the Disabled occupies
a great deal of the
Princess's time, so a
helicopter of The Queen's
Flight is very useful.

69. (*Below*) With Mrs. Thatcher, Mr. Whitelaw and the Princess of Wales in the official party to greet Queen Beatrix of The Netherlands.

70. (*Above*) Farnham Castle, 1982: the Princess Anne Awards are given by the the S.C.F. to youngsters who help the Fund in some way. The Princess likes to make the presentations personally if she can.

71. (*Above*) Her Royal Highness, as President of the British Olympic Association, visited Houston, Texas, in January, 1984 on a fund-raising tour. At the Petroleum Club she met oil millionaires and British film stars. (*Left to right*) Michael Ashley, Samantha Eggar, David Hemmings and his wife Prue, Tony Thompson, Chairman of BOA, his wife Marilyn, Patrick McNee and Mrs. Jack Hines, hostess for the evening.

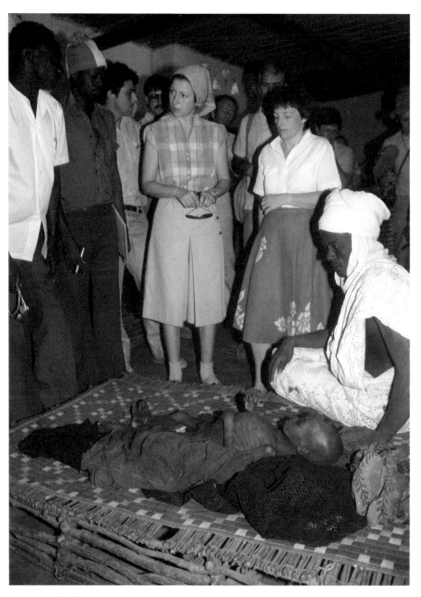

72. 'The toughest tour ever undertaken by a member of the Royal Family,' is how the press described Princess Anne's visit to Africa in February, 1984. Here in Upper Volta, said to be the 'poorest region in the world', she spent days with S.C.F. field workers in the most appalling conditions, seeing for herself the problems that have to be faced.

73. Captain Phillips resplendent in white tie and tails and the Princess in full-length evening gown, complete with tiara and the sash of the Grand Cross of the Royal Victorian Order. The occasion was a banquet at the Guildhall given in honour of President Kenneth Kaunda of Zambia in 1983 during his State Visit.

a remarkable record for longevity with regard to their respective titles. The Queen, the Prince of Wales and the Princess Royal each held their titles for sixty years – longer than any other members of the Royal Family even to the present time.

King Edward VII had been on the Throne for four years when he decided to create his eldest daughter Princess Royal. This was done by the simple expedient of announcing in the King's Birthday Honours of November 5th, 1905, that 'His Majesty's eldest daughter, Her Royal Highness Princess Louise Victoria Alexandra Dagmar (Duchess of Fife) shall henceforth bear the style and title of Princess Royal.'

Princess Louise was the third child born to the then Prince and Princess of Wales. Two boys, Albert and George (later George V), preceded the birth of the first female child in February, 1867, and two more girls followed – Victoria in 1868 and Maud in 1869 – so their mother Princess Alexandra of Wales had given birth to five children in six years, a splendid example of the procreative machinery that young royal princesses were required to be until recent times.

Because their father the Prince of Wales had little taste for public duties, and also the fact that their grandmother Queen Victoria retained a tight hold on affairs of State until well into old age, the Wales's children enjoyed a family life rare among royalty in those days. They lived at Sandringham where their parents indulged their every childish whim and grew up in a cocoon of Victorian comfort, finding their pleasures within the family and having no wish to meet outsiders, even cousins from the other royal houses of Europe. They were thoroughly spoiled, and the girls in particular became adept at playing practical jokes on members of the staff. Finally things got so much out of hand that the Prince of Wales gave permission to the servants to restrain the children, even going so far as to allow them to smack both boys and girls if their behaviour became too wild.

This democracy among the Wales's family did not endear them to the Queen who had brought up her own children in an atmosphere of rigid discipline and self-restraint, but the Prince of Wales, who spent a great deal of his time in enjoyable pursuits with his friends, continued his indulgent ways with his children when he was at home.

For more than twenty years the pattern of their lives remained unchanged. The three daughters were given no training to equip them for their future roles, and they were quite content to continue their pleasant but aimless existence, even the future Princess Royal remaining completely unprepared to take her place in public life.

When she was twenty-one and still an introverted, shy young girl, she fell in love with the man she was to marry. He was a commoner of immense wealth whom everyone called Macduff, though he was in fact the sixth Earl of Fife. He was very well known to the Royal Family and Queen Victoria was happy to give her consent to the marriage, even though Princess Louise's closest cousin, Princess Mary of Teck (later Queen Mary) was to write: 'For a future Princess Royal to marry a subject seems rather strange.'

At the wedding breakfast the Queen announced her intention of creating Macduff, Duke of Fife and soon after the wedding the bride became known as H.R.H. Princess Louise, Duchess of Fife.

Marriage did little to change the attitude of Princess Louise towards public life. She still preferred to find her companions from among her own family, and in this she was encouraged by her husband who was as reticent as she was when in the company of 'outsiders'.

But she was a devoted wife and mother to her two daughters, and even when her father, who had succeeded Queen Victoria in 1901, conferred the title of Princess Royal on her in 1905, there is no evidence that she welcomed the change in her status. It made little difference to her lifestyle and she accepted no more engagements than she had previously. When she was persuaded to attend an official function in her own right, she did so with such marked lack of enthusiasm that fewer and fewer invitations were forthcoming. Of course this was at a time when it was comparatively easy for a member of the Royal Family to retire into the privacy of the royal residences, and there was little criticism in the press, of the sort that today Princess Anne or Princess Margaret might attract if it was felt that they were not 'pulling their weight'.

The Princess Royal and her husband had been used to spending the winters in the warm climates of Egypt and in 1911 they set sail on the liner *Delhi*. Shortly after leaving the Bay of Biscay when they were off the coast of Morocco the ship ran aground and all the passengers had to be evacuated. The Princess Royal may not have been willing to accept a role in public life, but her lifetime of instinctive royal training came to the fore at this moment of peril. Both she and her husband refused to leave the ship until all the other passengers had been transferred to the lifeboats. Even then it was a precarious passage to the nearby shore with the Princess going under the waves several times before being able to stagger onto dry land.

This extraordinary adventure was undoubtedly the most dramatic event in the Princess Royal's life and there was to be a tragic sequel. Shortly after continuing their journey to Egypt the Duke caught pneumonia and within ten days he had died.

His widow survived him for twenty years during which time she retreated even more into private life, and when she died in 1931 at the age of sixty-three there were few members of the general public in Britain who remembered what she looked like or even that there was a Princess Royal.

So we come to the last member of the Royal Family to bear the title Princess Royal. We have already mentioned that of all six bearers of the title, Princess Mary, Countess of Harewood did more to enhance the style than any other. For thirty-three years she carried the title Princess Royal with dignity and grace. Her enthusiasm for good works manifested itself at an early age; even for her twenty-first birthday present from her parents, what she wanted was permission to work at the Great Ormond Street Children's Hospital, taking her turn in the operating theatre where the messiest jobs were always left to the youngest probationer. Also in that same year she became Colonel-in-Chief of the Royal Scots, a rank she was to hold for more than fifty years. And in 1983 when Princess Anne became the regiment's Colonel-in-Chief, they presented her with the same diamond brooch that had been worn by her relative during the First World War.

Princess Mary married Viscount Lascelles, Earl of Harewood in Westminster Abbey in February, 1922, and even during the wedding preparations she was thinking of the organisations with which she was associated. Her wedding presents were put on display at St. James's Palace and the receipts from the thousands of people who paid to see them all went to her favourite charities, thereby creating a precedent which has been followed at royal weddings ever since.

After her marriage the Princess Royal extended even further her list of patronages and she became one of the most active members of the Royal Family in terms of public duties. She was also the best loved within the family and the Abdication of her brother King Edward VIII in 1936 meant that she was torn between love for her favourite elder brother and her devotion to duty. Although she was totally in support of her other brother Bertie when he succeeded to the Throne as George VI, she still retained great affection for David, and she was the first member of the family to visit him abroad after his self-imposed exile following the Abdication.

Throughout her life Princess Mary continued to seek new horizons. She became the first woman in Britain to be appointed Chancellor of a university when she accepted the position at Leeds, and in 1948 she established a precedent when she became the first woman to register her own racing colours. So, if the previous Princess Royal had been a disappointment to the country by her unwillingness to accept a role in public life, her successor in the title more than made up for her during her thirty-three years tenure. When Princess Mary died suddenly in 1965 not only had the Royal Family lost one of its most beloved relatives, but the country a public servant of rare distinction.

And so to the present Princess Royal presumptive, Her Royal Highness The Princess Anne, Mrs. Mark Phillips. She is presumptive only in the eyes of observers for there has been no indication that the Queen wishes her daughter to be created Princess Royal, and as the title is conferred at the discretion of the Sovereign alone we all await the Queen's pleasure. Princess Anne's insistence that her children remain commoners and her husband's reluctance to accept a title on their marriage would seem to indicate that she prefers to maintain the 'status quo'. There is no doubt that she holds a unique and distinctive position as the Queen's only daughter. For more than thirty years she has been known simply as Princess Anne. Even if she were to be created Princess Royal it's doubtful if she would ever be called by the public anything other than Princess Anne. But if at some time in the future the Queen should request that she assume the title of Princess Royal, I believe Her Royal Highness's sense of duty and love for her mother would persuade her to accept. There is nothing her mother might ask her to do which she would not do willingly, and if it is to be the Queen's wish – it will happen.

Chapter 16

CONCLUSION

If there is a single quality that could be attributed to Princess Anne it is determination. She is determined to succeed in any thing she attempts, be it sporting or otherwise, and her own highly individual style is the result of her early and continued determination to be herself at all times.

This is not to confuse stubbornness with resoluteness, though on occasion she has been accused of the former by those who have not recognised that when she has stuck to a particular point of view it's because she has always been decisive in everything she does.

Princess Anne has been called her father's daughter because of her forthright ways and her reputation for being quick-tempered and arrogant. She is also very much her mother's child, inheriting from her courage, compassion and a deep-rooted sense of duty. Whatever else critics may say about the Princess, there is rarely an accusation that she does not pull her weight in royal duties. Carrying out more than 200 engagements a year at home and abroad, she is at last attracting the kind of publicity, other members of the Royal Family have enjoyed for years.

In her everyday dealings with the charities with which she is involved she demonstrates a practical understanding of their problems, and her in-depth knowledge of their work has made her so much more than just another royal figurehead. Carol Thatcher writing in the *Daily Telegraph* in October, 1983 about the changing image of the working Princess said 'Princess Anne has made her mark . . . as the good humoured, pragmatic face of royalty.'

Ever since she can remember she has been second to her brother Charles, whose destiny was predetermined from the moment of his birth. She has felt the need to prove herself throughout her life. She chose a sport where position and money count for little, and competitive three-day eventing has remained the most important part of her off-duty life. She accepted the position of President of the British Olympic Association because as a former Olympic competitor herself, she knows only too well what it means to be chosen to take part. She says 'if only those in authority realised what it means to a sportsman to train for four years and then to be told that they cannot go, they wouldn't be so fast to make decisions that can totally destroy someone's hopes. There is nothing like an Olympic Games; I know, I've been, and I want everyone who is capable of winning a place to be able to go. That's why I am willing to go anywhere and meet anyone to try and raise funds for our athletes.'

This is a side of Princess Anne's character that seems to be at odds with the usual picture we have of the ruthless, competitive horsewoman whose only aim is to win. Her view is that the Olympic Games are unique and that 'just to get there is an achievement in itself, even without the winning of medals.'

Hers has been the most remarkable of equestrian careers, rising to the top in just three years, during which time she showed all the qualities she inherited from her parents, courage, determination, an unwillingness to accept defeat and compassion for her horses when they have been injured. She has earned respect in a sport where there is scant regard for rank, and by proving to others that she is among the world's best as an equestrian she has proved to herself that being 'number two' does not have to mean being second best.

Could she achieve the same heights again? She believes that if the right horse came along in 'the next year or so it might be possible to do something, but otherwise perhaps I should think seriously about taking up another sport, such as sailing'. If she does decide to take it up competitively we could well see a sailor Princess flying the Union Jack in international events before long.

One of the biggest problems facing the Royal Family, and indeed any other public figure, is security. In Princess Anne's case it's something that has been with her for many years though as she explained 'things were rather different when I was at school. The detective lived outside the gates and he was not very much in evidence unless we were going somewhere'. These days she admits that she and her husband talk about the problem but they agree that 'if someone wants to do it there is little that anyone can really do to stop them. The difference now is that when I am on a "walkabout" I think and act like a policeman – my eyes are everywhere.' Her memories of the kidnapping attempt in The Mall are still sharp and clear.

Nevertheless, the Princess together with the other members of the Royal Family intends to carry on living as near normal a life as possible because the idea of 'living in a cage' simply isn't on.

Princess Anne's outlook on life has altered considerably in the past few years. When she first went away to school she was determined to get by with the minimum of effort. She surprised herself by going on to take her 'A' levels – she had intended to finish her education after 'O' level examinations. She did not want to go to university and even today she sticks by that decision. 'It was right for me at the time. Girls in the Royal Family did not have much chance of an outside career then, so there was no point in my going on. Today I would quite like to go to university, perhaps to read Geography or Geology – if time could be found.'

She still looks back on her schooldays at Benenden with affection. 'Noise and smells' – that's what school meant to me – cabbage and polish. Even today whenever I go into a school or a hospital I can still feel it.'

Princess Anne combines a wide variety of roles in her public and private lives, but the two main charities to which she devotes most of her time are still Save the Children and Riding for the Disabled. She doesn't think of herself as being particularly fond of children, but still believes that every child deserves a chance in life. In fact her views on the people who work with her in these two charitable organisations are quite definite. 'I think perhaps it's better that the workers are not sentimental about the children they are dealing with. It's so easy to become emotionally attached when there are so many deserving and appealing cases, it would be impossible to carry out the work properly if you did become too involved, so it's vital that the people at the sharp end are practical about their work. That's not to say they are not caring; they are, extremely so, otherwise they wouldn't be doing what they are doing, but the need is for someone to face up to the problems of disease and neglect, not just to wring their hands and say how sorry they are.'

Princess Anne was the first royal princess in 900 years who was able to marry the man she wanted to without any considerations of political or monarchial expediency. And the man she chose to accept was someone who shared her love of horses and who has managed to retain his independence in spite of sharing his life with one of the most public of figures. While the Princess carries on with her official commitments, Mark Phillips confines his activities, in the main, to running the farm at Gatcombe. To help finance his equestrian career he has accepted sponsorship from the Range Rover Company and on August 6th, 1983, he and Princess Anne opened the grounds of their house so that the first Gatcombe Horse Trials could be held under the sponsorship of a wine company, Croft Original. This was a successful business venture and several members of the Royal Family plus well known friends, such as Jackie Stewart and his wife, turned up to lend their support. The children were taken to Balmoral to be with their grandparents, because the Princess did not want them subjected to the publicity she knew the event would attract, indeed, need.

The whole question of protecting her children's privacy is almost an obsession. Princess Anne is determined that they will live as normal a life as possible despite the extraordinary circumstances of their birth. She sends them to local schools and they play with children from the surrounding area in exactly the same way as other youngsters, but the fact remains that no matter what the Princess and her husband want for them, they can never escape the fact that they are the grandchildren of the Queen and neither the public nor the press is ever going to let them forget it. Peter will probably end up at Marlborough, his father's old school and possibly Zara will go to Benenden, following in her mother's footsteps. Princess Anne says it all depends on the local schools and the way things work out in a few years' time.

One thing is fairly certain about the future. Princess Anne and her family will stay in Gloucestershire. They believe that the people of the county are good neighbours who 'accept you for what you are'. The area around Gatcombe has its fair share of eccentrics, including one elderly lady, who when wished good morning by the Princess while out riding subjected her to five minutes invective claiming that she, Princess Anne, had been talking about her behind her back. There was no harm done and Her Royal Highness tells the story without any malice – an amusing anecdote about life in the country.

Another activity she has taken up again recently is hunting. For some years Princess Anne devoted little time to hunting partly because of the controversial arguments stirred up by 'blood sports' but in the last couple of years she has managed to go out with a number of hunts, without attracting the kind of attention the Prince of Wales gets whenever he appears. It's a sport in which she once again has to compete, against obstacles both man made and natural.

Princess Anne is now one of the most senior members of the Royal Family and her devotion to the Queen and the whole idea of the Monarchy has never wavered. Unlike many other children of famous parents who have deliberately rebelled against everything their families stood for, she has never for a moment questioned the position of the Monarchy. She has accepted the hand which fate has dealt her without ever considering an alternative. When her natural impulses have been to live her own life away from the limelight, she has played her part in the 'Family Firm' as fully as any. If the world's press has concentrated on the occasional outburst from her notoriously sharp tongue, she accepts with resigned good humour the fact that they ignore her at hundreds of events when she is even-tempered, patient and conscientious to a degree.

When she has let fly with an incautious word to reporters, they are delighted. It always makes a better story. She is the Royal, who in the past, the press has loved to hate. She has provided them with more headlines than some of them deserve.

On the subject of titles Her Royal Highness sees no cause for discussion. 'There was no reason why Mark should be given a title when we married,' she says. 'He was never going to take part in public duties in his own right, so the question didn't arise.' By the same token the Princess sees no justification for the children being granted titles. She feels they are not royal and for this reason it is perfectly acceptable for them to remain as Master Peter and Miss Zara. They are not expected to take on roles in public life and they will undoubtedly have to earn their own living when the time comes.

But as things stand at the moment, Peter Phillips will have to accept certain royal responsibilities when he is eighteen. At that age he can expect to be made a Counsellor of State by the Queen, because of his place in the line of succession. If that happens he will be the first commoner to reach this innermost royal circle, and it's almost certain that the Queen would award him a title. But his mother feels that by the time her son is eighteen the matter will be purely of academic interest. 'The Council of State is restricted to six as far as I am aware' she says 'and as my brothers reach an age when they can be expected to take on more commitments, perhaps the need for Peter to act as a Counsellor of State in the future recedes.' Her feeling is that her own position as a Counsellor may change within a few years. It's a responsibility she takes very seriously but she accepts that the male members of the family take precedence, and when the time comes for her to hand over, she will do so willingly.

The Princess considers her role in public life to be something that was thrust upon her and she has devoted a large part of her time and energies to doing the best job she can, but she wonders if there will be a need for her to continue in twenty years or so. Will the people and organisations who approach her continuously now, do so in the future. As a younger group of Royals comes on to the scene will there be the desire on the part of the public to continue seeing the Queen's only daughter?

If at some time in the future she decides to retire from public life, what are the alternatives? Could she take a more active part in running the farm, which if well managed could provide a more than adequate income to compensate for any loss of revenue from the Civil List? Will she retreat to the shires enjoying the rural pursuits that she and her husband relish so much already?

Those who are involved with her organisations, both civil and military, are in no doubt about what they want from the Princess in the future. They want her to continue in exactly the same way as

she is doing today. They will not hear of any lessening of her partici-
pation in their affairs and some feel that the merest suggestion is
irresponsible and tantamount to treason.

Princess Anne has established herself as one of the most outspoken
personalities in the Royal Family and if it is true that they need the
press as much as the press needs them, then she has done more
than her fair share of attracting publicity to the Monarchy. The fact
that not all the publicity has been favourable does not detract in any
way from its value, and if she has been instrumental in opening up
a greater public awareness of the Royal Family, it can only be to the
common good. As she has matured, Princess Anne has grown into
a woman who is increasingly conscious of her responsibilities, and
her obvious love of her family and devotion to her duties, has made
her much more popularly accepted then she was in her early days.

There is one topic on which she refuses to be drawn however; the
question of her being created Princess Royal. Her great aunt, the late
Princess Royal, died in 1965 and there has been no successor to the
title since then. When I asked her for her feelings about it, she replied
briefly: 'The subject is nothing to do with me. It is entirely a matter
for the Queen and apart from the fact that it is the Sovereign's gift
I know little about the precedents.'

There are those who know and love her, particularly among her
Service connections who would be extremely happy if she were to
be created Princess Royal. She has reached the age and maturity
when she would bring to the title the same dignity and style carried
for so long by Princess Mary. If it is the Queen's wish, Princess Anne
will accept. If not she will remain what she has always been, a
courageous, determined forthright woman who is conscious of the
important role she has to play in British life in the latter part of the
twentieth century. The fact that she was born to position has not
changed the way in which she has worked all her adult life as an
active participant in all the organisations with which she is associated. Nothing will ever change that facet of her character and nothing
will force her to lose her independence or her own unique identity.

She is at her best when she is doing things and if she shows
impatience with others who are not quick enough to grasp what she
is trying to show them, it is simply because she is so fast to learn
herself. She recognises this impatience in herself but feels she is
getting better. She may never be the most popular member of the
Royal Family in the eyes of the public, but to those who have come
into the slightest contact with her, she is one of the most hardworking, conscientious and individual royal princesses there has ever
been. She is quite simply – herself.

APPENDIX

Official Appointments of HRH The Princess Anne

SERVICES
Colonel-in-Chief
9.6.69   14th/20th King's Hussars
9.6.69   Worcestershire & Sherwood Foresters Regiment (29th/45th Foot)
24.6.72 8th Canadian Hussars (Princess Louise's)
22.6.77 Royal Corps of Signals
         The Canadian Forces Communications & Electronics Branch
         The Royal Australian Corps of Signals
         Royal New Zealand Corps of Signals
         Royal New Zealand Nursing Corps
         The Grey & Simcoe Foresters Militia – Canada
30.6.83 The Royal Scots (The Royal Regiment)

1.7.74   Chief Commandant of the Women's Royal Naval Service (WRNS)
18.8.74 Patron of the Association of Wrens
18.8.74 Patron of the Army and Royal Artillery Hunter Trials
14.10.74 President of the Women's Royal Naval Service Benevolent Trust
18.8.81 Commandant-in-Chief of the Women's Transport Service (FANY)

         President of the Royal School for Daughters of Officers
         President of the Royal Navy and Royal Marines (Haslemere)
         Patron of Royal Corps of Signals' Institution
         Patron of Royal Tournament
         Hon. Air Commodore of RAF Lyneham
         Life Member of Royal British Legion Women's Section
         Life Member of Royal Naval Saddle Club
         Hon. Life Member of RNVR Officers' Association

GENERAL
1950   1,000,000 (millionth) Member of the Automobile Association
1.1.70   President of The Save the Children Fund (SCF)
10.11.70 Patron of Riding for the Disabled Association (RDA)
17.11.70 Commandant-in-Chief, St John Ambulance and Nursing Cadets
1.4.72   President of British Academy of Film and Television Arts (BAFTA)
12.9.72 Patron of Jersey (CI) Wildlife Preservation Fund
15.6.76 Visitor of Felixstowe College
27.2.76 Freedom of the City of London
27.10.79 Patron of Royal Lymington Yacht Club
17.2.81 Chancellor of London University
9.9.82   Patron of National Union of Townswomen's Guilds
14.4.83 President of the British Olympic Association

         President, Windsor Horse Trials
         President, The Hunters Improvement and Light Horse Breeding Society
         Hon. President, Stroud District Show – June 1981

         Patron, Gloucester and North Avon Federation of Young Farmers

Patron, Royal Port Moresby Society for Prevention of Cruelty to Animals
Patron, Horse of the Year Ball
Patron, Benenden Ball
Vice Patron, British Show Jumping Association
Vice Patron, Home Farm Trust
Vice Patron, Bourne End Junior Sports and Recreation Club
Hon. Member, Island Sailing Club
Hon. Member, British Equine Veterinary Association
Hon. Member, Royal Yacht Squadron
Hon. Member, Minchinhampton Golf Club
Hon. Member, Royal Thames Yacht Club
Hon. Member, Sussex Agricultural Society
Hon. Life Member of Flying Doctor Society of Africa 21.3.72
Hon. Member, 1970, Young Adventure Club
Member, Beaufort Hunt
Member, Reliant Owners Club – January 1971
Hon. President Royal Caledonian Hunt
Patron, British School of Osteopathy – February, 1984

LIVERY COMPANIES
30.11.71 Yeoman of the Saddlers' Company
 6.12.71 Honorary Freeman of the Farriers' Company
15.3.72 Honorary Freeman of the Loriners' Company
10.5.72 Freeman of Fishmongers' Company
 4.6.76 Honorary Freeman of Farmers' Company
29.4.82 Honorary Liverman of Carmens' Company

ILLUSTRATION ACKNOWLEDGEMENTS

Colour

Camera Press, London: Godfrey Argent 76; Camera Press: Baron 73; Camera Press: Lionel Cherruault, 235 top; Camera Press: Glen Harvey 240; Camera Press: Patrick Lichfield 234; Camera Press: Norman Parkinson 154, 156; Camera Press: Snowdon 233; Camera Press: Studio Lisa 74; Houston Chronicle 238 bottom; Anwar Hussein 159 bottom; Margaret Lavender 237 top; University of London 236 top; The Photo Source/Fox, London 75 top, 76–7 top, 76–7 bottom, 77, 78 top, 78 bottom, 79, 80, 153, 155 top, 155 bottom, 157, 158 top, 158 bottom, 235 bottom, 237 bottom; Rex Features, London 159 top, 160; The Save the Children Fund/Fritz Curzon, London 236 bottom, 236–7, 238 top, 239.

Black and white

Associated Press, London 200 bottom; Peter Boissier 197 bottom left; British Academy of Film and Television Arts, London 200 top; Public Relations, 4 Division, B.A.O.R. 114 top; Camera Press, London 38 bottom; Camera Press: Cecil Beaton 35; Camera Press: Srdja Djukanovic 196–7; Camera Press: James Reid 34 top; Camera Press: Snowdon 36–7, 113; Margaret Lavender 197 bottom right; The Photo Source/Central Press, London 40, 117, 118, 120 bottom, 193 top, 198 top, 198 bottom; The Photo Source/Fox, London 37 top, 199; The Photo Source/Fox: Norman Parkinson 194–5; The Photo Source/Keystone, London 33 top, 33 bottom, 34 bottom, 39, 114 bottom, 115, 116 top, 116 bottom, 119 top, 119 bottom, 120 top, 193 bottom, 196 top, 196 bottom; Press Association, London 38 top; Sport & General Press Agency, London 37 bottom.

AUTHOR'S ACKNOWLEDGEMENTS

The writing of a book of this nature invariably means dependence on the help of a large number of people. I am glad to be able to record my thanks to those who participated in its preparation and production.

When I first approached Buckingham Palace and suggested the idea of this book I was received kindly by The Queen's Press Secretary, Michael Shea, who warned me of the obstacles I might encounter and encouraged me to persevere. I am grateful to him for his initial and continued support. My thanks also to all the other members of the Press Office for their patience and courtesy in dealing with my never-ending queries; in particular Felicity Simpson, who provided me with much valuable information and Anne Wall who put me right on so many points.

Friends and acquaintances of Princess Anne who were kind enough to talk to me include, in no particular order: Elizabeth Clarke, Maj. General Peter Bradley, Maj. General J. M. (Mike) Palmer, Alison Oliver, Air Vice Marshall J. M. de Severne, Group Capt. Jeremy Jones, Brenda Matthews, Col. 'Bill' Lithgow, Pauline Charnock, Reginald Collin, John Cumber, Wendy Riches, Marjorie Langford, Lavinia, Duchess of Norfolk, The Hon. Verona Kitson, Dick Moss, Col. John Francis, Sukie Hemming, Sheila Parkinson, Ronald Allison, Maureen Baker, Malcolm McVittie, Lady Susan Hussey, Eric Grounds, Jackie and Helen Stewart, Elisabeth Craig-McFeeley, Voula McBride and a number of others who prefer to remain known only to themselves and to me.

Members of Her Royal Highness's Personal Household have been unstinting in their help, and I am truly grateful to Victoria Legge-Bourke, Celia Innes, Mary Carew Pole, Shân Legge-Bourke, Rowena Feilden and The Countess of Lichfield for their generosity and good-humoured tolerance, particularly when I have 'tagged along' on some of the visits. For the same reasons mention must also be made of David Robinson, Philip Robinson and Colin Tebbutt, those 'invisible' policemen who have eased my progress in the royal wake on many occasions.

In Princess Anne's office at Buckingham Palace, Alison Bush has dealt with unending patience with literally dozens of queries, while Brenda Hodgson, that 'fount of all knowledge' has shared her unique know-how in typically generous fashion. Peter Gibbs, the Princess's Private Secretary has been the sturdiest bulwark – never too busy to talk, always ready with advice and encouragement. I cannot rate too highly the contribution he has made.

For Country Life, Robert Owen, that most unfailingly courteous and considerate of men, has gently nursed me through the gestation period, having been present when the idea was first conceived and remaining steadfast until the birth – thank you Robert. My thanks to Patricia Pierce who edited the manuscript with tact and perceptive understanding, and to Judy Todd, who researched the illustrations. Lollie Duvivier and Doreen Lancaster laboured at the typewriters, for which my thanks.

My wife Diana has been a source of encouragement right from the beginning, even to the extent of allowing me to store volumes of research material in every corner of the family home – the house is yours once more!

Finally, Her Royal Highness, The Princess Anne, Mrs Mark Phillips GCVO, who's natural modesty made her somewhat reluctant when the idea of the book was first mooted. When she was persuaded that there is a great deal of interest in her activities she gave a tremendous amount of help. By allowing me to approach her friends and staff she invested in me a trust which I hope she will feel has been justified, and I am deeply grateful to Her Royal Highness for her hospitality and consideration at Gatcombe Park and Buckingham Palace.

The amount of cooperation I have received might give the impression that this is an authorized biography. It is not. The opinions expressed are my own and there has been no editorial control other than mine. If there is any disagreement with anything written on the preceding pages, the fault lies entirely at my door.

INDEX

N.B.: Numbers in *italics* are illustration numbers.

Abel-Smith, Lady *20*
Africa *67, 72*, 125, 126–7,
  146, 174, 177, 180
Albert, Prince Consort
  191, 192
Alexander, Brian 80
Alexandra, Princess 35,
  85, 94, 139, 159
Alice of Greece, Princess
  20, 23
Allhusen, Derek 49, 76
Allison, Ronald 79, 83,
  179
Anderson, Mabel 20, 27
Andrew, Prince *10, 64,* 6,
  16, 34, 64, 93, 136, 154,
  166, 168, 169, 176
Andrew of Greece,
  Princess 17, 23
Anne, H.R.H. The
  Princess birth *1,* 17–19;
  christening *2, 13,* 23–4;
  birthdays *3, 8, 14, 17,*
  25, 38, 37, 66; as
  Brownie and Girl
  Guide 30–31, 36;
  education *9,* 28–30, 35,
  37–47, 171, 183;
  engagement *40,* 70,
  77–83; wedding *42, 49,*
  50, 84–94, 161; birth of
  children 165–6, 168; as
  Champion of Europe
  66–69; as Counsellor of
  State 16, 188, 201; films
  and television
  interviews 6, 8, 79, 87,
  88, 109, 125, 132,
  177–80; Household
  148–9, 152–3, 154–6,
  176, 179, 185; kidnap
  attempt 109–18, 170;
  overseas tours 16, 94,
  124, 126–8, 146;
  relationship with
  parents 27, 170–71, 172;
  with Charles 26–7, 33,
  59, 171–2, 197; with her
  children 165–70; Service
  and other organisations
  8–9, 11–15, 52–4,
  122–43; sports *19, 24,*
  23, 31–2, 42, 68–9, 171,
  198; as Sports
  Personality of the Year
  68–9; as Sportswoman
  of the Year *24,* 69

Anne, Princess Royal 181,
  184–5, 187
Anne-Marie of Denmark,
  Princess 46
Armstrong-Jones, Lady
  Sarah *42, 48,* 92, 93
Army and Royal Artillery
  Hunter Trials 123
Army Horse Trials,
  Tidworth *55,* 7–8
Ashley, Michael *71,* 10
Australia *28,* 123, 126,
  134, 180
Automobile Ass'n 22, 122

Babington-Smith, Susan.
  See Hemming
Badminton Horse Trials
  15, 32, 46, 59, 63–4, 65,
  69, 70, 79, 81, 119, 175
Baker, Maureen 92,
  159–61
Ball, Ian 115–17
Banks, Trevor 70
Baylis, Sir Richard 168
Beaton, Cecil 24
Beaton, James *52,* 109,
  110, 113, 114, 115
Beaufort, Duke of *15,* 64
Beatrix, Queen 69
Benenden School for Girls
  12, 36, 37–47, 162, 199
Bliss, Sir Arthur 92
Bloodhound 19, 32
Booth, Hazel 64
Bosanquet, Reginald 7, 79
Boyd, John 160
Brabourne, Lord 133
Bradley, Peter 133–4, 135
Brassey, Rowena 78, 109,
  110, 115, 154, 157
Britannia 32, 33, 66, 94,
  100
British Academy of Film
  and Television Arts *59,*
  8, 122, 131–3
British Equine Veterinary
  Association 122
British Olympic Ass'n *60,*
  71, 10, 123, 124, 197
British Show Jumping
  Association 122
Buccleuch, Duke of 17
Bullen, Jane 49, 58
Burghley 7, *33,* 65, 66–7,
  70, 82, 119, 175
Bush, Alison 152

Callendar, Alexander 109,
  110, 113, 114
Canada 123, 126, 134, 182
Canadian Forest
  Communications and
  Electronics Branch 123
Canadian Hussars, 8th 9,
  54, 123
Carew Pole, Mary (*nee*
  Dawnay) 15, 154, 156
Chapman, Victor 176
Charles, Prince of Wales
  6, 8, 10, 29, 64;
  childhood 19, 20, 23,
  25, 26, 28, 36;
  education 27, 28, 35,
  171, 183; and family
  members 79, 112, 166,
  168, 172, 187;
  investiture 54, 181, 182;
  birthday 84; marriage
  63, 85, 88, 176; film 125
Charlotte, Princess Royal
  187–90
Checketts, Sir David 77–8
Churchill, Sir Winston 24,
  84
Clarke, Elizabeth *12,* 37,
  40, 41, 43, 44, 45, 46, 47
Coleman, David 54, 56
Collin, Reginald 132
Collins, Chris 7, 58
Columbus *36,* 69–70, 72,
  98
Commonwealth Games,
  Jamaica *44,* 33
Constantine, ex-King, of
  Greece 46, 80, 139
Cooke, Alistair 187
Craig McFeeley, Elizabeth
  136
Cromer, Countess of 20
Cumber, John 126, 127

Dean, Christopher 60
Diana, Princess of Wales
  69, 6, 85, 88, 175, 177,
  181
Doublet *32,* 7, 61–2, 63,
  66–8, 69, 70, 129
Duckett, Richard 143

Ede, Chuter 18
Edward VII, King 191–3
Edward VIII, King 143
Edward, Prince *37, 42, 64,*
  6, 64, 92, 93, 166, 168, 176